The Complete Guide

Mandolins
Mandolas, Mando-Cellos and Mando-Basses

by Paul Fox

FOREWORD BY WALTER CARTER

Cover Design by Roy "Rick" Dains
FalconMarketingMedia@gmail.com

ISBN 978-1-57424-339-0

Copyright ©2016 CENTERSTREAM Publishing, LLC
P. O. Box 17878 - Anaheim Hills, CA 92817
email: centerstrm@aol.com • web: centerstream-usa.com

About the Author

Paul Fox has two great passions – music and vintage musical instruments. He has been researching Gibson and Epiphone instruments for over 15 years. His first book *The Other Brands of Gibson (2010* Centerstream Publishing) is a chronicle of the over 40 different brands Gibson produced that did not carry the Gibson name. The author was inspired to write this new book because of the truly fascinating history of Gibson mandolins and vast array of superlative musical instruments made by that company for more than a century. He is also the author of an article about the "House of Stathopoulo Harp Guitar" published in *Vintage Guitar Magazine* in May 2010.

His company, Fox Guitars - **www.fox-guitars.com** is a great source of free information about the history of both Gibson and Epiphone. Fox Guitars also offers period-correct vintage replacement parts with an emphasis on pickguards for Gibson guitars and mandolins, plus those for Epiphone guitars as well. Beginning in the summer of 2016, Fox Guitars will also be offering a whole new line of other vintage replacement parts including intricately engraved pickguards, custom truss rod covers, mother-of-pearl and abalone inlay for fingerboards and headstock overlays and much more.

Please visit www.fox-guitars.com to see all of our products.

My sincere thanks and gratitude to all those who helped make this book possible.

Walter Carter, Roger Siminoff, Mike Newton, Rod McDonald, Alex Merrill and The Kalamazoo Public Library, Sarah Humes and The Kalamazoo Valley Museum, George Gruhn, Mark at Folkway Music, Lowell Levinger, Peter at Retrofret, Steve at Elderly Instruments, Buzz Levine at Lark Street Music, Alison Jay at Mandolin Brothers, Frank Ford at Gryphon Strings, Dan Beimborn, Darryl Wolfe, Joyce Brumbaugh, David Grisman, Rick Van Krugel, David Harvey, Tom Crandall, Jim Garber, Greig Hutton, Dick Boak and The Martin Archives and Ron Middlebrook.

Cover photo by William Ritter, courtesy of Gruhn Guitars

This book is dedicated to all Gibson-ites everywhere.

Table of Contents

Foreword

Gibson's role in the history of the mandolin is evident just by looking at mandolins of the late 1800s and mandolins of today. In the 1890s, as the mandolin was becoming the most popular fretted instrument in America, there were thousands of Italian-style bowlbacks and maybe a dozen Gibsons. Nowadays, bowlbacks are viewed as archaic conversation pieces – aka "wallhangers" – while the overwhelming majority of mandolin music is played on mandolins with an arched top and a symmetrical, pear-shaped body or a body with a scroll on the upper bass bout. In other words, most of the mandolins you see today are either Gibsons or they look like Gibsons.

It's a compelling story – how one company's instruments came to dominate an entire genre of American instruments – and Paul Fox tells it with a thorough chronicle of Gibson's models. Moreover, he digs deeper, going beyond production dates and specifications to provide insight and new information on the design of these mandolins, the people who made them, and even the various components of the instruments.

With The Complete Guide to Gibson Mandolins, Fox continues the fine research and presentation of historical material he is already known for, through his website and his previous book, *The Other Brands of Gibson*. As with all of Fox's work, this book is not only an excellent reference, it's a good read, too.

Walter Carter

Walter Carter is the author of *Gibson Guitars: 100 Years of an American Icon* and the proprietor of Carter Vintage Guitars in Nashville.

Introduction

In 2014, the Gibson Company celebrated the 120th anniversary of the most iconic musical instrument manufacturer in history. However, had it actually been 120 years since the company started? The answer is definitely no. The reason for this was derived from some original instruments built by Orville H. Gibson himself that are still in the possession of the company to this very day. They have plaques with the 1894 inscribed on them but the date has never been verified. As a company, Gibson was actually founded in 1902 by five investors who bought the rights to Orville H. Gibson's mandolin patent and instrument designs. The Complete Guide to Gibson mandolins, mandolas, mando-cellos and mando-basses proves conclusively that Orville H. Gibson starting building instruments much earlier than 1894 and it contains the most comprehensive account of his early career as an instrument maker.

Avid Gibson enthusiasts or "Gibson-ites" will also find the most complete collection of historical information ever assembled about the wide array of Gibson instruments in the mandolin family that have truly fascinated so many. For the casual reader, who may only be somewhat familiar with Gibson or their well-known F-5 mandolin, this book is not just a collection of data and pictures but tells the whole story about Gibson from the very beginning right. It answers some of the decades-old questions about the origins of Gibson including when Orville actually started making musical instruments. Who the made the "Handel" tuners? What did Lloyd Loar actually did while working for the company. It chronicles the growth of a company that started from a small one-man shop to a 160,000 square foot factory that made over 200 different kinds of musical instruments.

In addition to all the general information about these incredible instruments, this book also reveals some of the secrets behind many of the manufacturing methods used by Gibson throughout the decades, most of which have never been previously disclosed. Years of research has been culminated into this book's contents which are all well-documented, comprehensive and complete. It also contains information that has come from many of the world's leading authorities on the subject. There is also a large full-color section that contain some of rarest instruments known to exist including many custom-made and prototype models and many of the instruments built by Orville Gibson's own hands. As many of the world's greatest mandolin players and builders alike will tell you, no company has ever produced better mandolins than Gibson. Their legendary designs remain the most copied mandolins in the worl, from other large manufacturers all over the world to the small high-end boutique builders that number in the hundreds. The best mandolin players like Bill Monroe, Dave Apollon, James "Yank" Rachell, David Grisman, Ricky Skaggs and so many more always played Gibsons.

The most amazing thing about Gibson is the sheer breadth and depth of the instruments they have manufactured for more than a century. Not only their incredible mandolins, mandolas, mando-cellos and mando-basses but archtop and flat-top acoustic guitars, harp-guitars, banjos, ukuleles, archtop electric guitars, semi-hollow body electric guitars, solid body electric guitars and basses and many, many more. No other American musical instrument manufacturer can even compare themselves to Gibson, not only in terms of the number of different instruments, but the remarkable design innovations that makes Gibson such an iconic name. Even when studying just one type of Gibson instrument like their mandolins there were so many changes in designs, models, finishes, ornamentation right down to the finest details, that it is nearly impossible to cover every single nuance. However this book goes into great detail in hope of providing a complete and comprehensive source of information about these wonderful instruments.

 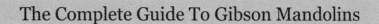

A Brief History of the Mandolin

The mandolin as we know it today is an eight-string fretted musical instrument with the strings in four pairs of unison strings tuned like a violin – G, D. A, E low to high. The mandolin is actually a descendant of the mandola and the name "mandolin" or "mandolino" in Italian, means "small mandola". The mandola's name is derived from the Italian word "mandoria" which translates as almond, undoubtedly a description of the shape of the body of the instrument. The mandola is a descendant of the lute, the first known fretted stringed instrument that can be traced back to the sevent century.

Prior to the 18th century there were dozens of other musical instruments that were variations of the lute that were being developed in other parts of Europe, Asia, and the Middle East. They include the mandura and mandore which were smaller treble lutes. The bandora, a large long-necked plucked string-instrument; and the gittern, a small gut string round-backed instrument that first appears in the 13th century in several parts of Europe. It was also called the guitarra in Spain, guiterne or guiterre in France, the chitarra in Italy and quintern in Germany. These are mostly considered to be ancestors of the modern guitar although their construction was similar to the 18th century mandola. In Arabian countries, there was the dambura and pandura. There is a bit of controversy about the name mandola, because the instrument has also been called the vandola in Spanish and mandörgen in German. However, for the purposes of this chapter, the focus will be on the Neapolitan instruments.

The mandola and mandolin were developed in Italy in the 17th and 18th centuries, primarily in Naples. The mandolin is to the mandola what the violin is to the viola, a smaller soprano or higher pitched version. Similar instruments were also being made by others in Italy, including the great Antonio Stradivari from Cremona Italy, who designed and built several variations of the instrument. The Neapolitan or bowl-back mandolin as we know it today was perfected by the Vinaccia family, in particular Giuseppe and Antonio Vinaccia.

One of the most significant differences of the Neapolitan mandolin design was that it used metal strings and was played with a plectrum or pick. Prior to its development, stringed instruments primarily used gut strings and were plucked with the fingers. These earlier instruments had a very soft tone and were generally played without accompaniment so they could be heard. In great contrast, the Neapolitan mandolin had a bright ringing tone and was much louder than its predecessors. This allowed the mandolin to be played in an ensemble with other instruments and even with a full orchestra. In the 18th century, many classical composers including Vivaldi and Mozart began writing music specifically for the mandolin. Mozart's legendary opera "Don Giovanni" contained some complex parts featuring the mandolin, including the accompaniment to the famous aria "Deh vieni alla finestra." The mandola and mandolin also became very popular in Italian folk music. Traditional songs like the tarantella were played using a rapid plectrum strumming technique called tremolo.

1779 Neapolitan mandolin made by Giovanni Vinaccia
Courtesy of Lorenzo Frignani

The Neapolitan mandolin is constructed from curved strips of hardwood wood or staves that make up the back or bowl of the body. It usually has a "canted" or bent soundingboard made of spruce. This design helps support the increased tension of metal strings, rather than gut strings. It has a hardwood fingerboard that held metal frets and was glued to the neck. The strings attached at the top of the instrument to tuners or tuning pegs, which are mounted on the peghead or headstock. At the bottom, strings attach to a tailpiece mounted on the body and are suspended between the nut and the bridge.

The Neapolitan Mandolin

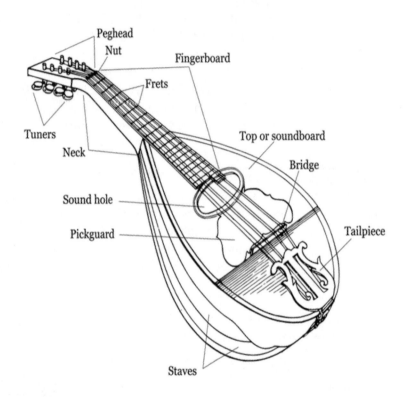

The Mandolin in America

In 1861 all the city states and regions of Italy were unified under one flag. Unfortunately economic conditions worsened in many parts of southern Italy and Sicily. This in turn caused millions of rural Italians to flee their homeland and seek a better life elsewhere. From 1880 to 1920, an estimated 4 million Italian immigrants came to the United States. America was the land of opportunity and was the main destination for Italian immigrants settling in the New York metropolitan area and Boston, but also Philadelphia, Chicago, Cleveland, Detroit, and Buffalo. Of course these Italian immigrants brought their cultural heritage wigth them, but it was not the aristocratic culture of Dante and Michelangelo, it was the poorer immigrant culture from smaller regions or villages. The various regional cultures had many similarities and established the basis of contemporary Italian-American life. Italian food and music still remain staples of modern America and what instrument is most closely associated with Italians? The mandolin.

Bohmann", a well-known violin maker. The date was 1883 or 1884. Partee, who was a mandolinist himself, noted that Bohmann's mandolins were larger than those imported from Europe, but also said that these early Bohmann mandolins were rather "crude" as compared to the instruments he made in the 1890s. Bohmann never patented his instruments, so it's hard to verify the date when he made his first mandolins.

The first patent for an American-made mandolin was awarded to George B. Durkee in September 1887 (Patent No. 370,732). Actually, the patent was just for improvements in the construction of the Neapolitan bowl-back mandolin that had been around since the 18th century. Durkee wanted to simplify the process of assembling the body of the mandolin using a metal form, as well as attaching each of the staves using clamps and internal braces instead of glue. He also claimed that eliminating the use of a paper or cloth backing material inside the body impeded the mandolin's tone. .

Joseph Bohmann c1885

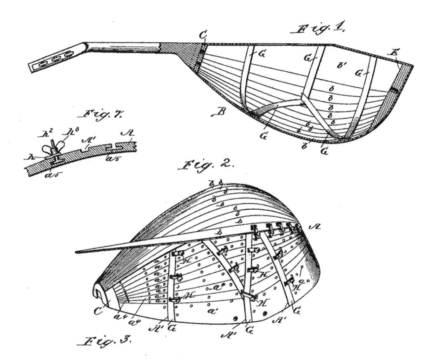

George Durkee was a prolific inventor and a brilliant engineer who patented many inventions for everything from improvements for mortising machines (Patent No. 152,473) to a machine for manufacturing barbed wire (Patent No. 281,653). In 1886, Durkee went to work for the Lyon & Healy Company in Chicago and was responsible for designing and patenting several musical instruments including a snare drum, zither, banjo and first American-made harp which L&H still manufactures to this day. Lyon & Healy had been importing and selling fretted musical instruments for many years, but were dissatisfied with their quality and decided to start manufacturing their own. They built a factory devoted to manufacturing musical instruments in 1885 and by 1886 or 1887, they were producing many different instruments including three different mandolin models. Lyon & Healy decided to call their new American-made mandolins "Washburn" named after George Washburn Lyon, co-founder of the company.

Enter the Spanish Students

The popularity of the mandolin in America is widely credited to a group called Estudiantina Fígaro Espanola or the "Figaro Spanish Students" (pictured above). They were already a sensation in Europe where they toured extensively giving

concerts. Their first performance in the United States was in 1879 when they appeared at Niblo's Garden, a theatre on Broadway in New York City (right). However the original group actually played bandurrias, a Spanish instrument that had six pairs of strings, plus guitars, a violin and cello Later, a copy-cat group was formed by Signor Carlos Curti, an accomplished Italian-American mandolinist. Curti had to use mandolins instead of bandurrias and used Italian-Americans instead of Spaniards. Since he was a mandolinist and could teach the members of the group how to play, he named the group the "Curti Spanish Students" and was quoted in 1899 as saying that "this bogus Spanish Students made a hit through the states." They had a tremendous impact wherever they played

and spawned a large number of other imitators. Since Curti's group actually played mandolins, they should rightly be credited with popularizing the instrument in America. Soon after mandolinists and mandolin groups began popping up all over the United States, particularly in cities like New York, Boston and Chicago where large numbers of Italian immigrants lived. It wasn't long before American musical instrument manufacturers recognized the growing demand for instruments in the mandolin family and stopped importing European instruments and started making their own. In an article published in 1902, in an issue of *The Cadenza* magazine, the author and publisher Clarence Partee, stated that "the first mandolin made in America was turned out in Chicago by Joseph Bohmann."

Signor Carlos Curti

By the 1890s, dozens of American manufacturers started making mandolins. They include F.H. Newell and C. Bruno & Sons, who actually called their instruments the "mandoline". C. Bruno & Sons was most likely the first American maker to produce a flat-back mandolin, a design that eliminated the Neapolitan bowl-back feature. H.A. Weymann & Son of Philadelphia made mandolins, manodolas and probably the first American-made mandolin-banjo, an instrument that had the body of a banjo and the neck of a mandolin. J.W. Jenkins of Kansas City, Missouri introduced the Harwood brand of musical instruments including guitars and mandolins. Their mandolins were very ornate with inlaid designs of mother-of-pearl, abalone, tortoise-shell and other materials. A.C. Fairbanks was a well-established banjo manufacturer but started making mandolins as early as 1894. There was also the Stratton brand, Biehl, W.A. Cole (Cole and Fairbanks joined forces in the 1880s), and John C. Haynes & Company, makers of the Baystate brand. Martin, the oldest American musical instrument manufacturer, didn't start making mandolins until the late 1890s. Others were experimenting with completely new designs like the Merrill aluminum mandolin, made by the Aluminum Musical Instrument Company.

With few exceptions, most of these new American-made mandolins were just copies of the Neapolitan or bowl-back mandolin. That is, until a clerk from Kalamazoo, Michigan came along.

Above right: 1894 Washburn ad. Below right: A page from an 1890 C. Bruno & Sons catalog. Courtesy of Jim Garber

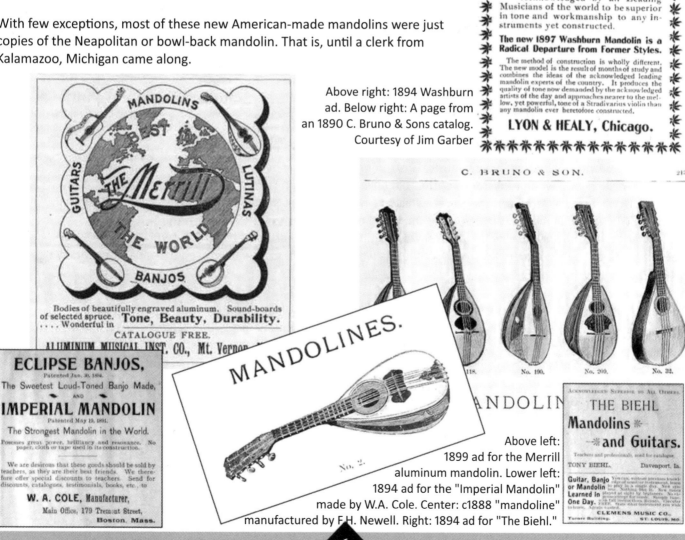

Above left: 1899 ad for the Merrill aluminum mandolin. Lower left: 1894 ad for the "Imperial Mandolin" made by W.A. Cole. Center: c1888 "mandoline" manufactured by F.H. Newell. Right: 1894 ad for "The Biehl."

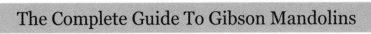

Orville H. Gibson – In the Beginning

Much has been written about Orville H. Gibson and yet to this day, no one knows for sure what the "H" stands for. Recently uncovered and well-documented information calls into question the validity of most of what has been widely accepted about Orville's life before the formation of the company that has carried his name for well over a century. Previously, most sources stated that he was born in 1856 in a small town in upstate New York called Chateaugay (pronounced like shadow-gay), came to Kalamazoo, Michigan sometime in the 1880s and started building musical instruments n 1894. This is all incorrect. Even the year of his birth may be wrong as all of the birth records that were recorded between 1850 and 1870 have been lost and an 1860 U.S. Census listed Orville as being six years old, making his date of birth 1854. The accuracy of the census information is somehwhat questionable because it lists "Orvil P" as the youngest of the five children of John W. and Emma Gibson and his brother Ozro's name is spelled wrong as "Asro." A very interesting and revealing article written by Henry Dornbush

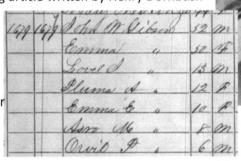

that was originally dated 1918 turns out to be the only first-hand account of Orville Gibson's life before 1900. In it Dornbush states that "I knew Orville when I was a boy and was in my teens." Dornbush was 19 years younger than Orville, so he was referring to the period between 1888 and 1895. His knowledge of when the older man

Above: c1880 portrait of a young Orville Gibson
Left: 1860 U.S. Census of the Gibson family

came to Kalamazoo and started making musical instruments must have been gleaned from several visits to Orville's shop and being regaled with wonderful stories of the "old days" by a veteran luthier. Dornbush also said that he knew Orville when he [Orville] was a clerk in a shoe store," which we now know was sometime between 1879 and 1891. It was also Dornbush who said that Orville was designing and building musical instruments "back in the 1870s and 80s," but also stated that "as a hobby or side line he [Orville] would utilize every opportunity to carve or whittle a piece of wood." For the longest time those who were aware of Dornbush's written account merely dismissed these dates as totally fictitious. But were they?

Next Stop Kalamazoo
Startling new evidence has conclusively proved that Dornbush was right about the dates, and in fact, Orville came to Kalamazoo much earlier than the 1880s and starting building instruments an estimated 10 years before anyone thought he did. Orville actually came to Michigan in 1873 when he was just 17 years old. More than likely, he came to Kalamazoo when his brother Lovel got married on March 16, 1873 to a gal named Hattie Morgan who was a Kalamazoo native. There is also one rather cryptic mention of Orville Gibson from a local newspaper that said simply "List of Letters – December 16, 1873." What Dornbush had written was just a bit confusing because it's likely that when Orville said he used to carve and whittle while not working at the shoe store, it was in back in the late 1870s and early 1880s. The first significant full-time job the young man got was working at A.P. Sprague's shoe store, originally located at 72 East Main Street in Kalamazoo. He was apparently a very good shoe salesman and by November 1879 ads started to appear in local newspapers featuring "O. H. Gibson – Salesman."

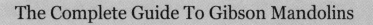

Apparently, "Fine Kid and Pebble Goat Buttons" were all the rage back then. Orville wound up working at the shoe store for over 10 years

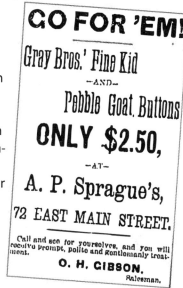

The New York Central Railroad had built a line to Kalamazoo in 1863, so it would have been easy for Orville to get there from upstate New York. He must have liked this thriving new city and wound up staying there for nearly 40 years. Orville liked Kalamazoo and Central Michigan in general. One reason was the multitude of furniture making and other wooden products manufacturing companies in that region. He was known for using a lot of reclaimed lumber for carving and there would have been dozens of places he could get old furniture or architectural salvage. Any number of lumber mills had cut-offs (short pieces lumber mills would discard or sell cheap). For someone who loved woodworking it was paradise. Another reason he must have been attracted to Kalamazoo was its growing theatre and performing arts community, something a small farming town certainly didn't offer. Some unsubstantiated information has suggested that he may have had relatives already living in Kalamazoo, but tracing his exact family tree has proved to be impossible.

The Guitar Player
The first mention of O. H. Gibson in print after 1873 was a review of a concert and variety show that took place in 1876. The April 6, 1879 edition of The *Kalamazoo Daily Telegraph* gave a rousing review of a show that took place the previous night and it described one of the acts as a vaudeville routine based on the story of William Tell, the legendary archer, with "O. A. Gibson" as a spectator in the scene. It also said that a song called "An Emerald Gem worth Erin" was "capitally sung in character by Gibson as Paddy." The truly astonishing thing is where the article talks about an orchestral piece near the end of the show with "O. H. Gibson" listed as one of two guitarists! Clearly the first instance where he was referred to as "O. A. Gibson" was a typo and all three mentions were referring to the same person. This new information reveals that at the age of 20 Orville was already an accomplished performer, singer, and guitar player. Dornbush's story also suggests that Orville was skilled woodworker as well, but what remains a mystery is where Orville learned music and how to play guitar. It is not out of the realm of possibility that he was somewhat of a youthful prodigy and had shown exceptional musical talent at an early age.

Henry Dornbush

As a side note Henry Dornbush is a very interesting character in Gibson history both during Orville's early career and also after the formation of the Gibson Company. He was a professional photographer and had a studio only a few doors down from Orville's workshop in the 1890s. The aforementioned article was finally published many years later in a 1937 issue of Gibson's in-house publication *Mastertone Magazine*. Dornbush became the Gibson Company's in-house photographer sometime around 1908 and later he even played the mandolin in a Gibson Company quintet that included two founding members, Lewis A. Williams and Sylvo Reams.

The Song and Dance Man
In the late 1870s and 1880s Orville was a charter member of an amusing-sounding group called "The Jolly Young Men's Unanimous Club" that was organized by Edgar E. Bartlett, a well-known local theatrical performer who was also mentioned prominently in the April 1876 newspaper review. The JYMUC was organized by Bartlett in 1874, so one could conclude that Orville joined the group when he was 18, only a year after he came to Kalamazoo.

In the 1880s, Orville performed regularly with several other local groups including the "Charity Minstrels" and "The Young Men's Musical Minstrels," and later he formed his own group called the "Orpheus Mandolin Club." He wasn't playing little honky-tonks but large theatres like the Academy of Music, a 1200-seat opera house, the largest such venue in Kalamazoo. He must have been the talk of the town as another newspaper clipping from September 1885, referred to him as "Prof. O. H. Gibson, the harpist," and yet another mentions him as part of a "mandolin and guitar duet," so it would appear that he was an accomplished multi-instrumentalist as well, playing guitar, mandolin and some kind of harp. An 1890 newspaper said that a group of other men "...and O. H. Gibson will be seen in their original song and dance, arranged by O. H. Gibson." A more prominent article was published February 18, 1893, entitled "Music and Jokes" with subtext that read, "The Musical Minstrels at the Academy" and "Ben Benallack and O. H. Gibson Make a Hit." Ben and Orville "rendered an excellent harp and mandolin duet and was loudly applauded being recalled." Even after the headline specifically mentioned "O. H." this particular reporter calls Orville "Chas. H. Gibson" when describing the duet later in the article. It also depicted an instrumental piece where "Misses Smith and O. H. Gibson with their mandolins, guitars and harps played excellent music and were recalled." Dare we ask, how many of these instruments Orville played? Maybe all three.

A Flare for the Dramatic

Apparently Orville's creativity knew no bounds. Two separate newspaper articles from 1889 stated that, "O. H. Gibson is constructing an elephant for the Charity Minstrels." Supposedly, it was a large mechanical elephant and Orville would be inside working various moving parts like the trunk. He arranged "a neat sketch song and dance" for other members of the Charity Minstrels that was described as being, "in the language of the Balloon Gallery Gods – it will be a 'pink'." One can only guess what that meant, but the article goes on to say that "D. M. [Daniel] Cohn and O. H. Gibson will introduce their trained elephant, 'Bolera'." Another newspaper article stated that, "the most ambitious undertaking of this sort is being planned by O. H. Gibson," and that "Mr. Gibson will have no less than 100 people on the stage of the Academy [of Music], forming a grand male chorus." Later in the article there's a wonderful depiction of the performance in which Orville's staging, "has the colonial in its makeup," including some of the solo performers in "full dress and white wigs." When the gigantic male chorus completed their part of the show, they remained seated on stage and specialty acts were paraded out in front of them, including vocal soloists, a trombone solo and a performance by the Grand Rapids Mandolin Orchestra. It must have been quite a spectacle indeed and certainly worth the price of admission.

Mr. O. A. Gibson has arranged a neat sketch song and dance for Bidwell, Sawyer, Drew and Davis, and it will be presented in the Charity Minstrel entertainment during the season, and in the language of the Balloon Gallery Gods it will be a "pink." D. M. Cohn and O. A. Gibson will introduce this season at the Charity Minstrels, their trained elephant, "Bolera."

One of seveal portraits taken of Orville wearing a fancy costume.

The Luthier

Webster's Dictionary lists luthier (pronounced lüt-ē-ər), as a noun derived from the French word "luth" or "lute," meaning one who makes stringed musical instruments (as violins and guitars) and the entry includes the date 1879. Someone must have invented that word just to describe a man like Orville H. Gibson. The most amazing new piece of information about his early life in Kalamazoo, that was only discovered very recently was a

Prof. O. H. Gibson, the harpist, went over to South Lyons Wednesday to assist Mrs. Scofield in an entertainment.

newspaper clipping from the *Kalamazoo Daily Telegraph* from October 17, 1888 and it stated:

"Mr. Orville Gibson of this city is not only a guitarist of more than ordinary merit, but a musical genius as well, and has conjured up several original instruments on which he performs skillfully. His latest production is a superbly finished guitar of a large size and peculiar form and arranged with a double set of strings. Inasmuch as Mr. Gibson made the instrument almost solely with the aid of a jackknife, the achievement is all the more remarkable."

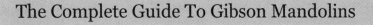

Yes, you read it right, a large and peculiar-shaped, multi-stringed guitar that Orville carved by hand in 1888! No other source of information has ever been able to put an exact date on when he built his first instrument, and for well over 100 years it was thought to be 1894. This could lead to the conclusion that he must have been building instruments for quite some time prior to 1888, since the guitar mentioned in the article was one of "several original instruments" Orville had made. It's therefore entirely possible that he started his career as a luthier in 1884 a full decade before anyone thought he made his first instrument. As anyone who has built or attempted to build a fretted musical instrument knows, nobody, not even Orville himself would have gotten it right the first time, and by the time you have completed four or five instruments you're just starting to get the hang of it.

An instrument as complex as a large hand-carved multi-stringed guitar would have been the work of an already accomplished luthier who had at least a few years of experience. The double-stringed guitar may also have been the first instrument Orville deemed worthy enough to be seen and played in public. It is also important to point out that in the Victorian era, things that were peculiar, odd or different were not considered attributes of people in polite society. Obviously Orville was not concerned about how polite society did things. Hewanted to break the mold and build wildly exotic and experimental instruments with radical new designs that were unusual, peculiar, but also bold, ambitious and beautiful. He was definitely pushing the envelope like no one had ever done before him. Further evidence to back up this supposition was found in a March 31, 1928 article from *The Music Trades* magazine which stated "It was back in 1885, that Orville Gibson opened the doors of his little shop in Kalamazoo." The July-August 1936 issue of *Mastertone Magazine* included an ad entitled "Half A Century of Carving" that stated "Almost 50 years ago Orville Gibson made his first carved top instrument. A mandolin." Could Orville have built his first mandolin in 1886?

The 1888 article clearly suggests that Orville was interested in building unconventional multi-stringed instruments and there are two existing Orville-built instruments that are proof of his willingness to experiment including a "peculiar"10-string instrument he made sometime in the early 1890s, but could possibly date to the late 1880s, and his very ornate 20-string harp-guitar built in 1894. Since Orville was a mandolin, harp and guitar player it seems to have been a natural progression to combine two instruments into one design.

Early Orville-built harp-guitar.
Courtesy of Gregg Miner

10-string guitar built by Orville Gibson sometime in the 1890s. Courtesy of Walter Carter

In August 1891, another newspaper story appeared that is also quite extraordinary. It read:

*"Orville Gibson has just completed a fine spruce guitar and the circular opening
[sound hole] is surrounded with inlaying of mother-of-pearl of exquisite workmanship.
It has taken his spare moments for eight months to do the work on the fine toned instrument."*

Wait, it gets even better. Another article from the November 7, 1892 edition of *The Daily Telegraph* reads:

> Mr. Orinville Gibson displayed last evening his most valuable and pure toned guitar, which was made entirely by himself. It is double the size of an ordinary guitar and as an expert piece of workmanship surpasses anything seen in this city. Mr. Gibson was offered $70 for it by a Grand Rapids firm but he values it at $100. The face of it is made of spruce, the back of cedar and the key board of sycamore.

Mr. Orinville [sic] Gibson displayed last evening his most valuable and pure toned guitar, which was made entirely by himself. It is double the size of an ordinary guitar and as an expert piece of workmanship surpasses anything seen in this city. Mr. Gibson was offered $70 for it by a Grand Rapids firm but he values it at $100. The face of it is made of spruce, the back of cedar and the key board of sycamore."

First of all, newspaper reporters never get anyone's name right. Secondly, it would appear that Orville had built many instruments that were not only much larger than other conventional designs, but were well-made, ornate and more importantly sounded good. This 1892 reference may have been one of the Orville-built guitar designs that became the more well-known factory-made Style "O" guitars of the early twentieth century (shown right). This begs the question: Could he have been experimenting with the idea of carving an arch in the tops and backs of his guitars as early as 1891? Anything is possible. This article also indicates that at the time, Orville was not interested in selling his instruments, but was only building them for himself.

"Orville Gibson has been engaged by the Barrows Music House, Saginaw to make guitars and mandolins exclusively for that firm. A mandolin which he recently made is beautifully inlaid, a central design of a butterfly in mother of pearl being quite exquisite. Mr. Gibson has adopted an entire new shape for the mandolin, what might be termed the half shell, perhaps. The result justifies the experiment as good judges say that his mandolins possess more resonance than any hereto made."

A "half shell?" It might have looked that way to this particular reporter, but most everyone who is reading this right now knows he was referring to the carved arch-top design that has made Orville Gibson a true legend. Strangely, there doesn't appear to be any other information about Barrows Music selling Gibson instruments other than this article. They were much more well-known as a piano retailer, so it's possible Orville thought twice about the agreement, and promptly pulled out of the whole deal. It doesn't appear that he was ready to start selling any instruments, let alone to a dealer. So one might ask: When did Orville start building mandolins? There is no concrete evidence that he had done so until 1895, ut could be as early as 1886. An August 9, 1895 newspaper article read that Orville had completed a mandolin in six weeks.

> O. H. Gibson has just completed a handsome mandolin which took him six weeks to make.

August 9, 1895 news article

 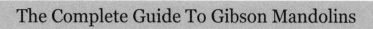

It is certain that O. H. started his own group, the aforementioned Orpheus Mandolin Club in 1894, and although there is no mention of him building a mandolin that early, it is safe to assume that he was playing one his own instruments in the group which means he started building mandolins sometime in 1894, or possibly earlier. The group, which was named after the mythological ancient Greek musician, poet and prophet, was very popular as numerous mentions of their performances appeared in local newspapers throughout the fall of 1894 into 1895 and beyond. Apparently, one of their songs was a little ditty called "Sick Indian Jig," but they also played more classical arrangements like waltzes, as well as accompaniment for other performers. It seems that sometime in 1895 Orville decided that he not only wanted to build instruments but sell them as well and he wanted to do it full-time.

Mr. Orville Gibson, who is at the head of the Musical minstrels, has shown THE TELEGRAPH a number of receipted bills and the statements of the amounts received in the box office during the performances of t[ ] minstrels two years ago. Claims havi[ ] been made that the money received fr[ ] the performances was not given to [ ] proper parties, Mr. Gibson wishes it unde[ ] stood that the receipted bills in his poss[ ] sion show positively that every dollar [ ] the money is properly accounted for. M[ ] Gibson says that the reports that have bee[ ] circulated have worked injury to him.

Feb. 19.—Opening day. Introductory remarks by Mayor J. W. Osborn and Col. E. M. Irish. Musical program in the evening in charge of Orville Gibson.

Orville Gibson has made a very fine lute for a lady in this city. The work occupied his spare time for six weeks. The tone of the instrument is excellent and it is beautifully finished. It is made of mahogany and other woods and the neck is beautifully inlaid with mother of pearl. The work was all done by hand.

stage. A. B. Sawyer, C. Holt, [ ] Drew and O. H. Gibson will be seen in their original song and dance, arranged by O. H. Gibson. That noble old Roman, Dr. Osborn, will deliver an

Orville H. Gibson – Musical Instrument Manufacturer

By 1892 Orville Gibson quit his full-time job at A.P. Sprague's shoe store and started working part-time at Butter's Restaurant so he could devote more time to instrument making. We do know that Orville hand-made various musical instruments of exceptional quality and craftsmanship. By 1895 he had built several guitars, at least one or two mandolins and harp-guitars, as well as a very large zither. In 1894 he also built a custom-made lute for a Kalamazoo customer that a September 17, 1894 article described as "made of mahogany and other woods and the neck is beautifully inlaid with mother of pearl." He was clearly a very gifted woodworker, but what's unclear is where he acquired those skills. Growing up in a rural area, Orville, like many other boys, probably had a pocket-knife and discovered how much fun it was carving pieces of wood.

c1896 photograph of Orville Gibson

The only known Orville-built concert zither with f-holes

Restless Luthier Syndrome (RLS)

Based on existing Kalamazoo city directories, Orville moved around a lot. He was listed at no fewer than seven different addresses between 1880 and 1895. Then in 1896, Orville set up a small workshop in his apartment in the rear of 114 South Burdick Street and the city directory now listed him as "manufacturer musical instruments." This must have been when he decided to start building instruments full time but within a year he needed more room and moved again to the second floor of 104 East Main Street (now called Michigan Avenue) sometime after March 1897. This location was big enough for both his residence and workshop and he stayed there for several years. Business must have been pretty good and it prompted him to place an ad in the Kalamazoo city directory which showed his newly patented mandolin. This is the only known advertisement for Orville's new business venture.

The Gibson Mandolin

was not on exhibition at the World's Fair but it is a world beater nevertheless.

Manufactured by Orville H. Gibson, 104 S. Main St.

Gibson Orville H. clk. bds 203 w South.

Gibson Orville H, clerk A P Sprague, bds 209 W Lovell.

bson Amos N. lab., bds. 899 Douglas Ave.
"   James W. att. Asylum.
"   John W. att. Asylum, res. 824 Village.
"   Linda, waitress, 107 E. Main.
"   Orville H. clerk, bds. 214 W. Main.

Gibson Cyrus,* lab. 232 E. Frank.
"   John W.* emp. Asylum, 824 Village.
"   Maggie M. Miss, 232 E. Frank.
"   Nancy Mrs. (wid.) 512 W. Walnut.
"   Orville H. clerk, 318 S. Burdick.

Above: Kalamazoo business directory listings from 1883 to 1896. Left: Orville Gibson's first advertisement placed in the 1897 Kalamazoo directory showing his newly patented mandolin. Courtesy of the Kalamazoo Public Library

O. H. Gibson – Violin Maker

There is the possibility that in addition to the instruments mentioned so far, Orville was also building violins. Julius Bellson, who was the Gibson Company's in-house historian for many years, stated in his 1973 book *The Gibson Story,* that before the turn of the century Orville had "won merited acclaim" for making a violin. A small article published in 1906 tells a remarkable story of Orville building a violin for world-renowned violinist Jan Kubelik. It also states that Gibson had made "many" violins and selected a special one for Kubelik as a gift. Yet another article published in the *Music Trade Review* in 1925 recounted the history of Gibson and referred to Orville's early career as "a violin maker and repairman." Unfortunately, no examples of these violins are known to exist, but there are numerous accounts of Orville's love for building violins. However, these printed news articles date to after the formation of the Gibson Company in the years 1903-1906. In the only known photograph of Orville's workshop there's a clearly visible violin body form is hanging on the wall. If Orville began making violins before 1895 then maybe it was the inspiration for his creative break-through that led to his most well-known invention, the carved top mandolin. It is clear that Orville had been working on and perfecting this radical new concept for quite a while because he actually filed for his mandolin patent on May 11, 1895. This supports the theory that he began building carved mandolins in 1894 or even earlier. It also suggests that he was applying this design to other instruments as well, but it appears that his mandolins were so sensational that he realized it was essential to secure the rights to this design as soon as possible.

The only known photograph of Orville Gibson's workshop at 104 East Main Street Kalamazoo. (V) violin body form;
(A) three Style "A" mandolins; (F) three Style "F" mandolins; (L) two templates for the lyre-mandolins;
(G) two arch-top guitars; (U) unknown guitar; (U2) possible Orville-built lute

The Patent

Finally, after nearly three years, O. H. Gibson was awarded his one and only patent on February 1, 1898 simply titled "Mandolin." The patent confirms that Orville knew he had invented something new and revolutionary and that he was using this new method of building instruments for "guitars, mandolas, and lutes." The patent contains some very important information about how he viewed his design versus the conventional mandolins that were essentially the same as those made in Italy beginning in the 18th century. He immediately criticized the design of the Neapolitan bowl-back mandolin by stating in the patent description that they "have been constructed of too many separate parts, bent or carved, glued or veneered and provided with internal braces, bridges and splices to that extent that they have not possessed that degree of sensitive resonance and vibratory action necessary to produce the power and quality of tone and melody found in the use of the instrument below described." He further states that "the object of this invention is to correct those objections and attain the results above." One of the oddest things about his patent is that figure 3 at the top clearly shows an arched top as well as an arched back, while figure 2 shows a more flat back in the shape of a "frying pan." All of the existing mandolins made by Orville were carved with the design in figure 2, so the reason for this inconsistency is unclear.

Orville was known for having great contempt for his competition and was quoted as saying that "they wouldn't know which end of a board to notch to make a boot jack." Conversely, he was clearly excited about his new invention describing it as being "alive at every touch of the instrument." His mandolin design had a rim (or sides), neck and headstock that were all carved from a single piece of wood in a manner that retained the grain pattern they occupied in their natural growth. His mandolins had absolutely no internal braces, blocks or supports, unlike the bowl-back mandolins, as he believed that any of these internal parts would impede the tone of the instrument. Orville carved the top and back pieces so their "resonance and vibratory qualities will be in accord with those of the integral rim, neck and head."

Another unusual feature of Orville's mandolins was an additional hollowed out neck cavity, which supposedly extended the resonating air chamber of the body. So, other than the fingerboard, strings, bridge and tailpiece, his mandolins had only three basic parts. Toward the end of the patent description, Orville seems to run out of ways to describe how great his new invention is and stated, "just the degree and the graduation of the thickness of parts comes to an expert almost intuitively by long practice and cannot be communicated to another in words." Obviously he felt like the average person couldn't even comprehend the magnitude of this radical new design.

The "graduation" of the parts referred to how he would carve the top and back so that the middle was thicker and would gradually get thinner toward the edges, just like a violin. Henry Dornbush said that Orville would "tap them with his knuckles" and then continue carving until the pieces produced their optimum tone and were "in tune with each other." This technique is now commonly referred to as "tap tuning" and Orville was probably the first American luthier to ever use this technique. It is important to note that he accomplished all of this without the use of any power tools and every part was hand-made using basic woodworking tools like chisels, gouges, rasps, saws and sandpaper.

Hollow neck design used by Orville Gibson. Courtesy of Rick Van Krugel

Orville Goes Green

Orville was fond of using reclaimed wood like old furniture and salvaged architectural woodwork in order to obtain high-quality hardwoods like walnut and mahogany. He also liked old seasoned wood because it was stable, dry and easy to work with, but also because it was readily available. Dornbush also said that Orville built him an "F" style mandolin out of black walnut that was salvaged from an old building in Kalamazoo. A news article from 1905 described how Orville used "spar wood" to build a one of his violins using the "true Maggini pattern." A spar is the mast of a sailing ship and Orville was able to procure a 100-year-old piece for the violin. Giovanni Paolo Maggini (1580 - 1632), is considered one of the great Italian masters of violin making, and apparently Orville was copying the carving pattern of a Maggini violin for his design. The article also contains another reference that Orville used some 90-year-old wood from an old town hall very close to his hometown in upstate New York to build one of his mandolins.

USED SPAR OF OLD SHIP

Violin on True Maggini Pattern Is Made from Century — Seasoned Wood by Kalamazoo Man.

A violin made of spar wood from an old sailing vessel said to date back more than a century has been turned out by O. H. Gibson for George Newell, leader of the Academy orchestra. The instrument is one of the finest examples of Mr. Gibson's workmanship, and is modelled after an original Maggini so accurately that experts have declared it to have the true Maggini quality of tone, mellow and sweet, with great carrying power. Mr. Newell is rather proud of his possession, which he says will make a fine solo instrument, the best he has ever played upon.

The latest piece of timber which Mr. Gibson proposes to work up into musical instruments is some of old wood taken from the town hall in Malone, N. Y., where it had seen for 90 years. A beautiful rich brown varnish is used in bringing the curly grain of this wood to the advantage.

The Master Luthier

The existing photo of Orville's workshop clearly shows that he made two styles of mandolins, as well as a very unusual lyre-shaped mandolin. The lyre-shaped mandolin was so unusual that it is further evidence that Orville was a creative genius and willing to experiment with ground-breaking designs. The two styles of mandolins he designed were the "A," which was basically the same design shown in his patent illustration, and "F" or "Artist," which was a more complex asymmetrical design including a large scroll on the upper treble bout of the body, a hook and scroll headstock shape, and three points that protruded from the rim (one on top and two on the bottom). Most likely, Orville did not use the "A" and "F" designa= tions, but did refer to the Style "F" as the "Artist Model." No one really knows how Orville came up with the "F" style mandolin or when he built the first one partly because he never patented this design even though it was very different from the "A." It's possible that he simply couldn't afford to file for another patent(s), as he was just starting out. These two designs would become the basis for all Gibson mandolins, mandolas, and mando-cellos for the next 115 years, and probably will be well into the future.

c1900 Orville "Artist" mandolin with star and moon inlay on heastock. Courtesy of Walter Carter

c1899 Orville Style "A" mandolin with butterfly guard-plate design. Courtesy of Walter Carter

Orville used a variety of woods for his instruments and made the back, rim, neck and headstock from hardwoods such as mahogany, birch, maple and walnut. The tops were usually spruce, but sometimes cedar. He used different finishes staining the instruments dark brown or orange, but he was particularly fond of a black finish. He probably used a clear shellac or varnish, which he applied over the stain as a clear top coat. He added many decorative features to his instruments including inlaid mother-of-pearl of various shapes and designs, inlaid tortoise-shell guard-plates or pickguards with intricate inlaid designs made of pearl, abalone and other materials. Around the body he added ornate edging or binding of alternating dark and light materials, usually white pearl and ebony. On his harp-guitar he carved a beautiful scroll-shaped relief on the front of the headstock, the fingerboard had mother-of-pearl flowers, vases and goddesses. Orville also seemed to be very fond of an inlaid crescent moon and star design that would adorn the headstock of most of his instruments. Henry Dornbush claimed that Gibson got his pearl inlay from a Turkish company in Grand Rapids, Michigan, which is where that design came from.

Orville affixed a label inside the body of some of his instruments and early examples simply stated "Made by O. H. Gibson – Kalamazoo, Michigan." Some were professionally printed and others were simply hand-written. Some included a picture of his newly patented mandolin and "The Gibson Mandolins and Guitars" was added. His most recognizable label featured a picture of Orville himself framed inside his lyre-mandolin with a little more marketing flare like "acknowledged by leading artists as world beaters" and "correct scale – easy to play – beautiful model – powerful tone." The "lyre label" design wound up being used by the Gibson Company for many years after that.

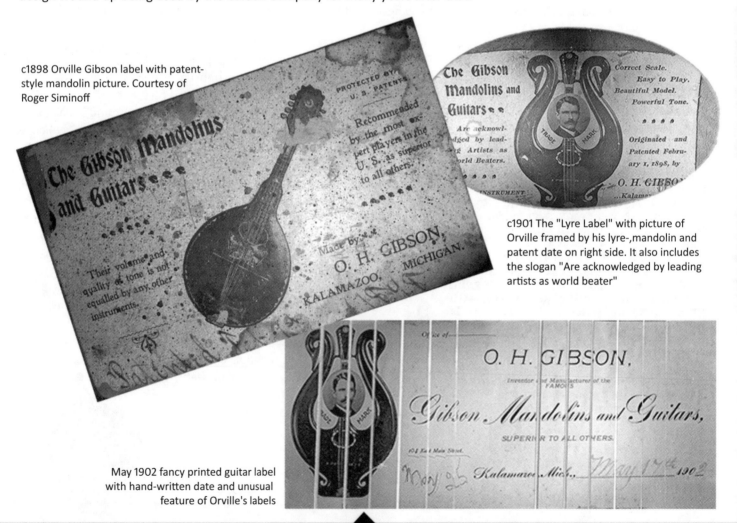

c1898 Orville Gibson label with patent-style mandolin picture. Courtesy of Roger Siminoff

c1901 The "Lyre Label" with picture of Orville framed by his lyre-,mandolin and patent date on right side. It also includes the slogan "Are acknowledged by leading artists as world beater"

May 1902 fancy printed guitar label with hand-written date and unusual feature of Orville's labels

Worldwide Recognition

During the period of time from 1895 to 1902, Orville was clearly at the pinnacle of his career and it wasn't long before his instruments were getting noticed by not only mandolinists all over the United States, but also around the world. Various newspaper clippings referred to Orville's mandolins as "world beaters" and his instruments were "acknowledged by the best experts in the United States as superior to all others." In 1900, he was awarded a gold medal and diploma by the Parisian Academy of Inventors, and the newspaper article about it mentions that "O. H. Gibson, the mandolin maker and inventor is constantly in receipt of letters and congratulatory remarks from musicians who know and appreciate his fine instruments."

GETS A GOLD MEDAL.

O. H. Gibson Honored by the Parisian Academy of Inventors.

O. H. Gibson, the mandolin maker and inventor, is constantly in receipt of letters and congratulatory remarks from musicians who know and appreciate his fine instruments. His skill is expended in a great variety of musical instruments and he holds letters patent covering his peculiar construction of the mandolin, mandola, lute, and guitar, all of which he makes of special design. The latest compliment to his genius is a communication which has recently arrived from the secretary of the Parisian Academy of Inventors stating that he had been elected to honorary membership, which carries with it an award of the first class of a great medal and diploma.

CITY IN BRIEF.

Gibson mandolin is a world beater.
Carpet opening—Gilmore's—all next week.
Did you read Rosenbaum & Speyers' ad.
O. H. Gibson's mandolins lead them all.
Fine custom shoes and repairing at Whipple's.

March 1897 newspaper clipping

In 1898 the *Kalamazoo Gazette* published an article about Orville sending a "12-string harp-guitar" to be entered in a competition against other well-known brands. The adjudicator, who was considered to be "one of the foremost guitar experts," had written to Orville that "he considers his [Orville's] instrument superior to an 18-string Washburn and a 12-string Bowman." In a November 1900 newspaper article, a well-known harp-guitarist, Professor Joseph Bistolfi, ordered a harp-guitar and Bistolfi was quoted as saying that "his [Orville's] was beyond compare." Orville may have been a one-man operation but was getting worldwide recognition.

O. H. Gibson of this city recently sent to Rochester, N. Y., a 12-string harp guitar to be entered in a competitive examination. Leo B. Moore, who is one of the foremost guitar experts, played the instruments in a theater; and he writes to Mr. Gibson that he considers his instrument superior to an 18-string Harwood valued at $150, and to a 12 string Washburn and a 12-string Bowman valued at $125 and $100 respectively.

December 1898 news clipping about Orville's harp-guitar being named "superior" to others

Up until very recently it was not known if Orville actually designed and built all of the various instruments that appeared in the Gibson Company's first catalog, but the harp-guitar articles as well as all of the previously mentioned information proves beyond a shadow of a doubt that Orville was responsible for designing every instrument that appeared in The Gibson Company's first catalog were in fact illustrated from existing instruments made by Orville himself.

GIBSON'S INSTRUMENTS

Subject of Compliment by New York Musicians.

A fine compliment for the musical instruments manufactured by O. H. Gibson of Kalamazoo is contained in a letter from Prof. Joseph Bistolfi and Louis C. Colombo of New York for whom Mr. Gibson made a harp guitar and an artist's mandolin during their recent visit in Kalamazoo and Battle Creek. The letter which accompanied a fine photograph of the two players and their instruments is as follows:

To O. H. Gibson:—

The peerless maker of musical instruments whose work is beyond compare and distinctly his own conception, thus blending the highest achievement of acoustic and artistic results.

Proud and delighted with the instruments he has made for us, we beg to offer him this slight token of our grateful acknowledgement with our best wishes for highly merited success and general recognition.

Admiringly and respectfully,
PROF. JOSEPH BISTOLFI,
LOUIS C. COLOMBO,
1214 Broadway, N. Y.

Jan. 15, 1902.

As his instruments began to draw a lot of attention, it appears that Orville was simply not equipped to handle the increasing demand. It seems that he did not foresee the possibility of mass producing his instruments and greatly disliked the idea altogether. He firmly believed that his instruments had to be hand-made, one at a time. Every known example of his work indicates that Orville never built any instrument the same way twice. Supposedly, a Boston-based company inquired about ordering 500 instruments and Orville's response was that it would cost them $100.00 per instrument and take 500 years for delivery. According to Dornbush's account as well as a newspaper article, it took Orville about six weeks to build a mandolin, and even longer to build a guitar.

His harp-guitars were so complex that it took at least three months to build one. This would indicate that his yearly output was roughly eight to ten instruments, but could have been as low as four or five. It simply wasn't enough to keep up with the orders he was receiving.

The Proposition

In 1902 a group of investors approached Orville with a proposition to start a company that would manufacture his instruments on a much larger scale. They paid him $2,500.00 for the rights to his patent and all of his instrument designs, an amount roughly equivalent to only $70,000.00* today . So, why did Orville accept such a modest amount of money for a lifetime of work? Orville was in his 50s and may have viewed this opportunity as an early retirement. He could free himself from the arduous tasking of trying to keep up with the huge demand for his instruments. From all of the accounts of his interest in building violins, he simply wanted to do something different. The newly formed company seemed only to retain Orville's services as a consultant and he had little or no input as to the day-to-day operations of the factory. He was neither included as a member of the board of directors nor as an officer of the company and only a short time after this the company decided he would only get paid for the time he worked at the factory. This gives the distinct impression that Orville spent little time there and he quickly became disillusioned with the whole idea of being an employee of a company he didn't control. Based on the fact that he had total disdain for the idea of mass producing his instruments, it is also likely that he simply wanted no part of the company that now bore his name. However, recently discovered documents paint a much more ominous picture.

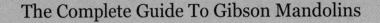

The hand-written first draft of the Gibson Company's "Articles of Association including each of the five founders investing an additional $500.00 to pay Orville Gibson $2500.00 for all the rights to his patented mandolin and all of his instrument designs. Courtesy of Roger Siminoff

* Available currency calculators yield varying results, so this is only a rough estimate

Orville H. Gibson – The Final Curtain

After the formation of the Gibson Company Orville continued to build musical instruments, but he clearly didn't want to be affiliated with the factory as evidenced by the labels on his post-1903 work that never included the company name. Sometime

around 1907, Orville began to have some serious health problems. He was suffering from an unspecified stomach ailment and was losing weight rapidly. Finally in June 1909, Orville Gibson suffered a complete nervous breakdown and was put in jail for his own safety because he had become violent. He was in jail for a week until a hearing could be scheduled to determine if he was in fact insane. In existing documents, his own brother Ozro, was the person who petitioned the probate court of Kalamazoo County to have Orville committed to the Michigan

INVENTOR GIBSON BELIEVED INSANE

N JAIL AWAITING APPOINTMENT OF COMMISSION TO MAKE EXAMINATION.

rooding over imaginary troubles, ll Gibson, music teacher and inr, occupies comfortable quarters he chapel of the county jail, awaithe appointment of a commission estigate into his sanity. Gibson een in poor health for some nd under the treatment of Dr. Crane for stomach trouble. weeks ago it was noticed that was losing his mind and on the of his friends and attending n, he was locked up. The inas violent at times. d lately been making his th the family of Cyrus Gib-East Lovell street. he taken before a commisobate court as soon as the egal steps can be taken. as at one time prominently with the Gibson Mandolin pany, which manufactured ons. He retired from acs some years ago and has ceen receiving royalties on his inventions.

SUFFERS MENTAL COLLAPSE

Orville Gibson, Guitar Inventor, Placed Under Restraint.

Kalamazoo, Mich.. June 16.—Orville Gibson, inventor of the Gibson guitar and mandolin, which has become popular all over the country and replaced the old style instruments, was taken to the county jail yesterday for safe keeping. He will be examined for his sanity. Mr. Gibson organized the Gibson Mandolin & Guitar company, of this city, one of the largest manufacturing companies in Kalamazoo. He is the beneficiary of royalties in this and foreign countries. His mental condition is due to a nerv-

State of Michigan, ss
County of Kalamazoo

At a Session of the Probate Court for the County of Kalamazoo, holden at the Pro... in said County, on **Wednes**day, the **23rd** day of **June** in the year one thousand nine hundred and **nine**. . 2 08865

Present, HON. GEORGE P. HOPKINS, Judge of Probate.

In the Matter of **Orville H. Gibson, Alleged Insane,**

On reading and filing the Petition, duly verified, of **Ozro M. Gibson** alleging that said

Orville H. Gibson of the fourth ward of the City of Kalamazoo, is insane, and praying that he may be admitted, on the order of this Court, to the Michigan Asylum for the Insane and there supported as a public patient.

June 23, 1909 Orville's brother Ozro Gibson pettions the probate court to have Orville commiteed. Courtesy of Roger Siminoff

State Asylum for the Insane. Ozro wrote that Orville was suffering from "pronounced delusions of persecution" and "imagines that different persons are trying to get at him, when nothing of the sort is true." Orville did spend about a month in the asylum while probate court judge George P. Hopkins investigated the matter further. Ultimately Orville was not judged to be legally insane but was deemed "mentally incompetent," which meant that he lost the right to manage his own affairs including his finances. The court had to appoint William R. Fox as Orville's legal guardian.

The Michigan State Asylum for the Insane
Kalamazoo, Michigan

From what can be pieced together from additional historical information, Orville sold his belongings including a Stanley Steamer automobile, left Kalamazoo about six weeks after his release, and moved back to upstate New York, where he lived alone in the Saranac Lake region of the Adirondack Mountains for three years. Apparently it did wonders for his over-all health and he returned to Kalamazoo and went back to probate court. Now he claimed that he had "practically regained his health" and after living a "largely out-door life," had gained 50 pounds, which indicates that he was a scant 100 pounds at the time of his nervous breakdown. In the court documents it also stated that Orville "believes and is informed by others that he is mentally competent." The court agreed and deemed him to be mentally competent which meant he was free to do as he pleased. Unfortunately, Orville's health problems had exacted a heavy toll and he decided to live out the rest of his life back in New York. He moved to Malone, a short distance from his hometown of Chateaugay, but continued to have health problems making it necessary for him to be hospitalized on more than one occasion. Finally, Orville was hospitalized in late 1917 for "endocarditis," an infection of the inner lining of the heart. One of the symptoms of endocarditis is un-explained weight loss, which may indicate that Orville had been suffering from this illness for many years. Finally, after five months in the Hepburn Hospital in Ogdensburg, New York, Orville died at the age of 62 on February 10, 1918.

While there is no concrete evidence that Orville had any mental health problems prior to 1908, it would go a long way in explaining his rather bizarre and erratic behavior during and after the formation of the Gibson Company (more on this in Chapter 5). In hindsight, the Gibson Company's board of directors must have been aware of his health problems and showed great compassion toward the inventor and saw fit to grant him a royalty agreement which paid Orville a small amount for every instrument sold both domestically and overseas. Even after five years, when the royalty agreement expired, the board of directors decided they continued to pay Orville a modest annual salary or stipend of $500.00 and sent him a check every month until he died. However Orville claimed that the court-appointed guardian, William Fox, never sent his royalty checks during the entire time he was in New York from 1909 to 1912.

Last Glimmer of Hope

In the 1950s, or so the story goes, a local antique dealer discovered some peculiar musical instruments that were apparently left at a Malone, New York home. One of them included a large harp-guitar and was described to a music store owner over the phone as being rather ornate with lots of mother-of-pearl inlay. Since these instruments have long-since vanished and supposedly had no clear evidence as to their maker, it is impossible to ascertain if they were in fact built by Orville after 1910. However, anyone who has admiration for the legacy of Orville H. Gibson, the world's most famous mandolin inventor, would like to believe that he continued to do what he was truly passionate about – building instruments.

Orville's Living Legacy

It is very difficult to verify how many instruments Orville himself. Approximately 20 or more instruments are known to still exist: two lyre-mandolins, four "F" mandolins, several "A"mandolins, three guitars, at least one or two harp-guitars, a 10-string guitar-mandolin and one concert zither. The guitar-mandolin is the earliest instrument Orville made and is dated 1894; then came the guitars, "A" mandolins followed by the "F" mandolins. Orville only used labels with his name on them, and none of the instruments he made after the formation of the Gibson Company have a label that identifies them as being made at the factory. Orville was building his instruments in his own shop and clearly did not want them associated with the company. An "F" mandolin that Orville built in 1903 only has a label with "Made by O. H. Gibson – Kalamazoo 1903" hand-written in ink with no graphics and no machine printed lettering. Another very ornate "F" mandolin has a simple hand-written label dated 1906, andis most likely the last mandolin Orville ever made.

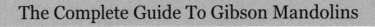

Orville made all the parts of his instruments by hand except for the hardware, including the tuners or machine heads, and tailpieces. Orville was fond of using "friction pegs," or banjo-style tuners and existing instruments with these types of tuners are stamped with a patent date of May 8, 1888. They were designed and patented by Lars Larsen Filstrup and George Van Zandt.

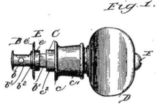

(No Model.)

L. L. FILSTRUP & G. VAN ZANDT.
TUNING PEG FOR STRINGED INSTRUMENTS.
No. 382,465.   Patented May 8, 1888.

The back of the headstock of one of Orville Gibson's lyre-mandolins showing the Filstrup and Van Zandt friction pegs.
Courtesy of Gruhn Guitars

Two different tailpieces Orville used on a lyre-mandolin and one of his guitars were made by Franz Schwarzer, a well-known zither manufacturer in Washington, Missouri. The patent for Schwarzer's original design was for a large metal zither tailpiece, but the lyre-shaped tailpiece on Orville's lyre-mandolin is stamped with the patent date October 26, 1886, referencing Schwarzer's original invention. The guitar tailpiece is closer to the zither design with a long flat metal strap that anchors the tailpiece to the bottom of the guitar.

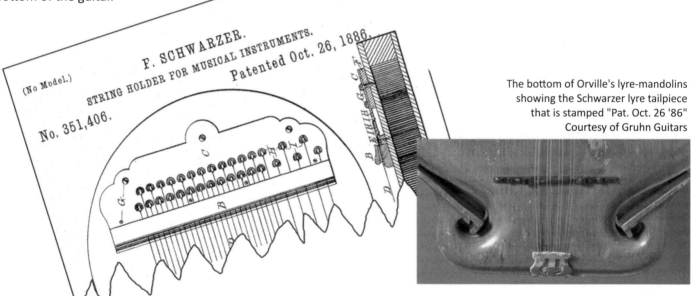

The bottom of Orville's lyre-mandolins showing the Schwarzer lyre tailpiece that is stamped "Pat. Oct. 26 '86"
Courtesy of Gruhn Guitars

The very ornate 1906 "F" mandolin has a "pineapple top" tailpiece that was commonly found on all factory-made instruments, but it has "O. H. Gibson" engraved on it, further proof that he did not want his instruments associated with the Gibson Company. Most Gibson historians believe that Orville did not make a lot of instruments, and some suggest that it may have been as few as 50. However, given what is now known about Orville's career as a luthier starting as early as 1884, that number could be considerably higher. Like Vincent van Gogh and many others before him, sometimes mental illness and great artistic genius go hand-in-hand. Orville was a man of great vision and his instruments will live on forever, because they changed the way fretted musical instruments are made to this very day.

Gibson Mandolin-Guitar Mfg. Co., Ltd. – The Early Years – 1902 -1909

The Gibson Mandolin-Guitar Manufacturing Company, Limited officially became an entity on October 11, 1902, although the actual paperwork was signed on October 10th. The company was formed using "Articles of Association" and it is interesting to note that they stated that the company would engage in the "manufacturing, buying, selling and dealing in guitars, mandolins, mandolas, violins, lutes and all other kinds of stringed musical instruments." There is some unsubstantiated information that Orville had built at least one mandola and the Gibson Company thought they could also manufacture and sell Orville's violins, lyre-mandolins and lutes, but did not wind up making any of these instruments once manufacturing commenced. Although early advertisements included lyre-mandolins as one of their products, they apparently had no real

intention of ever putting them into production. The five founding members included Judge John W. Adams who became the Chairman of the Board; Samuel Van Horn was named Treasurer; Sylvo Reams was a Secretary on the Board of Directors and Gibson's superintendent of day-to-day manufacturing operations; Lewis A. Williams became the Sales Manager as well as another Secretary on the Board of Directors. Strangely, LeRoy Hornbeck was not given any official title. Each of the five men put up $1000.00 each and received 100 shares of stock at $10.00 per share. They also had to put up an additional $500.00 each in cash that was used to buy the rights to Orville's 1898 mandolin patent, as well as all of his instrument designs for a total of $2500.00.

A judge, a dog breeder, a preacher's son, a businessman, and a loan shark walk into a bar…..
Judge John W. Adams came to Kalamazoo in 1887, became a lawyer in 1890, and by 1899 was elected circuit court judge. He had the reputation of being rather heavy-handed in his business dealings, but on the other hand, he had very little to do with running the Gibson Company. He attended board meetings and collected his stock dividends, but that was about it. Both Sylvo Reams and Lewis Williams had a lot of prior music industry experience and they were certainly the best candidates for running the business on a day-to-day basis. Reams and his two brothers Andrew and Arthur owned a music store in Kalamazoo, but in 1904 Reams resigned from the music store in order to devote his full attention to Gibson. Lewis A. Williams was the son of a Baptist preacher and prior to coming to Kalamazoo he had been a music teacher as well as a successful music salesman in New York. Samuel H. Van Horn was an attorney, but his real passion was breeding pureblood champion collies. He owned the Cragsmere Collie Kennels in Kalamazoo, and his dogs were so highly sought after that one of his prized collies sold for a whopping $8500.00. Hornbeck was also a lawyer, but spent more time buying and selling real estate and loaning money than he did practicing law. Apparently he wasn't exactly well-liked either. He and Samuel Van Horn had a law practice together, but a month before the formation of Gibson, Van Horn bought out Hornbeck and promptly dissolved the firm. Later, when Hornbeck ran for public office, a local newspaper ran the headline "Loan Shark Slated for City Attorney." Of course Hornbeck vehemently denied any wrongdoing which also included trying to persuade other elected officials to vote for him. How it is that these particular five men with such dissimilar backgrounds all came together to start a company is a real mystery.

| John W. Adams | Samuel H. Van Horn | Sylvo Reams | Lewis A. Williams | LeRoy Hornbeck |

What's in a Name?

In May 1904 Gibson officially dropped "Limited" as part of the company name and became the Gibson Mandolin-Guitar Mfg. Co. They had under-capitalized and needed to raise more money and the name change coincided with the addition of 17 new stockholders who invested $12,000.00 of much-needed capital. Then in January 1906 Gibson increased its capital stock again to $40,000.00 from $12,000.00 and changed the company name once more dropping "Mfg.," to become the Gibson Mandolin-Guitar Co. This name would remain the same until 1923 when even bigger changes in the company took place. By all accounts Gibson was in financial trouble right from the start as they completely miscalculated the amount of money needed to keep the company running. This is quite evident given the succession of capital stock increases in the first five years of operation. It is important to note that when the Gibson Company was formed, all they had was a little money, some paperwork and Orville's instrument designs. They didn't even have an address and had not secured any manufacturing space.

October 1902 article about the formation of Gibson

When Do We Get Started?

Two months later they rented space from the Witwer Bakery Company at 114 East Main Street but the company's first address was 100 Exchange Place a narrow street behind Witwer's. The two buildings Gibson rented were on the opposite side of Exchange Place Witwer's had used for baking, storage, and office space as well as an adjacent ice-cream factory. map clearly shows the exact location of the Exchange Place factory, including some interesting side notes in the left margin. The map does not contain the actual address, but designates the two buildings as "A and B Exchange Pl." It provides some basic information about the type of heat, number of fire extinguishers and that the building has electricity, but the really interesting part is a fairly detailed layout of the factory. The first floor of 100 Exchange Place or building "A" was used for turning the rough cut parts into components including all the shaping and carving or "body work." The second floor was designated "finishing" which was most likely where those parts were assembled into instruments. The first floor of the old ice-cream factory or building "B" housed the raw lumber and all the machinery to mill it into rough blanks, while the second floor was for applying the stains and varnish finishes. The total factory space of both buildings was just over 8000 square feet.

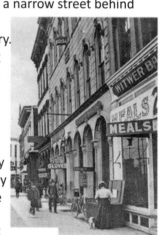

1906 East Main Street Kalamazoo showing partial facade of Witwer Bakery Company

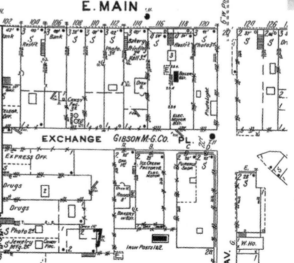

Right: 1906 city assessor's map of the area surrounding the Gibson factory at 100 Exchange Place. Above: Side margin notes describing factory layout.
Courtesy of Joyce Brumbaugh

Gibson had ordered machinery but didn't actually move into their first factory until the middle of December 1902. It would have taken at least a month or two to get the shop set up, hire some employees, as well as securing the materials needed, so Gibson probably didn't make their first instrument until February 1903. There is no evidence that the company published another catalog or brochure after February 1903 all the way up to 1906. The only known illustration of the Exchange Place factory appears in a small 1906 brochure and 1907's Catalog "E," with the Gibson Mandolin-Guitar Co. name on the side, coinciding with the name change that had occurred in 1906.

1905 Gibson factory illustration that that first appeared in a small brochure

Driven Out of the Factory

The company stayed in the Exchange Place location for seven years, but had outgrown it and as L. A. Williams put it, "we were driven out not only because of the lack of room, but because the cockroaches became so thick we could hardly prevent using them as bookmarks." One can only imagine the unintended ingredients in the ice-cream and baked goods Witwer's used to make there. So in 1909 Gibson had a new factory built on property they had purchased on Harrison Court. By 1909 Gibson had 25 employees and needed more space to increase factory output. Apparently they were turning down large orders because they simply couldn't build enough instruments. There are no known pictures or illustrations of the exterior of the new factory at 500 Harrison Court, but based on information that appeared in local newspapers, it was a two-story building that measured 55' x 125' or only 13,750 square feet, not much bigger than the Exchange Place facility. Apparently the lack of room, as L. A. Williams put it, was not as big a deal as the hordes of cockroaches. The new factory building designed and built by Thomas Foy, and was completed in only a few months, but Gibson ran into a major setback. The company did publish some pictures of various parts of the interior providing a rare glimpse of this new facility.

Various photographs of the interior of Gibson's second factory at 500 Harrison Court - Kalamazoo, Michigan

Out of the Old – Can't Get Into the New

In October 1909 Gibson began to move into the Harrison Court factory but the city council of Kalamazoo held-up Gibson's application for a permit to build a new sewer line from the new factory to nearby Arcadia Creek. George Laurian, who had become factory superintendent went before the city council to find what could be done about it. He was told that "the matter was under consideration by the board of health," but Laurian claimed that "members of the council" had led him to believe that they would be able to make the sewer connection. Laurian also insisted that Gibson had done everything needed to make the new factory a clean and safe work environment. The company's biggest concern was the lease on the Exchange Place facility would expire on November 4th. The mayor of Kalamazoo asked Laurian, "Who promised you could have sewer connections?" Laurian's response was "no one promised in particular," so he had made a potentially disastrous assumption before they had the actual permit. Luckily, in November, the city council resolved the sewer issue and Gibson was able to finish the new factory, but it appears that they weren't able to fully occupy it until mid-1910.

What Happened to Orville?

In 1902 Orville Gibson was the only person who knew how to build his instruments, so it was necessary for him to teach others how to do it. The earliest known factory-made mandolin is so similar to Orville's original design that it was either built by Orville, or by someone under his supervision. An article published in the *Kalamazoo Daily Telegraph* on February 7, 1903 stated that Orville had been named "superintendent" of the factory, the only known reference to Orville working in this capacity. The accuracy of the article is a little suspect, as its headline read, "7-String Guitars – Peculiar Kalamazoo Product," but the body of text stated that Orville was "the inventor and sole manufacturer of the only eight-string guitar ever put on the market." Either the reporter couldn't count or was just confused by this very unusual instrument. The article also staid that "the fingering is practically the same as the common guitar and the use of the additional eighth string is easily acquired." The instrument in question might have been some sort of small harp-guitar or more likely a standard-shaped guitar with eight strings instead of six. It went on to say, "the graduating of the instruments is done by experts under the personal supervision of Mr. Gibson," so it appears that Orville was in charge of training the new employees and possibly supervising the entire factory workforce.

Orville Gibson also became disillusioned with working for the Gibson Company because when they set up their factory, hired employees and started building instruments, the company wanted to change Orville's original designs. The factory quickly identified some inherent problems with Orville's method of construction that would not translate well into a production environment. Orville never liked building any instrument the same way twice. For example, the body of an Orville-built "A" mandolin could be anywhere from 10 3/4" to over 11" wide and the scale length could range from 14 1/4" to 15." One of the biggest challenges for the company was securing a source for wood of sufficient size to make the parts, while attempting to reduce the amount of wood wasted because of how Orville cut and carved the rim, neck and headstock from a single piece. The company needed to standardize the instrument designs in order to simplify the manufacturing process. Very soon they started making instruments that were smaller and shorter than Orville's designs. For example the "A" mandolin bodies were a uniform 10 1/4" wide with a 13 7/8" scale length. The neck and rim were changed so that the neck was made separately from a smaller piece of wood. They also changed the inlaid guard-plate on the body to a much smaller size than Orville's guard-plates which were much larger and more ornate.

 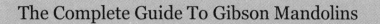

More Changes

Orville's neck design had large volutes, or raised spines, on the back of the neck and headstock. This design added strength to the angled transition from the neck to the headstock and worked well with the friction-style tuning pegs Orville used. Although the 1903 catalog illustrations of the "F" mandolins show the same friction pegs Gibson did not use them in production. All of their mandolins used four-on-a-plate style tuners, but they didn't fit quite right because of the volute. Gibson tried reducing the size of the volute to solve this problem, but it still required cutting off one corner of the tuner mounting plates. Finally, they just completely eliminated the volute.

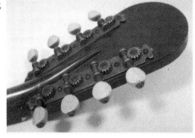

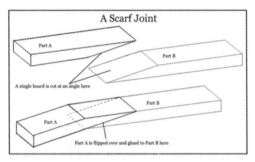

Another example of a cost saving measure were necks built using a "scarf joint." This allows the neck and headstock to be made from one thinner board cut at an angle. One piece is flipped over and both are glued back together to create the angle needed for the headstock. There are some examples of early Gibson mandolins with scarf joints, but it's not a good way to make a neck, so Gibson stopped doing it. Early production instruments show so many design variations that a lot of experimentation was going on in an attempt to simplify the manufacturing process, reduce labor and material costs while maintaining a high standard of quality and workmanship.

Within a few short months the company took Orville's big rounded "A" mandolin headstock design that looked like a canoe oar and changed it to a smaller and narrower shape with a symmetrical top design of curves and points (nicknamed the "paddle head'). This new design was used for more than 20 years on most of the mandolin models. They also added the iconic "The Gibson" logo inlaid in mother-of-pearl on the headstock, although some of the lower-priced "A" mandolins had no logo. The company kept the Style "F" headstock design and it has become one of the most recognizable features of Gibson mandolins. The company also completely abandoned Orville's hollow-out neck design, changed the body construction by adding a neck block that enabled them to shorten the pieces needed for the rim and back, and attach the necks to the block using a locking tapered dovetail joint. This method of construction would become the basis for all Gibson necks including mandolins, mandolas, mando-cellos, guitars and harp-guitars. One can only imagine the arguments that must have ensued between Orville and management about all of these changes to his designs and apparently on many occasions Orville either stormed out of the factory or just stopped showing up for work.

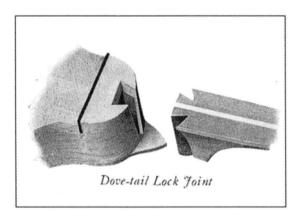

Dove-tail Lock Joint

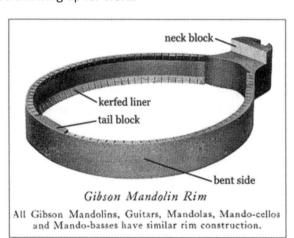

Gibson Mandolin Rim

All Gibson Mandolins, Guitars, Mandolas, Mando-cellos and Mando-basses have similar rim construction.

Based on some key facts Orville worked in the factory for only a couple of months, at which time the board decided to pay him only for the actual time he was there. Clearly, Orville was not happy about all the changes taking place nor was he interested in working in a factory environment. He was used to being a one-man show, free to do as he pleased. In addition to this, he was supposed to get 60 shares of stock in the company worth $600.00, but in July 1903, just as the official stock certificate was to be issued, Orville abruptly sold the shares to Charles Rickard, a local bartender. Based on what we now know about his mental health problems later on, this seems to indicate that he suffered type of "episode."

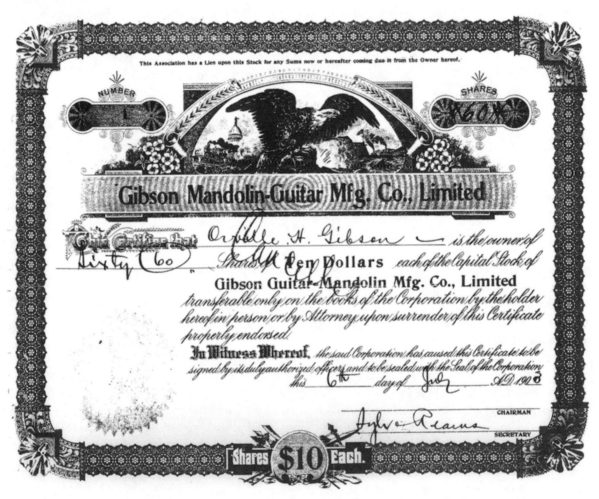

Orville Gibson's stock certificate that was supposed to be issued on July 6, 1903 but was cancelled just before that date because Orville had sold his shares to Charles Rickard. Courtesy of Roger Siminoff

What Do All These Letters Stand For?

As mentioned earlier, Gibson's first catalog was published in February 1903 and all of the illustrations were drawn using Orville-built instruments. It contained five different "A" mandolins, four different "F" or Artist mandolins, three different mandolas designated style letter "H," and three different style "K" mando-cellos. There were also the Styles "L" and "O" guitars and "R" and "U" harp-guitars. A number was added after the style letters which indicated how fancily the instrument was decorated. No number like the Style "A" was the plainest, and numbers one through four were used to identify each step up in ornamentation, with four being the fanciest and most expensive. Most likely Sylvo Reams and Lewis A. Williams came up with the style designations, but no one knows for sure why they picked those particular letters.

Catalog or Advertising

The first catalog Gibson published had illustrations of all five Style "A" mandolins and yet it only contained illustrations of the Artist models "F" and "F-2" and not the fancier "F-3" and "F-4." Also, it did not have any illustrations of the mandolas or mando-cellos as well as some of the guitar models. There wasn't enough time for Orville to build the fancier mandolins,

The cover of Gibson's first catalog published in February 1903

mandolas and mando-cellos, because the company had to rush to get the first catalog published by February 1903. They must have asked Orville to build two plain-looking "F" models, which he could complete in less time, in order for the illustrations to be drawn in time for the publication deadline. This also seems to confirm that Orville never actually built any mandolas or mando-cellos at the time the company bought the rights to his designs. So who decided to include these additional instruments as part of Gibson's first complete line of instruments?

The Complete Mandolin Orchestra

Lewis A. Williams envisioned making the different models of each style of instrument and came up with the idea of offering all the instruments in the mandolin family, as well as guitars and harp-guitars. Given his background in instrument sales, he had the foresight that a complete mandolin orchestra should mirror the string section of a classical orchestra. The mandolin would cover the violin parts, the mandola was the equivalent of the viola, the mando-cello was the cello, and the bass parts could be played by the guitars and harp-guitars. One early newspaper article actually stated that Gibson planned on building 29 different designs which now seems completely unrealistic. Williams and Reams were certainly aware of pre-existing variations in the mandolin family like the mandola and mando-cello, but it was a shot in the dark in terms of determining what if any demand there might be for them. This might explain why they delayed the building of the mandolas and mando-cellos and simply waited for the orders to come in.

Gibson's first catalog seemed to be more of an advertising piece rather than an actual catalog of instruments for sale, because it included several instruments that weren't yet available and a couple that may have never actually been made. The mysterious Style "H" mandola (no number followed the style letter), and the Style "K" mando-cello are described in the catalog, but completely disappear after that and no known examples exist. The first catalog stated that the back, sides and neck were maple, when in reality most early examples were used whatever wood was available like mahogany, walnut or birch. The supposed "ebony" fingerboards were mostly rosewood or some cheaper hardwood stained black to look like ebony, otherwise known as "ebonized." The "celluloid-tortoise guard plate [pickguard], inlaid with pearl ornament" was another typical catalog embellishment, as some "A"mandolins had no guard plate while others were plain celluloid with no inlay.

Based on surviving instruments from this early era Gibson probably didn't make any mandolas until late 1903 and no examples of a Gibson mando-cello can be dated earlier than 1905. Reams and Williams were keenly aware of the fact that their biggest sellers would be the mandolins and guitars and concentrated their efforts on those instruments.

A risque illustration of silent film star Paula Dean graced the inside of Gibson's first catalog

Gibson Mandolin-Guitar Co. – The Early Years Part 2 – 1904-1909

Early Innovators

The name George D. Laurian is not exactly legendary in the annals of Gibson folklore, but his contributions to improving Gibson's instruments cannot be overlooked. He was born in Kalamazoo in 1881 and was one of Gibson's first employees. It is entirely likely that Orville was the person responsible for getting the company to hire Laurian. Orville had played many concerts at The Knights of Pythias, a local fraternal organization that Laurian was a prominent member of, starting in the 1890s. By 1908 Laurian became the General Superintendent of Gibson, and co-founder Sylvo Reams became the General Manager. Laurian was a gifted engineer and inventor and left his mark not only on Gibson, but instrument design in general. He had been making many changes to the design and construction of Gibson's instruments as early as 1904, including a complete overhaul of Orville Gibson's original designs. He is probably the person responsible for discarding the one-piece carved rim design and replacing it with bent sides, internal blocks and braces. He also introduced the first necks to be attached to body using a neck block with a tapered dovetail joint.

c1898 George D. Laurian in his Knights of Pythias uniform Courtesy of the Kalamazoo Public Library

Orville's mandolins and Gibson's early factory-built mandolins had little to no neck angle. The end of the fingerboard was simply glued to a flat section on the top. The bridge height was only 5/16" to 3/8." From 1903 to 1908 Gibson used what is known as the "Stebbins Bridge" which was patented in 1896 by George R. Stebbins, for all of their mandolins, mandolas and mando-cellos . It was the first "compensated" fretted musical instrument bridge. A compensated bridge helps correct the inherent problem with all fretted musical instruments – intonation. Without going into a lot of detail about the science of acoustics, all fretted instruments require slight variations in the vibrating length of the strings or the distance between the nut and the bridge (commonly referred to as scale length) in order for fretted notes on each of the strings to be in tune with one another.

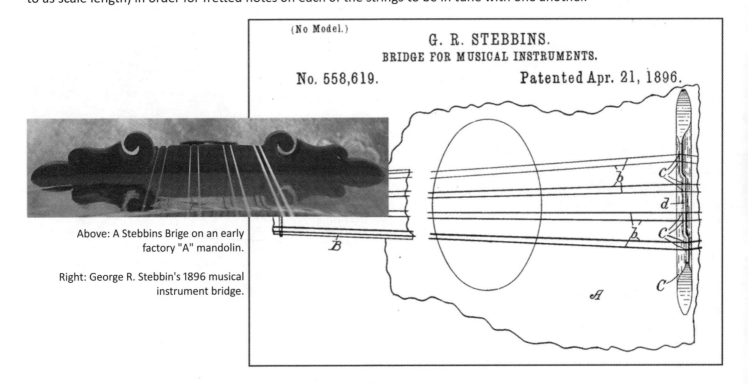

Above: A Stebbins Brige on an early factory "A" mandolin.

Right: George R. Stebbin's 1896 musical instrument bridge.

George Laurian began experimenting with increasing the neck angle and height of the bridge which resulted in greater string tension on the bridge. Higher string tension or down pressure resulted in a dramatic increase in top vibration making the instruments louder and brighter. These modifications seem to have evolved in a few stages from almost no neck angle and the low Stebbins bridge, to a neck angle of four degrees and a bridge height of nearly three quarters of an inch. These significant changes required an entirely new design and in 1909, Laurian finally perfected his bridge and was awarded a patent on September 21, 1909. It's interesting to note that some copies of Gibson's 1909 Catalog "F" still showed an illustration of the Stebbins Bridge, but were stamped "The bridge corresponding to this cut is discontinued for our new improved bridge, patented Sept. 21, 1909."

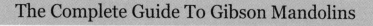

G. D. LAURIAN.
BRIDGE FOR STRINGED MUSICAL INSTRUMENTS.
APPLICATION FILED JUNE 14, 1909.

934,678.   Patented Sept. 21, 1909.

His design would easily accommodate the increased string height and was completely solid so the entire bottom of the bridge was in contact with the top. Laurian's idea was to have small movable saddle pieces on top of the bridge, capable of increasing or decreasing the scale length in order to correct intonation. The saddle pieces or "string rests"as he called them, sat in two slots and could be shifted from one groove to the other, as well being able to flip the saddle pieces around, additionally shortening or lengthening the distance between the nut and bridge. Laurian also describes his design as being capable of correcting intonation problems when using strings of different gauges, including wound vs. unwound strings and even the material they were made of like steel vs. gut, etc. The design evolved over time and although it was quite innovative for its time, Gibson eventually replaced it with a much better design in the early 1920s.

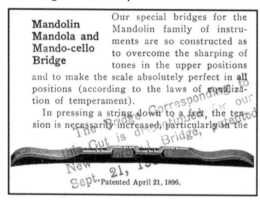

Mandolin Mandola and Mando-cello Bridge   Our special bridges for the Mandolin family of instruments are so constructed as to overcome the sharping of tones in the upper positions and to make the scale absolutely perfect in all positions (according to the laws of equalization of temperament).

In pressing a string down to a fret, the tension is necessarily increased, particularly on the Gut

Sept. 21,   Patented April 21, 1896.

The Visionary

Laurian's first patent application was filed on November 9, 1909, and the patent was awarded to him on July 19, 1910. Although this patent is not specifically for any improvements to mandolin design, it is a very important document. Laurian invents numerous revolutionary designs in a single patent, most of which are still in use. Probably the single biggest change to Orville's original design was eliminating the one-piece sawed rim and replacing it with thin bent side pieces that were reinforced by kerfed liners (strips of wood made flexible by multiple saw cuts), plus a separate neck block and tail blocks. A couple of existing instruments with this new method of construction can be dated to late 1904 or early 1905 and consequently all of Gibson's instruments are still made this way.

The patent shows that he completely redesigned Gibson's Style "U" harp-guitar, including bent sides that attached to a large neck block and smaller tail block, which confirms that he was responsible for introducing these construction changes on the mandolins as well. By redesigning the harp-guitar's tailpiece, Laurian was responsible for inventing the first "trapeze tailpiece" as it is known today. It had rods connecting a floating celluloid pin block to a metal tailpiece that was attached to the bottom of the instrument with screws. It was capable of pivoting where the rods attached to the tailpiece, or being able to swing like a trapeze.

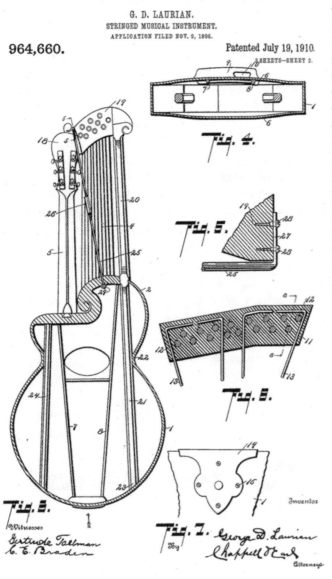

Almost as an afterthought, Laurian also includes a design for a new 6-string guitar which would become the Style "O" Artist model. It shows that he was clearly the person responsible for developing Gibson's top bracing that supported the bridge's increased down pressure. It would appear that he was the person who had added one short transverse brace (a brace that is below the sound hole and perpendicular to the strings) to the tops of the mandolins when they went to the bent-sides design. In the patent description, he specifies that the braces or "ribs" as he called them, had "different degrees of rigidity" and terminate at each end. This tapered top brace design is still used on Gibson arch-top or carved-top instruments over 100 years later. He also describes the hook-shaped upper treble bout design as "being cut away below the fingerboard...thereby permitting easy fingering" – effectively creating the first guitar ever to have a "cut-away." He also designs a new style of bridge where the center section is cut-away with feet at each end also the industry standard today.

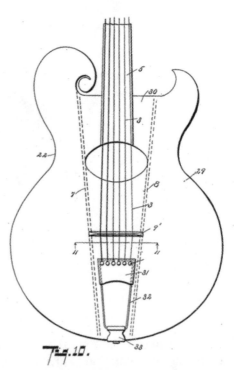

The third page of George Laurian's landmark patent was a design that became the Gibson Style "O" Artist guitar, the first to feature a "cut-away" and a "trapeze tailpiece."

Laurian's third patent is very significant in terms of Gibson's mandolins, mandolas, and mando-cellos. It is Gibson's iconic "pineapple" tailpiece that is as recognizable as any other part of a Gibson mandolin, and has been copied countless times for over a century. The big question is whether Laurian did in fact invent the whole design, because the patent wasn't awarded until September 30, 1910 nearly eight years after Gibson first started using it. Laurian is the only person to have patented this particular type of tailpiece, so it's possible that he did design it when he first started working for Gibson back in 1903 and made a number of improvements over the years until he decided to file for the patent. However, it's more likely that he did not come up with the actual pineapple-shaped removable cover or the angled base plate, but his patent clearly made improvements to how the strings attached to the tailpiece. Early versions of these tailpieces had rough bent metal hooks where the looped end of the strings attached to the base plate. One of the problems with this design is that it allowed the twisted section of the strings to slip and the loops to break very easily. Laurian solved this problem by adding a second set of four hooks for the A and E strings, so that the strings wrapped around the upper hooks and attached to the lower hooks at an angle The upper hooks held the twisted part of the strings locking them in place, as well as decreasing the tension on the looped end. He also mentions that his sliding cover design acted as an additional string clamp by holding the strings firmly against the hooks.

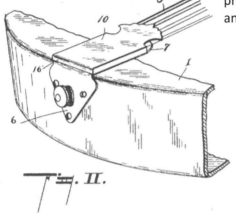

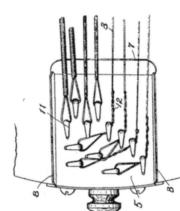

Laurian's fourth patent was awarded in 1911 for a pickguard clamp, an ingenious little device that will be discussed in more detail in Chapter 8. All four of George Laurian's patents were assigned to Gibson and the company retained all the rights to them in exchange for a flat fee paid to the inventor. He did not receive any additional royalties. For unknown reasons, George D. Laurian left Gibson in 1915 and became President of United Garage and Machine Shop. He also worked as an auto mechanic, a carriage painter and for the S. F. Everitt Company in St. Mary's, Ohio. By 1930 Laurian had returned to his home town of Kalamazoo where he stayed until he died. An article in the December 1909 issue of *The Crescendo* magazine stated simply:

"What George Laurian, Superintendent of the Gibson factory, doesn't know about mandolin construction, isn't worth knowing."

Salesman Turned Inventor

After Orville's original 1898 mandolin patent, the next patent Gibson was awarded was a milestone in early mandolin innovation. L. A. Williams proved to be not only a truly brilliant salesman, but was also quite adept at designing new improvements for the company's instruments. In 1907, Williams invented the elevated finger-rest as it was called, but it took two years before the patent was awarded on March 30, 1909. It was a revolutionary new accessory that is still used on every

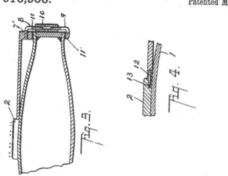

Gibson arch-top instrument till this day and has been copied by countless other manufacturers. One of the inherent problems with the earlier inlaid guard-plates was how labor intensive the process was coupled with the fact that it was more of a decorative design than a functional pickguard. The elevated finger-rest was made of faux tortoise shell celluloid and was attached to the instrument using three small pins and two clamps. Initially, Gibson used simple violin chin rest clamps to secure the outer edge of the finger-rest to the instrument body. Two pins attached it to the side of the fingerboard, and another pin at the bottom inserted into a hole in the treble side of the bridge. It was sturdy, durable and much less expensive to make than the inlaid guard-plates. Although the patent was applied for in 1907, extant instruments indicate that Gibson didn't start installing them until 1908. The finger-rests that Gibson used during the pre-patent era were stamped using a heated stamping iron that melted "Pat. Applied For" into the celluloid, while all subsequent pickguards were stamped "PAT.MAR.30.'09."

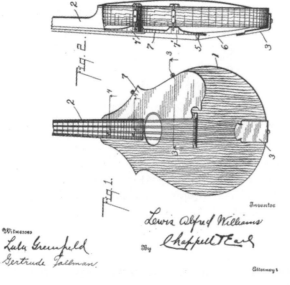

L. A. Williams 1909 patent for the elevated finger-rest

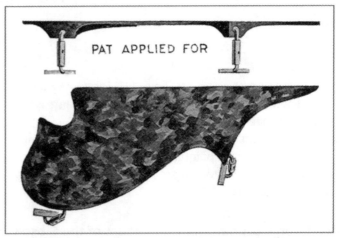

Elevated finger-rest illustration from Gibson's 1909 Catalog "F" which still says "Pat Applied For."

1909's Catalog "F" contained the first illustrations of Williams' new invention. The early versions used on the Style "F" mandolins look pretty much the same as the patent illustrations with the outer edge following the contours of the asymmetrical body. The company used this early design on the "F" mandolins for fewer than two years and by mid-1910 they completely redesigned it. It may have been George Laurian's idea to make the size and shape of the finger-rests more universal so it would fit both the Style "A" and "F" mandolins, while the mandolas, mando-cellos, guitars, and harp-guitars used similar shapes a littler larger than the mandolin finger-rests. Gibson continued stamping all their elevated finger-rests with the original patent date up until the early 1930s, even though the patent expired in 1926. Given the fact that Williams' basic design is still used, it was a remarkable achievement.

Closeup of heat-stamped finger-rest Gibson used prior to the patent being awarded.
Courtesy of Dan Beimborn

Sales and Advertising – 1903-1909

The pure genius of Lewis A. Williams's early sales and advertising efforts cannot be overstated. Right from the start he conceived a sales strategy that proved to be extremely successful. He decided that Gibson would only sell their instruments through teacher/agents and not music stores or other retailers. In April 1903, just six months after the company started, Williams actually resigned as a member of the Board of Directors. Instead, he would be paid a salary as Sales Manager. The reason for this seems to be that Williams was travelling so much that he would not be able to attend board meetings or effectively manage any of the day-to-day operations of the company.

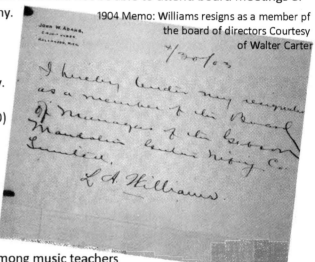
1904 Memo: Williams resigns as a member pf the board of directors Courtesy of Walter Carter

It was Chairman Adams who insisted Williams withdraw from the Board, so Williams simply wrote a note on Adams' stationery confirming his resignation. This indicates that he wasn't very happy about it but realized it was necessary to do his job more effectively. Ironically in 1904, when Gibson needed more working capital and increased the shares of stock, Williams owned as many shares (120) as Board Chairman Adams but Sylvo Reams was actually the majority stock holder with 132 shares.

Williams traveled all around the United States with samples of Gibson's instruments, enrolling local music teachers as agents for the company. In turn, the teachers would encourage their students to buy only Gibson instruments. Early advertisements clearly stated that "agencies for our instruments are established among music teachers exclusively." Very quickly, Williams was signing up teacher/agents and giving them exclusive territories, because his goal was having an "energetic agent in every town." Williams' early ads were aimed at getting more teachers interested in Gibson with phrases like "You Mr. Teacher will also wax warm with Gibson fervor."

Pop-Overs

Goodbye my little 'tato bug,
Your form is like a 'lasses jug,
You always were the bummest hug,
Goodbye.
The Gibson model, hully gee,
Is held as easy as can be,
There's no more 'tato bug for me,
Goodbye.

Williams also had a great sense of humor, a very colorful and flamboyant writing style, as well as greatcontempt for Gibson's competitors. Early ads called their competitor's instruments "crooked ribbed hump-backs" or "pumpkin back." Later he coined the phrase "potato bugs" describing the resemblance of the bowl-back mandolin to an insect. He referred to people who played bowl-backs as "potato buggists." He was constantly touting the virtues of Gibson instruments and even compared them to women wigth a "captivating form" and "it was love at first sight when seeing and hearing the "Gibson." Another early ad shows his wry sense of humor with a bold title "In Love? – We will send you a wife on approval – If you don't like her, send her back at our expense." He was so confident of the superiority of Gibson's instruments that the company offered a 30-day free trial and

November 1908 ad from *The Cadenza* magazine with the catch phrase "Not a potato-buggist among them."

The Gibson Artist Mandolin
Style "F2"
Net Price, $75.00
GIBSON MANDOLIN-GUITAR
MFG CO., Ltd.
Kalamazoo - - - Michigan

would pay for shipping both ways if the instrument was returned. "Not a potato-buggist among them" was another great Williams advertising catch phrase.Williams also saw the need for endorsements from prominent mandolin players as further proof of "The Gibson" mandolin's high quality and superior tone. Early endorsers included Hilda Hempel, Eugene Page, Fred C. Martin, Myron Bickford, Walter Boehm, Valentine Abt, and Dennis Hartnett, all well-known mandolinists at that time. On many occasions, Williams incorporated their actual statements into advertisements. Well-known Gibson teacher/agent Dennis Hartnett said, "permit me to add my name to the army of Gibson enthusiasts," Others included:

"There is nothing but praise to be said"
– Myron Bickford
"I take pleasure in recommending the Gibson"
– Hilda Hempel
"You simply have all the other mandolin manufacturers nailed to the cross"
– Harry S. Six

January 1913 ad with many enthusiastic Gibson endorsers including Lloyd Loar (bottom row, third from the left)

Williams came up with countless slogans that appeared in ads as well as Gibson's catalogs. He warned all about the dangers of using a competitor's instrument with phrases like:

"For now all see in part through a glass darkly. So, the whole truth is greater than the best and most told here"

"Cheapness diggeth the pit: the unwary fall therein"

"A picture too bright to be looked against by him who has mated with darkness"

"Before two seasons have passed the old bowl-back mandolin will look like relics"

"The misbegotten, deformed, ill-behaved ape is an instrument"

"A fool's paradise is a dangerous abode from which to direct or try to direct the public mind"

"How can an unsatisfactory tone be made satisfactory by decorating the instrument with fluma-diddles"

"When grey hairs applaud, progress may well ask, what have I done amiss?"

He was always raving about the virtues of "The Gibson" instruments with slogans like:

"Our instruments can make good in fast company"
"Right principles correctly applied invariably bring right results"
"The zenith of artistic excellence"
"Throughout the world the men behind Gibson are the brains of the profession"

He also came up with one of the catchiest slogans of all time *"Everyone a Gibson-ite."*

Gibson endorsers (left to right)
Hilda Hemple, Eugene Page, J. W. McLouth, Fredrick Martin, Walter Boehm and Dennis Hartnett

One of the most amusing advertisements Gibson published was a cartoon drawn by William Foster in 1908. It depicted a Gibson "F" mandolin character standing on the "eternal progress platform," sweeping away all the "potato-bugs" into the "Dead Sea" with the "New Era" broom. Some of the potato-bugs are labeled with the names of Gibson's competitors like Bay State, Brandt, Regal, and Waldo. The caption reads, "Mr. Potato-bug Mandolin (to his mate): Don't run dearie, we can dodge that 'Gibson' broom – (Swish) Help! Help! – Ker-splash."

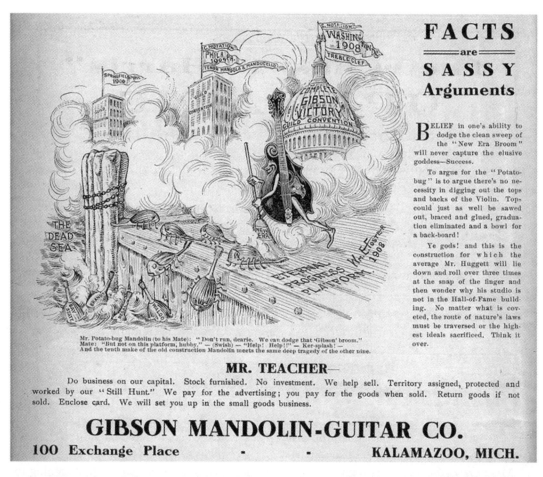

c1906 The Five Musical Noses, one of many mandolin groups to appear in a Gibson catalog.

c1909 The Aeolian Mandolin and Guitar Orchestra. L.A. Williams recognized the value of promoting women's groups.

Gibson Catalogs – 1903-1909

Lewis Williams was also responsible for all of Gibson's catalogs as well as writing the vast majority of the content. Their first catalog went into great detail about the tone, construction and the "distinctive features" of their instruments, but also claimed that "It is impossible to convey an adequate idea of the superiority of our product." Some of those distinctive features included:

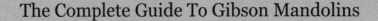

Title page of the "red cover" brochure from 1906

- No braces, blocks or cleats to impede vibrations
- Body made of finest selected and thoroughly air-seasoned woods
- Scale as near perfection as is possible to make
- Action easy and readily responsive
- Sonorous qualities and thickness of face and body
- Scientific preparation and fitting of same

One important aspect of the first catalog as well as many of Gibson's subsequent catalogs is they were often inaccurate when describing the exact details of each model. There's an old saying that "the only consistent thing about Gibson is their inconsistency" and that would apply to Gibson instruments right from the very start of the company.

There is no evidence that Gibson published any catalog after 1903 until their first full-line catalog came out in 1907, designated Catalog "E." Many Gibson enthusiasts have been puzzled by this, because there were no catalogs A, B, C or D. In 1906, they only issued two small brochures. One, referred to as the "red cover" brochure had just 12 pages and only contained illustrations of the "A-4" and "F-2" mandolins and no mention of Gibson's mandolas or mando-cellos. The second was an even smaller four-page harp-guitar brochure. Catalogue "E" (with the "ue" like the British spelling), was a modest 16 pages, half the size of their first catalog. It did have beautiful illustrations of all the mandolin models, but like the first catalog, there were no illustrations of mandolas or mando-cellos.

In 1909 Catalog "F" was triple the size of "E" with 48 pages, plus the cover, inside front cover and inside back cover. It was the first catalog to show illustrations of every Gibson instrument, as well as an accessories section and many photos of Gibson players and mandolin groups. It was also the first catalog to show all of the instruments with their new patented elevated pickguards.

Above left: Cover of Gibson's 1907 Catalogue "E" Lower left: Cover of Catalogue "F" Lower right: the Three Masqueria Sisters, also known as the "Gibson" Girls

The Ozburn Quartet. Courtesy of Rick Van Krugel

Gibson Instruments – 1903-1909

Style "A" Mandolin – 1903-1904

It is necessary to divide early Gibson mandolins into two separate time periods. The early factory models from 1903-1904 and 1905-1909. The early factory "A" mandolins adhered pretty closely to Orville's original design. The earliest known factory-made mandolin is an "A" and has the serial number 2506. It is almost certain that Gibson started their serial numbers at 2500 meaning this mandolin was the sixth instrument built at the Exchange Place factory around February 1903. It is so similar to Orville's original design that it must have been built by Orville himself or under his direct supervision.

List Price: $44.32*
Net Price: $25.00
Wholesale Price: $12.50

Gibson included a "List Price" in their early catalogs which seems to have no relationship to the actual selling price. "Net Price" was the actual retail price and "Wholesale Price" was what their teacher/agents paid.

Label of the earliest known factory-built "A" mandolin with serial number 2506

Style "A-1" Mandolin – 1903-1904

Early versions of the A-1 were pretty much the same as the "A" except the top was bound with a single strip of ivory-colored celluloid or "ivoroid," and had an inlaid celluloid faux tortoise shell guard-plate with an inlaid pearl design. The early factory instruments did not have the model number on the label making it difficult to determine the correct model designation for mandolins any fancier than the entry-level "A." One of the earliest examples of such a mandolin appears to be a 1904 A-1 with serial number 2858. It has the redesigned headstock shape with the small points and curves and the inlaid mother-of-pearl "The Gibson" logo. It has two soundhole rings and an arched back unlike the early factory "A" models with the Orville-style "frying pan" back. It also has a celluloid guard-plate with an inlaid pearl fleur-de-lis and decorative pearl border.

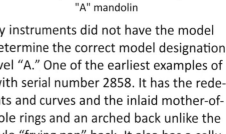
1903 catalog illustration of the Style "A" mandolin

List Price: $53.19
Net Price: $30.00
Wholesale Price: $15.00

1903 catalog illustration of the Style "A-1" mandolin

Style "A-2" Mandolin – 1903-1904

It is possible that Gibson never made any A-2 mandolins or there is no discernable difference between the A-1 and A-2, because the catalog descriptions are nearly identical, so the aforementioned A-1 could be an A-2. The only difference between the two catalog descriptions is the A-2 had a "veneered headpiece, inlaid with pearl ornament," but the illustration shows an eight-pointed star and no extant Gibson mandolins have this design. The 1903 catalog also stipulates that the A-2 had a celluloid guard-plate with a pearl border and a pearl inlay design, but the illustration does not show these features.

List Price: $62.05
Net Price: $35.00
Wholesale Price: $17.50

Style "A-2" mandolin

Style "A-3" Mandolin – 1903-1904

The A-3 is very similar to the A-2 except for the addition of an ivoroid-bound fingerboard, and a bound back. Like the A-2, the 1903 catalog also stipulates that the A-3 had a celluloid guard-plate with a pearl border and a pearl inlay design, but the illustration only shows the faint outline of a dark guard-plate. Early factory A-3 mandolins do have an inlaid guard-plate with the pearl border framing a fancy pearl design, "The Gibson" inlaid on the headstock, as well as a pearl floral design below the logo, plus fancy pearl fingerboard inlays of various shapes. It had an orange top finish or "pumpkin top" with dark mahogany stained back, sides and neck.

Style "A-2"

A-2 List Price: $70.91
Net Price: $40.00
Wholesale Price: $20.00

Style "A-4" Mandolin– 1904

It appears that Gibson did not make any A-4 mandolins until late in 1904. The A-4 was the top-of-the-line Style "A," and had several design features that set it apart from all the other "A" models. Top finish was "ebonized" or jet black, double soundhole rings with inlaid ivoroid in between, celluloid guard-plate with a mother-of-pearl border and an inlaid design in the center of the guard-plate (designs varied, including shells, butterflies, fleur-de-lis, or other various shapes). The earliest known example has the redesigned headstock shape, inlaid mother-of-pearl "The Gibson" logo at a slant, and a pearl fleur-de-lis below the logo. The most striking feature of this example are the pearl fingerboard inlays that are different shapes at each position, starting at the first fret. Even though the catalog describes the machine heads (or tuning machines) as just "finest quality," this existing example has tuners with ivoroid buttons inlaid thin wire swirls and pearl or abalone dots, diamonds, leaves, and flowers which are commonly known as "Handel tuners"

Additional Style "A" specifications:

Carved spruce top (catalog says Norwegian spruce)

Back, sides and neck were usually birch, but some were mahogany

Ebony Stebbins bridge

Nickel-plated brass "pineapple" tailpiece with a hole near the top, "The Gibson" logo is stamped on the cover; base-plate has five mounting screws and no end pin hole

Catalog states that the fingerboards are "oval" or having a radius. While there are examples with this feature, it appears Gibson did this early on then used flat fingerboards after 1904.

19 narrow nickel-silver frets

4-on-a-plate nickel-plated machine heads with ivory-celluloid buttons (except A-4)

Inlaid pearl fingerboard dots at 5th, 7th, 10th and 15th frets, with a double dot at the 12th fret (except A-4)

Style "A-4"

Style "F" Artist Mandolin – 1903-1904

The Style "F" (no number) only appears in Gibson's first catalog and is also the only model described as having "celluloid-ivory binding inlaid on the outer upper edge of rim," aka a single-bound top. There are no "F" mandolins from the pre-1905 era that have these two features. The earliest known factory-made "F," with a single-bound top (s/n 2790), was significantly altered at the factory in the 1920s, so it's far from being all original. The only other example (serial no. 2803 – see instrument gallery) has the single-bound top, but also an ivoroid bound fingerboard, "ebonized" or "black top" finish, and a fancy inlaid guard-plate with pearl ornamentation. These inconsistencies are quite common on all Gibson instruments from the very beginning, so determining the exact model can be very difficult. Case in point, the "F" catalog description also says the "F" has two soundhole rings, a small celluloid-tortoise guard-plate with a pearl border, but the illustration shows none of these features. All of the Style "F" mandolins had an "Artist Extension Fingerboard" above the soundhole increasing the total number of frets to 24 vs. 19 on the "A" models.

List Price: $106.38
No net price or wholesale price information available

Style "F-2"Artist Mandolin – 1903-1904

The F-2 is the only other Style F mandolin illustrated in Gibson's first catalog, and is so similar to Orville's design that it must have drawn using his instrument as the model. Like the "A" mandolins, the earliest factory F model bodies are narrower than Orville's design, but did have the rim, neck and headstock made from one piece, and the necks had a hollowed out cavity. Factory-made F models did not have the wide fancy guard-plate, star and crescent moon headstock inlay, or the banjo-style friction pegs. The most distinguishing Orville design feature the factory did use was the "cord pattern pearl and ebony inlaying" around the top, usually referred to as "rope binding" which looks just like the illustration

List Price: $132.98
Net Price: $75.00
Wholesale Price: $37.50
.

Style "H-2" Mandola - 1905-1909

The H-2 was roughly comparable to the A-4 including the ebonized or black top finish, inlaid pearl "The Gibson" logo with a fleur-de-lis below it, and the top, back and fingerboard were bound with ivoroid.

Recent research failed to locate a single pre-1910 H-2, making it difficult to confirm the exact specifications as compared the illustration and description in Catalog F.

Style H mandola dimensions:
Body width: 11 1/4"
Body length: 15 7/8"
Overall length: 28 1/2"
Scale length: 15 3/4"
Nut width: 1 7/32" +/- 1/32"

Additional Style H specifications:
Bone nut
Ebony bridge
Nickel-plated pineapple tailpiece with "The Gibson" stamped on the cover
Ebony end pin
21 nickel-silver frets including the fingerboard extension
Single mother-of-pearl fingerboard dots at the 5th, 7th, 10th, and 15th frets and a double dot at the 12th fret. Both models also had side dots or position markers on the upper edge of the bound fingerboard
4-on-a-plate tuners – H-1 had plain ivoroid buttons and H-2 had Handel tuners

Artist's rendering of a c1905-1908 H-2 mandola

1909 catalog illustration of the JH-2 mandola

Gibson's prices for all the instruments stayed about the same from 1903 till 1909. Strangely, Catalog F provided both List and Net prices, but also contained the following: Where but one catalog is given and that not marked Net, it is usually a fictitious price called List which is not the regular selling price and It is a lively, alluring bait that gives a customer a lot-of-pork-for-a-shilling smile, as he bites quick, is hooked and landed. It further states that the list price policy of duplicity and misrepresentation to get orders eventually proves a boomerang to the agent and a post-graduate course on 'How to Spend Money' to the customer. Why do catalogs E and F have List prices? Only L. A. Williams could answer that question.

All teacher/agents received a confidential wholesale price list which showed that they paid one half of the Net price for every instrument.

Style "K-1" Mando-cello - 1905-1909

Catalog E gives a very brief description of the K-1 and states that In general appearance this instrument is the same as the Style H-1. The few existing examples of pre-1910 K-1s do not have an inlaid guard-plate despite the catalog description. However, like the H-1, they had the fingerboard extension and the top, back and fingerboard were bound with ivoroid. The tops were spruce, back and rim were birch, and the three-piece necks were Spanish cedar or mahogany, with the ebonized center strip. The headstock had "The Gibson" logo inlaid with mother-of-pearl. The K-1 was quite a bargain at $35.00.

Style "K-2" Mando-cello - 1905-1909

The K-2 was similar to the H-2 only much bigger. The K-1 had the pumpkin-top finish while the K-2 had the black top finish. Surviving examples of the K-2 have the same decorative features as an H-2 including The Gibson and fleur-de-lis pearl inlay on the headstock, inlaid celluloid tortoise guard-plate with pearl border and fleur-de-lis, and ivoroid binding on the top, back and fingerboard. Pre-1910 K-2 mando-cellos are very rare and it appears that Gibson did not sell many partly because of its $50.00 price tag.

Style K mando-cello dimensions:
Body width: 14 1/4"
Body length: 19"
Overall length: 38"
Scale length: 24 3/4" (same as a guitar)
Nut width: 1 3/4"

Additional Style K specifications:
Bone nut
Ebony bridge
Nickel-plated pineapple tailpiece with "The Gibson" stamped on the cover
Ebony end pin
24 frets including the fingerboard extension
Single mother-of-pearl fingerboard dots at the 5th, 7th, 10th, and 15th frets and a double dot at the 12th fret.
Both models also had side dots or position markers on the upper edge of the bound fingerboard
4-on-a-plate tuners –
K-1 had plain ivoroid buttons and
K-2 had Handel tuners

Gibson Finishes – 1903-1909

The types of finishes and processes used by Gibson to achieve their superlative results have been the subject of countless debates. The information contained here is a combination of close examination of many extant instruments, information Gibson published in their catalogs, and the opinions of several veteran luthiers who have spent decades analyzing and re-creating vintage Gibson finishes.

Varnish

From 1903 until 1924 Gibson always used a varnish finish for the top-coat, or the clear coat that was applied last on top of other layers of material. Starting with 1909's Catalog G, L. A. Williams published some colorful information about varnish. He wrote that Gibson's instruments are finished by experienced workmen under the supervision of one who has made a life study of varnish as used on the violin. He probably was not referring to anyone in particular, but like so many of his flowery embellishments, it was just good marketing. As he continues, "let the reader first eliminate the notion of staining wood with acids, corrosives, or other inventions of the age..." This was not marketing mumbo-jumbo, but just plain common sense. He also included some very helpful information about the benefits of the varnish used like it's the first and greatest function is preservation of wood and without varnish no instrument can attain an age of more than a few years without losing its tonal sweetness and power. Williams added that varnish is a preservative, not a causative of tone and it should be tender and in a manner soft; that is, yielding to the movement of the wood. Absolutely spot on.

The yielding qualities of oil varnish give it a vast superiority over spirit varnish or French polish. – L. A. Williams

This is where the big debate begins. Every expert consulted agreed that Gibson actually used spirit varnish, which is essentially some type of resin dissolved in alcohol (or spirits). In layman's terms French Polish is shellac applied by hand with multiple thin layers using a small bag or rubbing pad made by wrapping a ball of wool with a piece of linen cloth. This process produces a beautiful glossy finish, but it's extremely time-consuming, so Gibson definitely did not French polish any of their instruments. The word varnish is still used as a broad term to describe many types of finishes. Spirit varnish can be made using different resins like copal, sandarac, or mastic, all of which are produced by various species of trees. It can also be made with shellac, but shellac is not actually a resin, it is an organic material excreted by the female lac bug on trees found in Asia. Varnish formulas can be a mix of shellac and one or two kinds of resin like sandarac and mastic. Most likely Gibson used a clear varnish formula that consisted of 80% light-colored shellac flakes mixed with 10% sandarac and 10% mastic powder dissolved in denatured alcohol of at least 90 proof or 45% pure alcohol.

The easiest way to verify if a vintage instrument has a varnish finish is to look closely at the checking pattern. The small cracks that form in the top coat over many years as the varnish continues to harden is called checking. Varnish finishes usually have a very small crisscrossed pattern that looks like hundreds of perpendicular lines. This is very common on Gibsons made before 1924 because the varnish was so thin that for the most part, the thinner the finish, the smaller the checking will be.

Applying Varnish

Most experts agree that Gibson sprayed the spirit varnish top-coat right from the start and did not brush it on because brushing took too much time and put too much varnish on the instruments. In 1907 Thomas DeVilbiss had designed the first commercially viable hand-held air-powered spray gun and soon after, they were in common use in many wood products manufacturing industries like furniture and musical instruments. This early design is sometimes referred to as a "blow gun" because the air power was supplied by the person doing the spraying. Blowing into a tube, connected to a nozzle, lowered the pressure and a siphon tube submerged in liquid varnish rushed upward to fill the partial vacuum. When the varnish hit the air stream, tiny atomized particles of the finish sprayed out of a tip located on the nozzle. It's likely that Gibson used this type of sprayer to apply a fine, thin coat of material quickly and evenly.

Wood Dyes

Just about every Gibson instrument had the back, rim and neck dyed a shade of brown. There are many variations of the stains used by Gibson resulting in shades that ranged from very dark brown (almost black) to a lighter brown with a reddish hue. The company's early catalogs always referred to this as "dark mahogany." The variations depended on the dye-to-solvent ratio or the number of coats applied. Most experts agree that Gibson used water-based stains and probably used aniline dyes which come in a powder form in a wide variety of colors and dissolved in water. One of the reasons for the wide variety shades was a finisher would mix a batch of stain for several instruments but once that was used up, another batch would be mixed and so on, so there was always differences in the color of each batch. The stain was wiped on the wood with a rag and vigorously hand-rubbed to ensure the stain penetrated deeply and evenly. One of the most distinctive qualities of the hand-rubbed finish is it greatly enhances the wood's natural variations in color and grain pattern, especially figured woods like curly maple.

The Pumpkin-top Finish

The light orange/yellow finish Gibson used on the tops of their instruments has been nicknamed pumpkin top although Gibson called it "golden orange." Orange shellac was the most commonly available shellac flakes and were a yellow/orange color. The vast majority of shellac finishes were made by dissolving the flakes in denatured alcohol and wiping it on the wood with a cloth. Shellac is a natural wood preservative as well as an excellent sealer that forms a base coat that allows the varnish top coat to adhere strongly and level out more easily. Gibson also used shellac on top of the water-based stains as a sealer.

The Ebonized Finish

Gibson called their jet black finish ebonized and it was used on the tops of several early models. Experienced luthiers believe that Gibson produced this finish in several steps. First they put a generous amount of water-based black stain on the surface allowing it to really soak into the wood and then they added two or three additional layers of bone black. Bone black is made from dried animal bones that are cooked at such a high temperature that it burns away all of the remaining organic material, leaving nothing but charcoal which is basically pure carbon. Originally it was used for purifying sugar and water filtration, and then as a dye for things like India ink and shoe polish. Bone black was dissolved in a small amount of alcohol so it would not be diluted too much. It's important to note that the spruce tops were a light color, so getting them to look jet black was not an easy task. The more expensive instruments had real ebony fingerboards and veneered head-pieces, but even the best quality ebony usually has some lighter colored streaks so they would be ebonized. The lower-end instruments were advertised as having ebony fingerboards but most were some cheaper hardwood that some refer to as "cheese wood," Because it was any inexpensive hardwood that was available. The ebonizing process was used on these cheaper fingerboards and headstock veneers.

Early Sunburst Finishes

Sunburst is a term that Gibson didn't start using until 1918 and has since become synonymous with their finishes because no other instrument manufacturer past or present has ever come close to matching the beauty and artistry of these finishes. Before 1910 Gibson referred to this finish as "violin shading of red to brown" and the earliest known instrument that with it is an F-4 mandolin that dates to late 1905 or early 1906. It appears that Gibson decided only to use the violin shading on the backs of the F-4 which highlighted the figured maple grain pattern. The finish was accomplished by dyeing the back a semi-red color (sometimes almost orange) then the edges were shaded brown by wiping the darker color over the red and vigorously hand-rubbing it to get the two colors to blend giving the appearance that the red gradually got darker toward the edges.

Gibson Parts & Accessories – 1903-1909

The Mystery of the Handel Tuners

From early on Gibson decided to use completely different tuning machines than the friction-style tuners Orville was fond of. The basic design of these tuners that had the shaft, worm-gear, and string post mounted on a plate had been around for more than 100 years. Gibson's lower priced instruments had 4-on-a-plate tuners with plain ivoroid buttons; the more expensive instruments had tuners with very fancy inlaid buttons. The ones with the inlaid buttons are commonly known as "Handel tuners," but no one seems to know where that name came from. For the longest time the prevailing theory has been that the tuners were imported from Germany, mainly because Gibson stopped using them around the same time the United States entered World War 1 at a time when heavy restrictions were put on almost everything imported from Germany. Gibson did describe the decorative buttons as being "inlaid with German silver," but this was just another name for an alloy of zinc, copper and nickel, or nickel silver and had nothing to do with Germany. The biggest problem with confirming who made these early tuners is they had no maker's mark or patent date stamp, making it nearly impossible to be 100% sure.

Recent research has confirmed that these tuners were actually made by the Louis Handel Co., located in New York City, and that's where the name came from. The company made a diverse array of products including musical instrument parts like tuning machines and tailpieces and inlaid celluloid guard-plates and headstock veneers with all types of patterns and designs. They even made automobile parts. Handel had a fully equipped machine shop for fine metal fabrication like scroll-saw cutting for small parts, stamping and engraving and many other types of metal products and services. They also had a screw machine shop that produced threaded screws, bolts and worm gears, as well as fine metal lathes for tuning out small parts like the shafts and posts used for the instrument tuners. They were supplying both the tuners with plain buttons, and ones with inlaid buttons to other manufacturers like Martin Guitars and Lyon & Healy.

No. 301

No. 300

Catalog illustration of the No. 301 Handel tuners with inlaid buttons and the No. 300

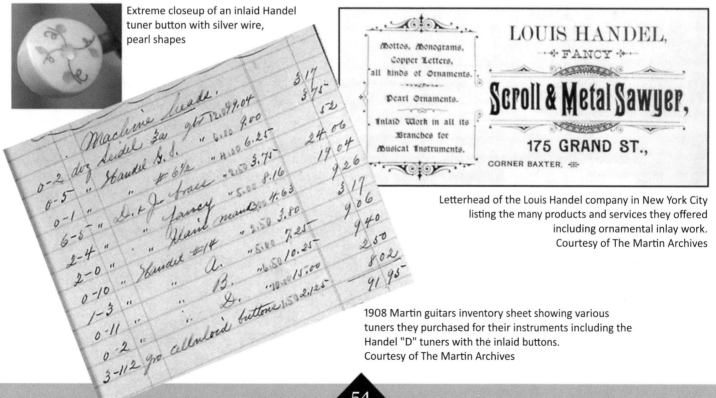

Extreme closeup of an inlaid Handel tuner button with silver wire, pearl shapes

LOUIS HANDEL,
FANCY
Scroll & Metal Sawyer,
175 GRAND ST.,
CORNER BAXTER.

Mottos, Monograms, Copper Letters, all kinds of Ornaments.
Pearl Ornaments.
Inlaid Work in all its Branches for Musical Instruments.

Letterhead of the Louis Handel company in New York City listing the many products and services they offered including ornamental inlay work.
Courtesy of The Martin Archives

1908 Martin guitars inventory sheet showing various tuners they purchased for their instruments including the Handel "D" tuners with the inlaid buttons.
Courtesy of The Martin Archives

Healy for guitars and mandolins. From documents found in Martin's archives, Handel made four different tuner designs, including the Style "D" which had the fancy inlaid buttons and were the most expensive set they made.

In addition, Gibson required specially made tuners for their "F" style mandolins, because they required shafts of varying lengths to fit the asymmetrical "hook and scroll" headstock shape. Handel also supplied this design with plain buttons for the lower-priced "F-2" mandolins; the more expensive "F-4s," had the inlaid buttons. Gibson also used 4-on-a-plate tuners with uniform length shafts for the Style "A" mandolins, Style "H" mandolas and Style "K" mando-cellos, each of which had plain or inlaid buttons depending on the model. Gibson did stop getting the Handel tuners with the inlaid buttons in 1917 or 1918, but it appears the reason for this was a cost-cutting measure instituted by L. A. Williams shortly after he became General Manager. Actually, Gibson continued using tuners made by the Handel Co. until 1922. More on this subject in Chapter 17. However Martin Guitar's internal inventory sheet from 1918 does show the Handel "D" tuners, but the 1920 sheet does not. In 1918 these tuners were $1.80 per set wholesale, more than triple the price of the tuners with plain buttons, so it appears that they were just too expensive and were discontinued by Handel.

c1908 back of an F-4 headstock showing the fancy Handel tuners with dissimilar length shafts to fit the asymmetrical shape of the headstock.

Instrument Cases

Before 1911 Gibson used two basic styles of instrument cases, a light duty canvas case and a heavy duty embossed black leather case. Both of these were made by Maulbetsch & Whittemore, which was founded in 1886 in Newark, New Jersey by John Maulbetsch and George Whittemore. In 1893, M&W trade-marked their "Bull's Head" brand of cases and most of the embossed

leather cases from the early 1900s had their new trademark "bull's head" logo.

Maulbetsch & Whittemore's "Bull's Head" trademark logo

Gibson catalog illustration of the Maulbetsch & Whittemore embossed leather mandolin case.

Strings

It's almost certain that Gibson did not actually make their own strings until 1929, but it is interesting to note that Gibson's 1909 Catalog "F" stated that "the exclusive manufacture of these special strings is held and controlled by the Gibson Company." Ironically, the company also stated in Catalog "F" that "it must, therefore be understood that the above named strings are manufactured for quality of tone rather than for exceptional service." Apparently string breakage and unraveling was a major problem with these early strings. Gibson just repackaged strings from another manufacturer and the strings were made to their own specifications. One of the most likely companies that could have supplied the strings was the V.C. Squier Company, which was located in nearby Grand Rapids, Michigan. V.C. Squier was mainly known for their violins and violin strings, but they did produce strings for other fretted musical instruments as well. The company was established in 1890 by Victor Carroll Squier and was eventually sold to Fender in 1965, the same year that CBS bought Fender. Apparently CBS did not see the need for having their own string manufacturing company and soon after the acquisition they shut down the V.C. Squier plant. Even though the "Squier" string brand became defunct, Fender reused the name for a line of lower-priced instruments still being made.

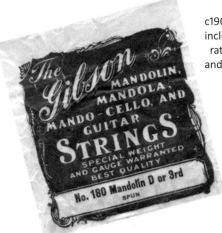

c1909 Gibson string envelope with one-color dark blue graphics, including the instrument and type of string printed on the envelope rather than ink-stamped. This required every envelope for each string type and gauge to be printed separately.

Note:—There is nothing known to the science of string manufacturing that will prevent Mandolin wound second or A, Guitar wire wound second or B, Mando-cello wound first, or A from raveling. The winding has to be so fine on the smaller wound strings that it shortly wears through on the fret which causes the raveling or unwinding. It must, therefore, be understood that the above named strings are manufactured for **quality** of tone rather than for exceptional service.

No order filled for less than one dozen Strings, or by the Set. Gut strings and Contra-Bass strings excepted.

Some additional information about Gibson strings that was included in Catalog F from 1909

Tailpieces

Gibson used several variations of the "pineapple" tailpiece early on, but by 1906 settled on a standard design. Tailpieces c1903-1905 are slightly longer than the later designs, usually with a hole near the top of the cover and holes for five mounting screws. Many of these early tailpieces had no hole for an end pin. The tailpieces Gibson started using in 1906 were shorter, had three mounting screw holes, and a hole for an end pin. Most of the pre-1910 tailpieces were made from nickel-plated brass and "The Gibson" logo was stamped rather than engraved. Around the same time that Laurian's patent was issued in 1909, Gibson switched to a nickel silver alloy that eliminated the need for plating.The design also changed from the pineapple-shaped top to more of a crown-shaped top which is the same design still in use.

c1904 pineapple mandolin tailpiece with hole in the center

c1906 pineapple tailpiece without hole

c1909 new style crown-top tailpiece

Gibson Mandolin-Guitar Co. - 1910-1919

A New Era

In 1910, Gibson had settled into their new factory located on Harrison Court and were producing about 2500 instruments a year. Their production totals increased steadily throughout the decade and by 1919, they were making over 6700 instruments per year. 1910 also marked the beginning of a whole new era for Gibson because they made some significant changes to their instrument line and within a couple of years added several new models. The single biggest change that occurred in late 1910 or early 1911 was the complete redesign of the Style "F" mandolins. Gibson completely stopped making the three-point body style that was such an integral part of Orville's original design and the new "F" bodies had only two-points. They eliminated the body point on the bass side at the waist and also changed the lower point on the treble side upper bout making them slope upward, rather than downward like the three-point design.

Orville Fades from the Picture

Another big change that happened in 1910 was when the company stopped using the "lyre label" with the picture of Orville on it and started using a new oval-shaped "guaranteed" label as it's commonly called. The label boldly proclaimed that all of their instruments were now "guaranteed against faulty workmanship or material" and should anything "go wrong, we agree to repair it for free" or "replace it." However someone made a huge mistake and put the wrong patent date on these labels. The "Mar. 30" patent date printed at the top corresponded to L. A. Williams' elevated finger-rest, but the year should be '09, and not '06. One of the reasons for these particular changes seems to reflect the company's desire to distance themselves from Orville. Given the new information about Orville Gibson's nervous breakdown in July 1909 coupled with the fact he had left Kalamazoo seems to indicate

Above left: An early 1910 3-point F-2. Courtesy of The Mandolin Bros. Upper right: 1915 F-2 with the new 2-point body design. Courtesy of Elderly Instruments.

that the Gibson Company no longer wanted to be associated with Orville's legacy, at least not publicly. The earliest existing mandolin with the new "guaranteed" label is a three-point black-top "F-2" with the Williams' style elevated finger-rest, serial number 9967 confirming this change took place in mid-1910, but before the change to the two-point body style.

A blank "lyre-label" with Orville Gibson used from 1903-1910

Center: The earliest known "guaranteed" label from an early 1910 F-2 with serial no. 9967. Courtesy of The Mandolin Bros. Below: The "guaranteed" label with the incorrect year for the patent date.

Gibson Management

After George D. Laurian left Gibson in 1915, Thaddeus Joseph McHugh or "Ted," as he was known by his colleagues, was appointed the new plant superintendent. McHugh was born and raised in Kalamazoo and became friends with Orville Gibson in the 1890s when on many occasions they performed at concerts together. Ted was a very good singer as well as a talented woodworker, but by all accounts didn't play a musical instrument. Frequently, he was one of several musicians that "hung out" at Orville's shop playing music and talking shop. He went to work for Gibson in 1911 as a shop foreman and was promoted to factory superintendent by Sylvo Reams. A short biography from 1944 that was written by one of his family members stated that "since 1922, he has been doing experimental work, designing, drafting, etc. and still holds his position doing special work." There's no doubt that McHugh left an indelible mark on the company's history and he remained at Gibson until his death in 1945. (more on Ted McHugh in Chapter 13)

1909 Thaddeus "Ted" McHugh

One of Gibson's major blunders was the that Harrison Court factory should have been much bigger. It was barely larger than the Exchange Place facility and the company grossly miscalculated the amount of room they needed. As early as 1912, Gibson was already in the early stages of planning a third factory that was eventually built in 1917 (more on this in Chapter 11). Also in 1917 Sylvo Reams, Gibson's General Manager and co-founder died and Lewis A. Williams became the new General Manager. Williams hired Sylvo Reams' brother Andrew Jay or "A.J." Reams Jr. who became Williams' right hand man as Associate General Manager. Unfortunately A. J. Reams died only two years later in 1919, which may have been the reason why Williams had McHugh take over the engineering and designing position.

The Rise of the Mandolin Orchestra

Andrew "AJ" Reams Jr.

Mandolin groups of various sizes had been around since the 1880s after the success of the second incarnation of the "Spanish Students." Around the turn of the twentieth century many mandolin groups started forming on college campuses like Harvard, Princeton, Yale and Vanderbilt. The mandolin and most fretted musical instruments were easier to play compared to instruments in the violin family because the frets aided in fingering notes correctly, and a pick or plectrum was easier to use than a bow. The mandolin was an instrument of the "average Joe," and it attracted would-be players from all walks of life. Mandolin groups grew in size to become large orchestras sometimes consisting of 50 or more members.

Early 1900s mandolin trio

c1911 Mandolin Orchestra.
Courtesy of Centerstream Publishing

The Buffalo Symphonic Mandolin Orchestra

Gibson was quick to realize the potential sales boom that could be generated by promoting and endorsing these groups. L. A. Williams started off advertising just Gibson's instruments in small simple ads then started to use sales and promotional materials that catered to music teachers, whom he enrolled as sales agents. After the tremendous success, his initial sales strategy, Williams shifted the focus of his advertising efforts to featuring mandolin orchestras. One of the first such ads appeared in the June 1912 edition of *The Cadenza* magazine featuring the "Gibson Mandolin Orchestra, Dallas, Texas," with Williams' iconic slogan, "Everyone A Gibson-ite." Almost every month Gibson was placing full-page ads in magazines featuring yet another mandolin orchestra, every member of which played only Gibson instruments, as well as featuring them in many catalogs. Williams appointed himself the leading authority on how to organize and promote mandolin orchestras and even went so far as to dictate the correct instrumentation needed to be considered up to his standards qualifying to be featured in an advertisement or catalog.

HE HAS NOT THE CONVICTION BUT THE SIGHT

THE GIBSON MANDOLIN ORCHESTRA, DALLAS, TEXAS
"EVERY ONE A 'GIBSON -ITE!"

The Gospel According to L. A. Williams

Nay-sayers that didn't do things according to Williams' way of thinking would incur his wrath and were lambasted with criticism. He would write things like "The teacher who aims to speak only as books instruct, as custom insists, and as interest commands – babbles. Let him Hush" and "They are proud of everything of which they should regret. Proud of the antiquity of their opinions; proud of adhering to an outgrown musical orthodoxy" and so on. Williams' incessant critique, would get down-right biblical at times. He once wrote, "Let that which shows God within fortify thee instead of placing divinity without and making of thyself a wart and a wen." His way was the right way and wrote that one "must have a string quintet completed in the mandolin orchestra" and "these instruments must be accurately   voiced by one individual or concern (which necessitates using one make)." In other words, buy only Gibson instruments.

THE CADENZA

For Now All See in Part as Through a Glass Darkly. So, the Whole Truth is Greater than the Best and Most Here Told

EVOLUTION or DEVOLUTION

NOT A POTATO-BUGIST AMONG 'EM.

Then Grey Hairs Applaud, Progress May Well Ask "What Have I Done Amiss?" THE PROFESSIONAL MICE.

Some ads were simply a whole page with nothing but text where Williams would seemingly go on and on waxing poetic about the right way for teachers, players and groups to be considered innovators and not imitators. Williams started to expand his advertising into much larger publications like *Popular Science*, *Popular Mechanics* and even *Cosmopolitan Magazine*. He toned down the rhetoric for these more mainstream magazines and promoted Gibson's unbeatable deals like "5 Cents A Day Buys a Gibson" and the tremendous opportunities to "Teach and Sell The Gibson – Big Money." Whatever one's opinions are about his tactics, he was successful in turning Gibson into the 800 pound gorilla of the mandolin universe.

1912 example of an ad with a full page of the Gospel According to LA Williams

After 1917 Williams was unable to work on sales and marketing and hired Clarence Vincent or "C.V." Buttelman as the new Sales & Advertising Manager. Buttelman had been working for a Boston-based publisher, Walter Jacobs, writing for

their well-known music industry magazine *The Cadenza*. Buttelman actually lived in Jackson, Michigan only 65 miles from Kalamazoo, so when the opportunity to work for Gibson came up he jumped at the chance. Buttelman had a completely different writing style than his new boss, L.A. Williams. He wanted to romanticize Gibson instruments with cute little catch phrases like "Companionship and Music – A Delightful Combination" and "It's easy to play the Gibson way." His ads showed romantic couples rowing "the old canoe" down a gentle stream on a "redolent moon-flecked evening" while playing their Gibson mandolins. He wrote that "Gibsons furnish that indefinable 'something' which eliminates formality, makes

C.V. Buttelman

hearts lighter, eyes brighter, friendships dearer, and love sweeter." Who could say no to that? Buttelman also came up with Gibson's newest catch phrase, "Music Pals of the Nation."

"The Old Canoe" ad appeared in the September 1919 edition of *The Cadenza* Magazine

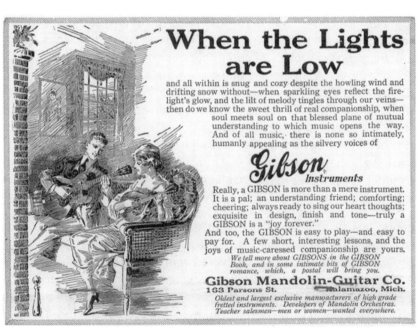

Another 1919 ad is a good example of how C.V. Buttelman wanted to romanticize playing music and in particular, a Gibson instrument

Gibson Mandolin-Guitar Co. – Part 2 - 1910-1919

More Innovations

On July 4, 1911 George Laurian was awarded a fourth patent for his pickguard mounting clamp, His main objective was to design a lightweight clamp that adjusted easily for instruments of varying depths without the aid of any tools. The clamp

was attached to the side of the instrument and was screwed into a celluloid riser and support arm (Figures III & IV - #s 6 & 7).

The clamp had three main parts; two interlocking bent plates slid back and forth and locked in place using a cam lever. When Gibson changed their finger-rest a smaller size than L. A. William's original design, almost all of their instruments only required one clamp. The clamps were all stamped with the July 4, 1911 patent date and Gibson used Laurian's clamp design from 1911 till 1925.

Gibson catalog Illustration of the new elevated inger-rest clamp

Patent No. 996,652 for George Laurian;s elevated finger-rest clamp

In 1911 Gibson introduced a completely new mandolin, the Style "D – Alrite." Previously, it was thought that Gibson only made the "Alrite" in 1917, but they started advertising it in 1911 and it appeared on their 1912 price list. The Style "D" certainly has an amusing name and the company probably figured that since it was fairly inexpensive ($17.00 vs. $25.00 for an "A" mandolin) and had a simple flat "pancake" body, it could be considered a genuine Gibson, it was just "alright." Gibson never included the "Alrite" mandolin in any of their full-line catalogs and only advertised it very sparingly. Gibson also referred to it as the "junior" model, a name that would re-emerge in the 1920s. Its body was almost perfectly round and had a round soundhole, instead of oval shape all other mandolin models had. Gibson added purfling, a ring of alternating dark and light inlaid wood around the edges of the top between the binding and the spruce sounding board. It also had a soundhole ring or rosette of dark and light wood that matched the purfling. The Style D was the only mandolin Gibson ever made that had purfling. They only made the Style D for a little over five years until it was discontinued in 1917.

More than three and a half years later a second patent was awarded to Williams and Reams on December 7, 1920 . They had taken their previous design patent and turned It into a whole new invention. Although Gibson never built any mandolin using this design, the patent did contain some significant new ideas that would be incorporated into Gibson's radical new Style "5" Master Models within a couple of years. Their idea was to try a radically new soundhole design. The shape became known as the "cat's eye" and Gibson did use it for a couple of prototype guitars in the 20s. The patent also specifically describes its new headstock shape which tapered from wider at the bottom to narrower at the top. This was

the basis for Gibson's "snake-head" design they started using in the 1920s. Although it is not mentioned in the patent, the illustration clearly shows that for the first time, they had conceived of the idea of an elevated fingerboard, which would be a significant feature of the all the Master Model instruments.

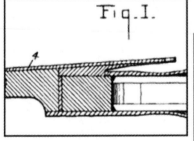

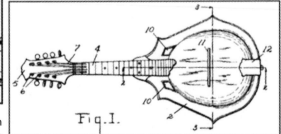

Two sections from Williams and Reams Patent No. 1,361,182. Above: Design for an elevated fingerboard. Right: The tapered mandolin headstock shape

New Instruments

In 1911 the company also introduced the mammoth Style "J" mando-bass, although it didn't appear in a catalog until 1912. Gibson clearly saw the need for a bass instrument to cover the low end of the mandolin orchestra. The mandolins played the soprano or violin parts, the mandola covered the tenor/viola parts, and the mando-cello, the baritone/cello parts, but Gibson wanted to add a bass instrument. Other manufacturers had made similar instruments before Gibson, but the Style J was just the right design for the times. Gibson called it "the colossus of tonal power" and that the mandolin quintet (including guitar) was "now complete." When posed with the hypothetical question of "how can I afford a mando-bass," in classic form, Lewis Williams responded "how can you not afford it" and called any-one that didn't clearly see the need for the mando-bass as a "false economy's foot-licker" and questioned their very worthiness asking, "Is thy greatness real or a feigned preten-tion?" You could get a Style "J" for only $5.00 down and $3.00 per month. How could anyone resist?

In 1914 Gibson introduced two new members of the mandolin family, the Style "H-4" mandola, and the Style "K-4" mando-cello. Although Gibson had made a prototype mando-cello with an "F" style mandolin body in 1906, the design was fully realized becoming a regular production instrument. Similarly, the "H-4" mandola had a post-1910 two-point "F" mandolin-style body, only smaller than the K-4 mando-cello that was nearly 40" long and 14 1/4" wide. A lot of other interesting changes took place between 1912 and 1918, especially the new types of finishes Gibson started using as well as modifications to inlay designs and fingerboards. Gibson discontinued the A-1 mandolin in 1917 and replaced it with the A-2, a model designation that had not been used since 1903.

The Style 'J' mando-bass
The colossus of tonal power

April 1919 *Popular Science* ad

Also in 1917 Gibson raised its prices for the first time since the company started, but also raised prices in 1918 and again in 1919, a direct result of L. A. Williams becoming the new general manager who was trying to increase profit margins and stock dividends. The price difference between 1918 and 1919 equaled nearly a 23% net increase which may have increased profit margins, but had a deleterious effect on overall sales. On their September 1919 price list, Williams tried to bolster sales by including new sales slogans like "7 2/3 cents a day buys a Gibson" and "NO GIBSON is more than 35 cents a day."

In 1918 Gibson manufactured its first banjo, but the company was the "Johnny-come-lately" to the banjo party. There were many competitors who had been in the banjo manufacturing business well before 1918, including William Lange of Rettberg & Lange, makers of the Orpheum and Paramount brands, S.S. Stewart, who started making banjos in the 1800s, and Bacon Banjos, founded by banjo virtuoso and pioneer, Fred Bacon (later called Bacon & Day) and many others. Gibson's early banjo model was a basic "open-back" design and the model designation was simply "TB" or tenor banjo. In 1919 the company added three additional variations of the banjo including the "CB" cello-banjo, "GB" guitar-banjo, and the "MB" mandolin-banjo.

October 1919 ad for Gibson's new 'TB' tenor banjo

The New Factory

In July 1917 Gibson moved to its third factory located at 225 Parsons Street in Kalamazoo. For several years prior, the company had been buying up several parcels of land where Parsons Street abutted the Grand Rapids and Indiana (G. R. & I) railroad tracks in anticipation of a location that was ideal for the new factory. On July 17, 1917 Gibson hosted a "House Warming to Celebrate the Opening of [the] New Factory," which was by invitation only. The Parsons Street factory had three floors with a total of 45,000 square feet of production and office space. The first floor, which was partially a basement, housed the furnace room, a rough lumber storage room, the wood steaming room, pattern-makers shop, machine shop, and the repair shop. On the second floor, huge windows provided plenty of daylight for the main assembly room including the binding and gluing departments. It was also where Gibson did banjo assembly, but also contained all the administrative office and an employee lunchroom. On the

July 1917 invitation to Gibson's new factory "house warming." Courtesy of Rod McDonald

Gibson's landmark factory at 225 Parsons Street that opened in July 1917

third floor were the staining and finishing rooms and the final inspection area. The machine shop was responsible for milling and cutting the rough lumber into blanks for all the various instrument parts, as well as rough carving the tops, backs and necks. The pattern-makers shop built all the templates, the body molds which were used for bending the rims, as well as the body molds that were used for assembling the bent rims together with the neck and tail blocks and kerfed liners. The main assembly and gluing departments took the finished rim assemblies and glued on the tops and backs, and rough-fitted the necks, then sent them to the binding room for the bindings to be glued on, and final sanding in order to prepare the instruments for finishing. Also on the second floor were Gibson's administrative offices including the engineering department and a large showroom where they displayed samples of all the various instrument models they manufactured as well as promotional materials like banners, posters, catalogs and pictures of all the Gibson endorsers.

On the third floor the staining and finishing rooms were the final stage of manufacturing, before the instruments were sent for final inspection. In 1917 Gibson was still hand-staining their instruments and using clear varnish for the top coat. The final inspection department closely examined every instrument and if necessary, sent some instruments back for re-work if they found any flaws. They were also responsible for stringing and playing the instruments. Next to final inspection was the shipping department. They were responsible for packaging and crating the instruments for shipment all over the world. It was not unusual for the shipping department to send out over 100 instruments per day.

The Parsons Street factory was expanded several times during the 67 years that Gibson occupied the premises. It had approximately 170,000 square feet when Gibson left in 1984 and moved all manufacturing to Nashville, Tennessee. The building still stands and is called the Kalamazoo Enterprise Center. In 2015, the iconic smoke-stack with "Gibson" in huge letters on it was in danger of being demolished, but attempts are being made to declare the building a national historic landmark, and rightly so.

c1918 main assembly room

c1930 gluing and binding department

c1918 factory workers with guitar, harp-guitar and banjo rims

All photos courtesy of the Kalamazoo Public Library

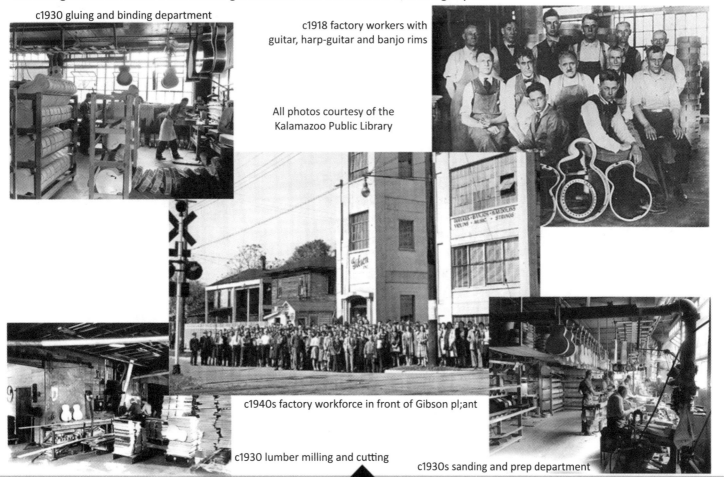

c1940s factory workforce in front of Gibson pl;ant

c1930 lumber milling and cutting

c1930s sanding and prep department

Gibson Instruments - 1910-1919

Style "D - Alrite" Mandolin – 1911-1918

The Alrite was Gibson's first flat-top and flat-back mandolin. Previously most sources believed that Gibson only made the Alrite for one year – 1917, but it was actually first introduced in 1911 and wasn't discontinued until 1918. The Alrite never appeared in any Gibson catalog, but did appear in the first edition of the company's in-house publication *The Sounding Board* magazine in 1911 as well as appearing on Gibson's 1912 price list. It's difficult to date these mandolins because Gibson used different serial numbers. Early examples have a non-standard three-digit number starting around 100 through 600; then they decided to use regular six-digit numbers later on. The highest serial number recorded is 47038 which dates to 1918. Its body was round and also had a round soundhole, unlike the standard oval holes on all the other mandolin models. The Alrite was the first Gibson mandolin with a flat top and flat back as well as the first to have a 12-fret neck (12 frets clear of the body), as compared to the standard 10-fret necks on all of their other mandolins. In order to strengthen the thin flat top of this totally new design, Gibson used internal top bracing that was completely different from the carved-top instruments. The Alrite also had alternating dark and light wood purfling (inlay between the binding and the top) around the edge and around the soundhole, a feature that no other Gibson mandolin has ever had before or since. Although the Alrite had a different label that was round as opposed to the standard oval-shaped "Guarantee" label, it did have the company's name printed on it. The majority of them had a plain black headstock overlay with no logo similar to the Style "A" mandolins.

1911 Price: $17.00
1917 Price: $20.00
1918: Discontinued

An example of a Style "D - Alrite label

D - Alrite dimensions:
Body width: 9 1/4"
Body length: 11 1/4"
Overall length: 22 3/8"
Scale length: 13 7/8"
Nut width: 1 1/8"

Additional D-Alrite specifications:
Flat spruce top with golden orange finish
Flat mahogany back and mahogany rim
  (brown finish)
12-fret, 1-piece Spanish cedar neck c1911-14 and
  mahogany neck 1915-1917
Ebony nut vs. bone
Ebony Laurian-style bridge
Ebony end pin
Nickel-plated "cloud" tailpiece (more on this in Chapter 13)
4-on-a-plate tuners with ivoroid buttons
18 nickel-silver frets
Ivoroid bound soundhole and top edge
Alternating dark and light wood purfling around the top
  edge and soundhole
Fingerboard with inlaid pearl dots at 5th, 7th, 10th, 12th and
  15th frets (double dot at the 12th)

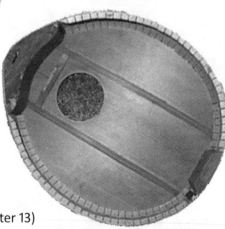

Interior showing top bracing pattern

Model "DY - Army/Navy" Mandolin – 1918-1919

It has been a common assumption for many years that the Army/Navy models "GY" guitar and "DY" mandolin were sold strictly to the military for veterans returning from World War I. However Gibson made them available to any of their sales representatives and sold to the general public. The reason for this stems from the fact that the DY never appeared in any Gibson catalog or price list with the exception of a January 15, 1921 "Confidential Wholesale Price List." Like the D – Alrite mandolin, the DY was a round flat-top and flat-back mandolin and although it was much less ornate than the Alrite, its price tag was only slightly less. L. A. Williams had just become General Manager and was implementing many cost-cutting measures, so in the case of the Alrite, Gibson was able to re-use the same body molds and bending forms as the Alrite which cost nothing and still charged about the same price. The company marketed it as the embodiment of "Gibson workmanship" but was "made to sell at a moderate price" and "puts to rout the excuses of the 'Can't-afford-it' prospects." The DY had no binding, purfling, or the Gibson logo on the peghead, but it did have the company's name on a round label similar to the Alrite labels. It had a spruce top, birch back and sides, and a mahogany neck, and was finished in "Sheraton Brown" which was a brand new finish Gibson introduced in 1918.

1918 Price: $17.50

DY - Army/Navy Mandolin dimensions: Same as D – Alrite

Style "A" Mandolin – 1910-1919

The Style "A" mandolins went through some changes between 1910 and 1919, but with the exception of the three-piece mahogany neck in 1914 and the elevated finger-rest, the "A" stayed pretty much the same as pre-1910 examples. In 1911 Gibson changed the elevated finger-rest support clamp to the newly patented Laurian cam clamp. Gibson's 1918 Catalog K stated that the "A" mandolin had the new Sheraton Brown finish, but existing examples had the earlier pumpkin-top finish. More on finishes at the end of this chapter.

1910 Price: $25.00
1917 Price: $27.50
1918 Price: $30.25
1919 Price: $37.00

Left: Pre-1910 violin chin-rest clamp Gibson used for their new elevated finger-rests. Courtesy of Dan Beimborn
Right: The George Laurian patented cam clamp Gibson used from mid-1910 until 1925. Courtesy of Gregg Miner

Style "A-1" Mandolin – 1910-1917

Gibson discontinued the A-1 in 1917 and introduced the A-2 as its replacement. Almost all A-1s from this era stayed pretty much the same with the exception of the change to a 3-piece mahogany neck in 1914. Most had the pumpkin-top finish but there are examples with the black-top finish.

Style "A-2" Mandolin – 1918-1919

1910 Price: $30.00
1917 Price: $32.50

Gibson decided to introduce a whole new model as a replacement for the A-1, because it had the new Sheraton Brown finish. They also changed the soundhole rings from alternating dark and light inlaid wood, or marquetry, and replaced them with two soundhole rings that had four plies or stripes of alternating ivoroid and black celluloid, sometimes referred to as "ebonoid."

1918 Price: $38.50
1919 Price: $47.00

Style "A-3" Mandolin – 1910-1919

1910-1917 A-3 mandolins also stayed relatively the same as the pre-1910 versions with the exception of the same changes to the "A" and A-1. However, in 1918 Gibson introduced a whole new A-3 design nicknamed the "Ivory-Top." Rather than changing the model name like the A-2 the company opted to keep the same model although the post-1917 A-3s look nothing like the previous ones. Gibson referred to the top finish as "beautiful old ivory" but the back, rim and neck retained the dark mahogany finish as well as the headstock design with "The Gibson" logo and floral design inlaid in pearl. The top was bound with two plies with a thicker ivoroid piece on the outside and a thinner ebonoid layer in between the ivoroid and the top. It had a single-bound ivoroid back and fingerboard, a "grained ivoroid" (a type of celluloid made to look like real ivory) elevated finger-rest and a matching ivoroid finger-rest mount that had a threaded metal rod support arm attached to a threaded ivoroid block under the finger-rest.

1910 Price: $40.00   1918 Price: $46.75
1917 Price: $42.50   1919 Price: $57.00

The "Gibson" Mandolin, Style "A-3"

Carefully selected, straight grain, graduated spruce top (sounding-board), beautiful old ivory finish; thoroughly air-seasoned maple rim and back; dark mahogany finish; highly polished throughout; straight grain British Honduras mahogany neck, reinforced and non-warpable; neck finished in shading of mahogany; head-piece veneered front and back, front inlaid with "The Gibson" in pearl, and pearl ornament; ivoroid bound, solid ebony finger-board, with twenty ovaled narrow frets; pearl position dots inlaid on finger-board and position dots on upper edge of neck; ebonoid bound, oblong sound-hole inlaid with two rings of purfling of colored woods; top bound on outer edges of rim with ebonoid and ivoroid; back bound on outer edge of rim with ivoroid; elevated guard-plate or finger-rest with white copper clamp (Patented July 4, 1911. See cut, page 106); compensating bridge preventing sharping of tones in upper positions; best quality of machine-head, onyx-ivoroid buttons; bone nut; "Gibson" extension white copper string-holder.

Pat. Mar. 30, 1909
Pat. Sept. 21, 1909
Pat. Sept. 20, 1910

Gibson instruments may be purchased from Gibson Agents, or, in territory where we are not represented, direct from us. Responsible parties may arrange for monthly payments to suit their convenience. For prices and terms see price list attached to inside of front cover. Price list of strings, supplies and parts furnished on request. Prices quoted are Net and not subject to further discount.

Style "A-4" Mandolin – 1910-1919

In 1912, Gibson changed the A-4 design to include a fingerboard extension, a feature that no other Style "A" mandolin had. In 1914, the company started offering the A-4 with three different top finish options including ebonized (black), golden orange (pumpkin-top), or "golden red to a beautiful dark mahogany," otherwise known as a sunburst. Almost all existing 1910-1914 A-4s have the ebonized finish, but after that Gibson seemed to transition to mostly sunburst finishes. There appear to be no existing A-4 mandolins from this post-1914 era with the pumpkin-top finish.

1910 Price: $50.00
1917 Price: $52.50
1918 Price: $57.75
1919 Price: $70.00

1917 A-4 fingerboard extension
Courtesy of Folkway Music

"A" mandolin dimensions:
Body width: 10 1/4"
Body length: 13 1/4"
Overall length: 25 1/2"
Scale length: 13 7/8"
Nut width: 1 1/8"

Additional "A" specifications:
Carved spruce top
Birch back and rim (some A-4s were maple)
10-fret three-piece Spanish cedar neck 1910-1912
Three-piece mahogany neck 1913-1919
Ebony heel cap 1913-1919 (except "A")
Bone nut
Ebony bridge
Ebony end pin
Nickel-plated crown tailpiece with "The Gibson" stamped on cover
4-on-a-plate tuners – Models "A" and "A-1" had plain ivoroid buttons and "A-3" and "A-4" had fancy inlaid tuner buttons until 1918
19 nickel-silver frets

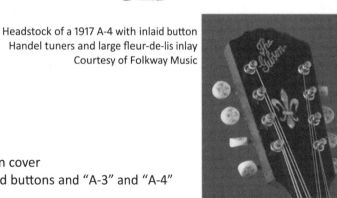

Headstock of a 1917 A-4 with inlaid button
Handel tuners and large fleur-de-lis inlay
Courtesy of Folkway Music

Single mother-of-pearl fingerboard dots at the 5th, 7th, 10th and 15th frets (double dot at the 12th fret). Models "A-3" and "A-4" also had side dots or position markers on the upper edge of the bound fingerboard

Note: Style "A" mandolins did not have laminated three-piece necks. They had one-piece necks with wings glued to the side of the headstock.

Style "F-2" Artist Mandolin – 1910-1919

1910 Price: $75.00
1917 Price: $80.00
1918 Price: $88.00
1919 Price: $108.00

In mid-to late-1910 Gibson discontinued the Williams-style elevated finger-rest design and changed the F-2 and F-4 finger-rests to a smaller tear-drop shape with a hook tail that wrapped around the bridge. All of Gibson's post-1910 elevated finger-rests were stamped with the patent date – Sept. 21,'09. Around 1916 the pickguards lost the hook tail feature and the new ones had a simpler rounded bottom. The F-2 retained most of the same specification and ornamentation as the pre-1910 versions. F-2 customers had the option of the pumpkin-top or ebonized top finish, but after 1914, Gibson transitioned to a sunburst finish. The F-2 did not have a back binding.

Near right: c1908-1910 Williams-style "F":
finger-rest. Courtesy of Dan Beimborn
Far right: c1910-1916 "F" finger-rest with
hook-tail feature around the bridge

Style "F-4" Artist Mandolin – 1910-1919

In 1911 Gibson changed the headstock inlay on the F-4 mandolins and discontinued the torch & wire design with no logo, to a headstock inlay that did have "The Gibson" logo. Below it was a new inlaid floral design known as the "flowerpot." Later, in the teens, Gibson added a lower section to the inlay design, which has earned the nickname "double flowerpot." Gibson did not refer to their inlay designs using names like torch & wire and flowerpot. These nicknames became part of the Gibson vernacular many years later. Most sources believe that Gibson only used a style number for each design, but that information has never surfaced. As mentioned above, Gibson offered three top finish options on the "F-4" and existing examples from 1910-1914 show they used all three, but after 1914 Gibson transitioned to all sunburst finishes on this model including the top, back, rim and even the back of the neck.

1910 Price: $100.00
1917 Price: $110.00
1918 Price: $121.00
1919 Price: $148.00

F-2 and F-4 mandolin dimensions:
Body width: 10"
Body length: 13 3/4"
Overall length: 25 1/2"
Scale length: 13 7/8"
Nut width: 1 1/8"

Additional "F" specifications:
Carved spruce top
F-2 had a birch back and rim, 10-fret,
  3-piece Spanish cedar neck 1910-1912,
and 3-piece mahogany neck 1913-1919
F-4 had tiger or figured maple back, rim and 10-fret 3-piece neck
Ebony heel cap 1913-1919

Bone nut (F-4 had a mother-of-pearl nut)
Ebony bridge
Ebony end pin
Nickel-plated crown tailpiece with stamped
4-on-a-plate tuners – both models had Handel
  tuners with inlaid buttons until 1918
24 nickel-silver frets including fingerboard
  extension
Single mother-of-pearl fingerboard dots at the
  5th, 7th, 10th and 15th frets and a double dot
  at the 12th fret.

 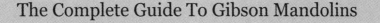

Style "H-1" Mandola – 1910-1919 (right)
Just like the "A" mandolin, very little changed on the 1910-1919 H-1 mandolas, with the exception of the elevated finger-rest, which was similar in shape to the mandolins only larger and cam clamp added in 1911. Gibson's 1918 Catalog K stated that the H-1 also had the new Sheraton Brown finish, and existing examples confirm this change did occur in 1918.

1910 Price: $35.00
1917 Price: $37.50
1918 Price: $41.25
1919 Price: $50.00

Style "H-2" Mandola – 1910-1919 (below)
The differences between these two mandola models are the H-2 had a bound top, back and fingerboard, and a fleur-de-lis pearl headstock inlay below "The Gibson" logo. 1910-1914 H-2s had black-top finishes with dark mahogany backs, rim and neck, but after that Gibson start using a new "red sunburst" finish, they described as "a shading of golden red to beautiful dark mahogany." The rosette* had inlaid ivoroid in between the two rings of alternating black and ivory celluloid.

1910 Price: $50.00
1917 Price: $52.50
1918 Price: $57.75
1919 Price: $70.00

H-1 and H-2 mandola dimensions:
Body width: 11 1/4"
Body length: 15 7/8"
Overall length: 28 1/2"
Scale length: 15 3/4"
Nut width: 1 7/32" +/- 1/32"

Additional H-1 and H-2 specifications:
Carved spruce top
Birch back and rim
10 fret, 3-piece Spanish cedar neck 1910-1912
3-piece mahogany neck 1913-1919
H-2 - ebony heel cap 1913-1919
Bone nut
Ebony bridge
Nickel-plated crown tailpiece with stamped logo
Ebony end pin
21 nickel-silver frets including the fingerboard extension
Single pearl fingerboard dots at the 5th, 7th, 10th, and 15th frets
 double dot at the 12th fret. Both models also had side dots or
 position markers on the upper edge of the bound fingerboard
4-on-a-plate tuners – H-1 had plain ivoroid buttons and H-2 had
 inlaid buttons

* The terms rosette and soundhole rings can be used interchangeably

Note: Style H-1 mandolas did not have laminated/3-piece necks. They had one-piece necks with wings glued to the side of the headstock.

Style "H-4" Mandola – 1914-1919

1912 Price: $125.00
1917 Price: $115.00
1918 Price: $126.50
1919 Price: $155.00

First introduced in 1914 the Style H-4 had the same basic ornamentation as the F-4 mandolin including the pearl "The Gibson" logo and inlaid flowerpot or double flowerpot inlay design on the headstock. It also had an ivoroid bound top, back, fingerboard and headstock. Gibson offered the H-4 with same three top finish options as the F-4, but most existing examples have a sunburst finish. It's very difficulty say who came up with the idea of manufacturing a mandola with an "F" mandolin-style body but the H-4 became Gibson's top-of-the-line mandola from 1914 to 1924.

H-4 mandola dimensions:
Body width: 11 1/4"
Body length: 15 7/8"
Overall length: 28 1/2"
Scale length: 15 3/4"
Nut width: 1 7/32" +/- 1/32"

Additional H-4 specifications:
Carved spruce top
Curly maple back and rim
10-fret, 3-piece mahogany neck
Ebony heel cap
Single-bound ivoroid on top, back, fingerboard and headstock
Mother-of-pearl nut
Ebony bridge
Nickel-plated crown tailpiece "The Gibson" stamped on cover
Ebony end pin
21 nickel-silver frets including the fingerboard extension
Single mother-of-pearl fingerboard dots at the 5th, 7th, 10th and 15th frets and a double dot at the 12th fret. Both models also had side dots or position markers on the upper edge of the bound fingerboard 4-on-a-plate Handel tuners with inlaid buttons (until 1918)

1916 ad for Louis Handel Company's screw machine shop which made the worm-gear, shafts, cogs and string-posts for their musical instruments machine-heads

Style "K-1" Mando-cello – 1910-1919 (right)
Like the Style H-1 and H-2 very little changed on the 1910 to 1919 K-1 and K-2 mando-cellos, with the exception of the additional upgrades mentioned earlier. Like the "A" mandolin, Gibson's 1918 Catalog K stated the K-1 came with the Sheraton Brown finish, but extant instruments from this era have the pumpkin-top finish. The one noticeable difference between the catalog illustrations of most of the mandolins, mandolas and mando-cellos is the shape of the elevated finger-rest. The catalogs show a bigger, rounder lower section around the bridge but extant instruments have a small hook tail design as shown on page 69.

1910 Price: $35.00
1917 Price: $40.00
1918 Price: $41.25
1919 Price: $55.00

Style "K-2" Mando-cello – 1910-1919 (below)
The differences between the K-2 and K-1 were the same as the H-2 vs. the H-1. In addition to the inlaid mother-of-pearl "The Gibson" logo on the headstock, the K-2 also had a large fleur-de-lis below the logo. 1910-1914 K-2s had the black-top finish but after that Gibson transitioned to the red sunburst. There is much more information on Gibson finishes at the end of this chapter.

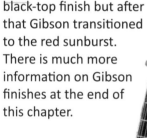

1910 Price: $50.00
1917 Price: $55.00
1918 Price: $60.50
1919 Price: $75.00

K-1 and K-2 Mando-cello dimensions:
Body width: 14 1/4"
Body length: 19"
Overall length: 38"
Scale length: 24 3/4"
Nut width: 1 5/8" +/- 1/16"

Additional K-1 and K-2 specifications:
Carved spruce top
Birch back and rim
12 fret three-piece Spanish cedar neck 1910-1912
Three-piece mahogany neck 1913-1919
K-2 - ebony heel cap 1913-1919
Bone nut
Ebony bridge
Nickel-plated crown tailpiece with "The Gibson" stamped on cover
Ebony end pin
24 nickel-silver frets including the fingerboard extension
Single mother-of-pearl fingerboard dots at the 5th, 7th, 10th, and 15th frets and a double dot at the 12th fret.
Both models also had side dots or position markers on the upper edge of the bound fingerboard
4-on-a-plate tuners – K-1 had plain ivoroid buttons and the K-2 had inlaid buttons until 1918

Note: Style "K-1" mando-cellos did not have laminated/3-piece necks with the ebonized center strip. They had one-piece necks with wings glued to the side of the headstock.

Style "K-4" Mando-cello – 1914-1919

Like the H-4, the K-4 was introduced in 1914 with all the same ornamentation as its mandola counterpart. It was the new top-of-the-line mando-cello with a fairly hefty price tag. The large two-point body of the K-4 was similar to the H-4, but the body points were larger in proportion to the mandola body. The K-4's was wider than several of Gibson's guitars. It's hard to describe the sound of a K-4. Its tone is deeper than that of a guitar and does not have the same timbre of a typical eight-string instrument, but has a tone unlike any other instrument.

1912 Price: $140.00
1917 Price: $125.00
1918 Price: $137.50
1919 Price: $168.00

K-4 Mando-cello dimensions:
Body width: 14 1/4"
Body length: 19 1/4"
Overall length: 39"
Scale length: 24 3/4"
Nut width: 1 3/4"

Additional K-4 specifications:
Carved spruce top
Curly maple back and rim
12-fret three-piece mahogany neck
Single-bound ivoroid on top, back, fingerboard, and headstock
Double flowerpot pearl inlay below "The Gibson" logo
Mother-of-pearl nut
Ebony bridge
Nickel-plated crown tailpiece with "The Gibson" stamp
Ebony end pin
24 frets including the fingerboard extension
Single mother-of-pearl fingerboard dots at the 5th, 7th, 10th, and 15th frets and a double dot at the 12th fret.
Side dots or position markers on the upper edge of the bound fingerboard
4-on-a-plate Handel tuners with inlaid buttons

Style "J" Mando-bass – 1911-1919

As stated in Chapter 8, the Style "J" mando-bass was introduced in 1911. At first the Gibson mando-basses had the pumpkin-top finish, but a few rare examples from 1915 to 1917 have a red sunburst top. In 1918 and after, they were all finished in Sheraton Brown. The Style "J" mando-bass was essentially a fretted version of an upright bass. The 42" scale length was the same as a three-quarter size upright bass and it was tuned the same as well – E-A-D-G (low to high). However, it could not be played with a bow because the strings were not arched like an upright bass but it did have an exstendible steel rod that raised the playing height just like a regular bass. Gibson illustrated different ways to hold the mando-bass and even offered an optional arm-rest that stretched across the body.

1912 Price: $100.00
1917 Price: $90.00
1918 Price: $99.00
1919 Price: $120.00

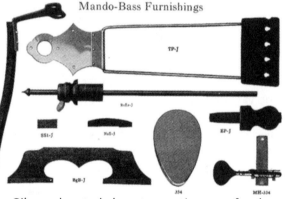

Mando-Bass Furnishings

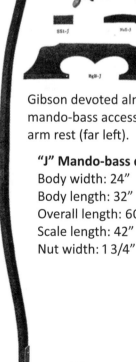

Gibson devoted almost an entire page for the mando-bass accessories including the optional arm rest (far left).

"J" Mando-bass dimensions:
Body width: 24"
Body length: 32"
Overall length: 60"
Scale length: 42"
Nut width: 1 3/4"

"J" Mando-bass specifications:
Graduated carved spruce top
Carved maple back and maple sides
Mexican mahogany neck
Dark mahogany finish on the back, rim, and neck
Ebonized veneered headstock with pearl logo
Ebonized fingerboard with slight treble-side extension
17 nickel-silver frets
Inlaid pearl fingerboard dots at 3rd, 5th, 7th, 10th, 12th and 15th frets (double dot at 12th)
Round soundhole with ivoroid binding and inlaid with two rings of fancy colored wood
Ivoroid bound top   Maple bridge with adjustable ebony string saddles
Ebony nut   Exstendible steel rod floor stand
Extension string holder
  with celluloid cross piece and four ebony pins

Gibson Finishes

Gibson offered three different top finishes on most of their instruments from 1910-1914 – ebonized or black, golden orange and sunburst, although sunburst was reserved for the higher-end models like the A-4, F-4, H-4 and K-4. This changed around 1914, when Gibson transitioned to a new sunburst, and for the most part, used it on a majority of these models without the option of the other two. In 1914 the company started offering a new finish that Gibson referred to as "a shading of golden red to beautiful dark mahogany," which is now commonly called a red sunburst. Early examples of the shading on these finishes tend to be rather subtle and almost appear to be entirely a reddish-orange hue, with just a slight bit of brown around the outer edges, then progressed to a more vivid sunburst a bit later.

Sheraton Brown

In 1918 Gibson introduced another new finish called "sheraton brown." This name seems to reference a style of English furniture most notably made by Thomas Sheraton. Strangely he died in 1806, so it's anyone's guess if that is the true origin. Almost all of Gibson's lower-priced instruments, including the newly introduced A-2 mandolin came with this finish. It's possible that it was another cost-cutting measure like the elimination of the Handel tuners with the inlaid buttons, and the discontinuation of several styles of instrument cases that was instituted by L. A. Williams after he became the new General Manager. Sheraton brown was a quick and easy finish to apply because it was simply one or maybe two coats of brown wood dye, plus a clear varnish top-coat. Gibson referred to it as a satin finish, because it didn't get as much buffing and polishing as the other finishes required. On the spruce tops, the dye would soak into the wood a little deeper in between the grain lines, leaving the top of the grain lighter for a kind of striped effect.

Ivory Top

In 1918 Gibson introduced an entirely different finish on the A-3 mandolins and called it a "new, piquant old ivory finish, the most distinctive, eye-popping ever used on string instruments." The vast majority of instruments with this finish were the A-3s, but was also available by special order on the H-2 mandola, K-2 mando-cello, and the L-3 guitar. The general consensus is that it was another water-based wood dye that was applied directly on the unfinished wood surface with a clear varnish top-coat. The ivory top is much more opaque than the Sheraton Brown, so it's likely that Gibson used multiple coats of the wood dye. Without a doubt it remains one of the most unusual and interesting finishes the company ever used. Gibson also included the following description of these new finishes:

Please note: None of this information is absolute because there are so many variations of the finishes on extant instruments that it is difficult to make any universal statements about it, or for that matter, make any such statements about any particular design specification. This is one of the aspects of Gibson instruments that is so fascinating to many. All of the hand-rubbed finishes were unique to each instrument, based on many factors like the batch of dye used, who was doing the finishing, as well as the time period of a particular instrument.

Advantages of the New Finishes

In the Beautiful Sheraton Brown, Satin Finish and the New Piquant Old Ivory Finish are secured:—

1. Varnishes that are not brittle, and do not flake—they are a new process, thoroughly tested and of proven advantage.

2. They do not readily show scratches.

3. Are permanent in color.

4. Are not liable to hair check.

5. Do not enter into the pores of the wood, but leave the wood free and sensitive.

6. Are the happy medium between the two extremes of soft, yielding oil varnish, and the hard, flint-like French polish.

7. The Sheraton Brown, satin finish is particularly light in body of coating, and is, therefore, splendid for tonal purposes.

8. Said satin finish hardly shows a finger-mark, and may be cleaned by a damp chamois skin.

9. The ivory finish shows less finger-marks than the brown, and is polished to a beautiful, glistering luster.

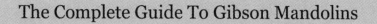

Gibson Parts & Accessories – 1910-1919

Instrument Cases

Gibson had two suppliers of instrument cases from 1911 to 1923. Maulbetsch & Whittemore made their light-duty canvas cases, as well as their heavier embossed leather ones. In 1911 Gibson started carrying cases made by Geib & Schaefer a luggage manufacturer that was founded in Chicago 1899 by Jacob Schaefer and Charles Geib. G&S called their new hard-shell cases "Mastercraft," but Gibson always referred to them as "Faultless." These cases were made from several layers of crisscrossing wood veneer molded into two halves that opened like a suitcase. They were covered with a faux leather material called Keratol which was a thin fabric covered in a coating of black celluloid and linseed oil and embossed with a pattern roller to give it the appearance of real leather. They were available with three types of lining – purple flannel, purple velvet and red plush.

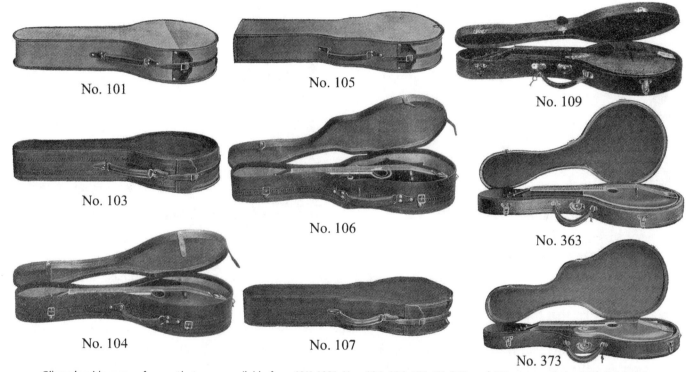

No. 101

No. 105

No. 109

No. 103

No. 106

No. 363

No. 104

No. 107

No. 373

Gibson's wide array of cases that were available from 1911-1921. Nos. 104, 106, 109, 111, 363, and 371 were made by Geib & Schaefer. Nos. 101, 103, 105, and 107 were made by Maulbetsch & Whittemore.

M&W cases had a hinged flap that opened at the bottom of the case, and the instrument would have to be pulled out, rather than lifted out. The M&W cases were good quality, but the hinged flap cases are often referred to as "bottom dumpers" because instruments had the tendency to just fall out of the case.

In 1918 Gibson stopped carrying the M&W embossed leather cases as well as the G&S purple velvet-lined ones. Like the Handel tuners with the inlaid buttons, these cases were probably dropped as a cost-cutting measure put in place by L. A. Willams who had just become General Manager allowing the company to reduce inventory by eliminating several models of cases. In 1920 M&W was bought out by The Felsberg Company but Gibson stopped carrying their cases in 1924 and G&S became their sole supplier of instrument cases for the next 20 years.

The hinged flap design of M&W cases became known as "bottom dumpers"

Tuners

Starting in 1903 Gibson was using tuning machines made by Louis Handel Co. In 1918 Gibson stopped using the #302 Handel tuners with the fancy inlaid buttons. Gibson's 1917 Catalog J still showed the #302 tuners as well as the other tuners made by Handel, but 1918's Catalog K no longer showed the #302. Just to confuse matters even further, Gibson's tuner part numbers in Catalog K had an "MH" prefix which stood for "mandolin head." However neither the illustrations nor the basic designs changed indicating that they continued using Handel as their main supplier until 1922. Based on documents from Martin Guitars' archives, Handel was also supplying tuners to Martin beyond 1918. But by 1922 Martin was only getting inlaid headstock veneers from Handel, so it's entirely possible that Handel closed or sold-off their metal fabrication shop at that time.

Mandolin accessories from Gibson's 1917 Catalog J including the #302 Handel tuners with the fancy inlaid buttons

Mandolin accessories from Gibson's 1918 Catalog K without the #302 Handel tuners but now showing the new #299 economy tuners

A new style of machine heads appeared in Catalog J, part #299 (second row down, in between the picks and the pickguard). These tuners were only used on the inexpensive models like the DY Army-Navy and early 1920s A-Jr. mandolins. It has been assumed for decades that they were made by Waverly Musical Products in New York City, but according to Stewart-MacDonald, the company that now owns Waverly, they [Waverly] weren't in business until 1918, a year after Catalog J was published. It also appears that Waverly didn't start making tuners until the early 1920s. Once again there are no maker's marks or patent dates stamped on these tuners so determining the true manufacturer has been nothing but guesswork until very recently.

These "economy" tuners were actually made by an obscure company called Dinsmore & Jager. John H. Dinsmore and Frederick G. Jager founded the company in the 1890s and set up a small factory at 29 Walnut Street in Northampton, Massachusetts. John Dinsmore died in 1901 and Frederick Jager decided to sell D&J to George H. Drury. Jager went into the automobile dealership business and started the Springfield Automobile Company, the first car dealership in western Massachusetts. The 1900 U.S. Census lists George Drury as a bookkeeper, but the 1910 census lists his occupation as "violin trimmings," so it appears that Drury was D&J's book-keeper prior to 1901 then took the opportunity to buy the business from Jager. As early as 1901 D&J was supplying machine

Above: Dinsmore & Jager letterhead. Courtesy of The Martin Archives

Left: A set of #299 D&J machine-heads on a 1919 Gibson DY Army/Navy mandolin.

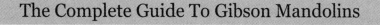

heads to C. F. Martin & Co. D&J's prices were very competitive, but apparently the quality of their machine heads was not that good. In 1923, Martin Guitars wrote a letter to D&J stating "We are having increasing trouble with lost motion in your patent heads" and threatened to "place all our business with other manufacturers. In response to the complaint D&J's letter was rather surprising. It said that "You [Martin] evidently require machines that are made with great care so that every part will be perfect" and "when we are very busy it would not pay us to take the great care to make them perfect, and would interfere with our production." This letter dated March 24. 1924 was signed:

> Yours truly,
> Dinsmore & Jager
> Per Drury.

"Per Drury" indicates that George Drury had dictated the letter to his secretary rather than handling the situation himself. Despite the apparent lack of quality, Martin continued to use them well into the 1930s.

February 1923 letter
from Martin to Dinsmore & Jager
complaining about the quality of their machine-heads.
Courtesy of The Martin Archives

Strings

In 1910 Gibson changed the design of their string envelopes, dropping the printed string number and type and ink-stamping that information below the graphics. Unfortunately, no one realized that the word "gauge" was misspelled on these new envelopes. In fact, Gibson didn't catch the mistake for two years until they corrected the error in 1912. The corrected version with "Best Quality" in large type was used until about 1922.

c1910-1911 mandolin string envelope with "gauge" misspelled.
Courtesy of Rod McDonald

c1912-1922 mandolin string envelope with corrected spelling.
Courtesy of Rod McDonald

Pickguards

Initially the designs of Gibson's new elevated finger-rests were the same as the illustration that appeared on L. A. Williams's patent. These early "patent pending" pickguards were only used from 1908 to 1910 and by mid-1910 the "patented" pickguard was redesigned to a smaller tear-drop shape, which reduced the amount of celluloid needed and eliminated one of the pickguard clamps, making them less expensive to manufacture. This design would stay the same until 1916 when Gibson changed the pickguard shape and the support design. The new shape was slightly wider than its predecessor and did not have the "hook tail" that wrapped around the bridge. The celluloid support arm was replaced with a threaded metal rod that extended from the half-moon-shaped riser block to another mounting block glued to the bottom of the pickguard. The new version still attached to the side of the instrument using the Laurian clamp, but eliminating the celluloid arm helped extend its life because they had the tendency to breaking. The company also experimented with a transitional design that replaced the mounting pin that inserted into a hole in the bridge and replaced it with a rather bulky celluloid block with a bent metal bracket that had a point on the end. Gibson never included any illustrations of this new design in any catalog and it appears from surviving instruments that Gibson couldn't seem to decide which design was better.

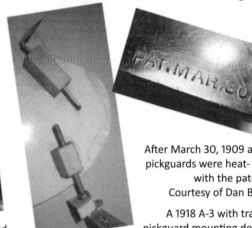

Left: c1910-1916 mandolin pickguard with "hook tail." Right: c1917-1923 pickguard without the tail. Courtesy of Folkway Music

The Laurian patented clamp attached to half-moon riser on top

After March 30, 1909 all Gibson pickguards were heat-stamped with the patent date. Courtesy of Dan Beimborn

A 1918 A-3 with transitional pickguard mounting design with grained ivoroid mounting blocks and bent metal hook. Courtesy of Lowell Levinger

Tailpieces

In late 1909 or early 1910 Gibson changed their tailpiece design from the "pineapple top" to the "crown top." The new tailpiece design still had "The Gibson" logo stamped on the cover as well as swirls and scrolls that adorned the top and is still used today. The only other mandolin tailpiece they used was on the Style D – Alrite mandolin. The shape of its cover prompted the nickname "cloud tailpiece," and the assumption has been that they were made by Waverly, but newly discovered information confirms that they were actually made by the Louis Handel Co. Martin Guitars was using the identical tailpiece on their lower-priced mandolins and documents from their archives confirm that Handel was the manufacturer. This indicates that Handel also made Gibson's pineapple tailpieces and could have been the company's supplier from the very beginning.

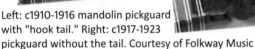

The "cloud" tailpiece on a pre-1917 D - Alrite mandolin made by Handel Co.

Researcher Greig Hutton uncovered inventory records in Martin Guitar's archives that verified that Handel made the "cloud" tailpieces Martin used on their mandolins which are identical to the Alrite.

Transition from pineapple to crown-top tailpiece cover

Courtesy of The Martin Archives

Picks

Although the term "plectrum" was in common use for any small flat tool used to pluck or strum a stringed instrument. Gibson almost always called them picks. They carried a few picks which were mostly flat celluloid tortoise shell but they also offered picks made out of a dense fiber material which were branded the William Place Jr. pick, named after the famous mandolinist and avid Gibson endorser. In 1918 Gibson added a newly patented "Kork Grip" pick which had thin layers of cork on both sides of the top of the pick to prevent it from slipping from a player's fingers. The "Kork Grip" pick was invented by Richard J. Carpenter and Thomas G. Towner and they were awarded a patent on January 22, 1918.

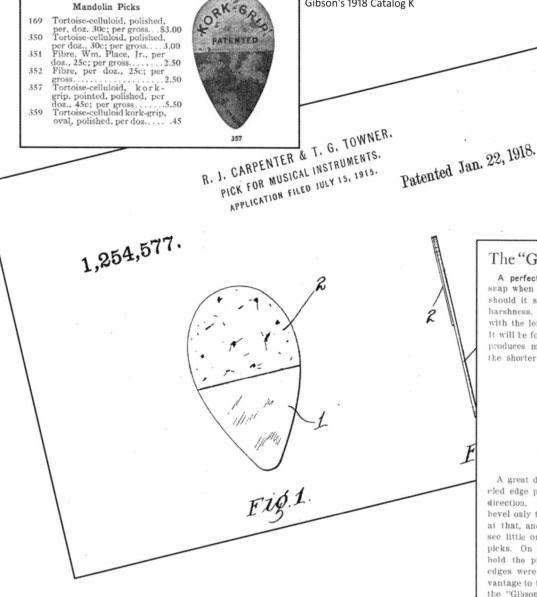

Illustration of the patented Kork-Grip pick from Gibson's 1918 Catalog K

Mandolin Picks

169	Tortoise-celluloid, polished, per, doz. 30c; per gross...	$3.00
350	Tortoise-celluloid, polished, per doz., 30c; per gross....	3.00
351	Fibre, Wm. Place, Jr., per doz., 25c; per gross.......	2.50
352	Fibre, per doz., 25c; per gross..................	2.50
357	Tortoise-celluloid, kork-grip, pointed, polished, per doz., 45c; per gross.......	5.50
359	Tortoise-celluloid kork-grip, oval, polished, per doz.....	.45

357

R. J. CARPENTER & T. G. TOWNER,
PICK FOR MUSICAL INSTRUMENTS.
APPLICATION FILED JULY 15, 1915.

Patented Jan. 22, 1918.

1,254,577.

Fig.1.

The "Gibson" Mandolin Pick

A perfect plectrum should not click nor snap when passing over the strings, neither should it stick nor grate, nor produce any harshness. To test a pick, muffle the strings with the left hand so that no tone is heard. It will be found that the long or pointed pick produces more clicking and snapping than the shorter and slightly oval pick.

A great deal has been said about the beveled edge pick. This is a step in the right direction, but some manufacturers who bevel only two edges, bevel the wrong edges at that, and no wonder the performer can see little or no advantage by using beveled picks. On the other hand, some performers hold the pick wrong, so that if the right edges were beveled, there would be no advantage to the player. We, therefore, believe the "Gibson" pick will fill a long-felt want, for all edges are beveled so that the pick is adapted to meet the demands of every performer.

Gibson Mandolin-Guitar Co.
515 Harrison Court, Kalamazoo, Mich.

1911 ad for Gibson's celluloid picks with "The Gibson" company name heat-stamped on both sides. One of the only instances where Gibson used the term plectrum.

Gibson Publishing - 1910-1919

Gibson Catalogs

During this decade Gibson published the largest catalogs in their entire history. From 48 pages in 1909's Catalog F, their 1910 Catalog G was nearly twice the size with 82 pages. Each successive year the catalogs grew even larger reaching the pinnacle in 1918's Catalog K that was a whopping 112 pages. 1914's Catalog "I" was the first catalog to have full-color illustrations of some of Gibson's instruments. Every catalog was filled with photographs of prominent musicians who endorsed "The Gibson" as well as dozens of mandolin groups and orchestras. L.A. Williams was at the top of his game writing pages and pages of catalog content that continually bashed the non-believers and sang the praises of "Gibson-ites."

Gibson's 1912 Catalog H had the illustrations of the "A" and A-1 mandolins reversed, but had an ink-stamped explanation of the error. They also continued to use the same illustrations from the 1909 catalog until 1914 when they published Catalog "I." This catalog had illustrations with the standard front views but also included side views of each instrument.

Gibson Publications – 1910-1919

In 1911 L.A. Williams started publishing a new in-house magazine called *The Sounding Board* and appointed himself editor and manager. Williams guaranteed a circulation of 10,000-15,000 copies of each issue and sold them for 10 cents each or 30 cents for four issues. Although the first issue of the magazine was solely dedicated to the Gibson Company's interests, "all remittances" were payable to Lewis A. Williams and "NOT to the Gibson Co." Apparently General Manager Sylvo Reams immediately put a stop to that and all subsequent issues were payable to Gibson. Williams also published two songs that he wrote and if anyone had any doubt about his fervent belief in Gibson the song titles laid that to rest. He wrote a little march called "The Gibson Is King" that had "a melody that's contagious" and would "stir the soul of every 'Gibson' patriot."

The name of the magazine was changed in 1915 to *The Sounding Board Salesman* and its focus shifted toward Gibson's teacher/agents to keep their efforts squarely on selling more instruments and abreast of all the latest news from the home office. The inside title page of many issues were addressed "to the 'Gibson' Agent," but was "not meant to entertain, but rather to suggest, help and instruct," and was "written for the salesman who uses his head to get ahead."

Front cover of the first issue of
The Sounding Board published in 1911

Lewis Williams frequently took the opportunity to write about one of his pet peeves – stationery. Many long-winded articles would go on and on about this particular subject where he wrote rather demeaning and even insulting remarks like:

"...almost every male biped on the 'Gibson' agency list wrote us for cuts for their stationery, or had new stationery printed," *"But oh, you lady agents! Your stationery still indicates (with but few exceptions) that you are like the foolish virgins who had lamps, but without oil."*

"Every 'Gibson' agent should use a letter-head that not only answers the purpose of [the] correspondence paper, but that creates prestige; emanates sound professional and business worth.." *"No, Winifred, your delicately scented and tinted note paper with its dainty monogram isn't the kind that impresses its receiver with your sound professional and business worth."*

His writing knew no bounds and he often wondered into an eccentric and bewildering arena that seemingly had nothing to do with Gibson or anything related to business matters. He once wrote an article entitled "Surfaces and Depths" which contained the following:

"I see a black monster laying traps for me. Across his forehead, that all may see, is indelibly inscribed his name, Relative Truth [surfaces]." *"...another leader of an entirely a different family of truth. His name is Absolute Truth [depths]."*
"When self-adornment and fineries, trinkets, pomp, ostentation, appearances have drawn one's thought exclusively to surfaces without regard for depths - for beauty of soul and stalwartness of character, we are forced to think of many gods, not the one God."

To say that Williams's prose were bizarre would only be scratching the surface and they appeared to be the reveries of a man who had appointed himself god of Gibson. It is no surprise that he was the son of a preacher.

After C.V. Buttelman took over as editor, he decided to lessen the stern tone of the magazine's content, much the same way he did with Gibson's advertising. He included many little cartoons and informative articles like "Timely Tips" and amusing little quips like the Gibson staff will "beat it out to the backroom to help the janitor build soundholes for mando-basses, while the editorial chair is occupied by the Gibson agents themselves," all of which were intended to bolster more enthusiasm from its readers. *The Sounding Board Salesman* was not without some intrinsic value and it showed new and innovative ways for agents to advertise. "Are you using Gibson Slidevertizing?" was a clever way for teacher/agents to "augment and emphasize [their] personal efforts." And the company had the foresight to also offer "screen slides" that could be projected in movie theatres.

Are You Using Gibson Slidevertizing?
Three Slides in a Set. Single Slides, 50c; Set of Three, $1.25.
G. M.-G Co., Kalamazoo, Michigan.

INTRODUCING THE RESISTLESS MANDY LINN.

Bill O'Sa'e is a'fickle cuss but he sure couldn't resist Mandy Linn. Ol' Man Dolin says she should be Bill's favorite wife because he can *string* her easily, and he can come home nights and *pick* on her without hurting her disposition, but if she does get sore, Bill can always *get her number* from the guarantee label. Oh gosh !

Gibson Screen Advertising

The new slides we have been waiting for so long are now being prepared. The first of them is illustrated above and is a very striking pose of Priscilla Dean, the Universal Film Star. Other slides will be announced in the next issue of the Sounding Board.

Single slides 50c; set of three postpaid $1.25
GIBSON MANDOLIN-GUITAR COMPANY

different Gibson banjo and its steady growth in popularity seems to be proof that they are on par with the long-famous Gibson guitars and mandolins." Although Gibson had used the name "Mastertone" in 1924, the Mastertone banjos made from 1925 to the early thirties are still considered be the best banjos ever made and now command very high prices among collectors and banjoists.

However Guy Hart had the reputation of not being the nicest person to work for and was rumored to be particularity harsh on his factory workers. One story in particular recounts an incident where Hart threatened to fire someone for discarding an oily, dirty rag, rather than reusing it. Be that as it may, Hart was a shrewd businessman who also realized that he needed an equally brilliant sales-man to bring Gibson's new banjos to market. In January 1925 Hart appointed Frank B. Campbell as Sales and Advertising Manager, which made him Hart's second in command. In March 1925 Hart was unanimously re-elected General Manager by the Board of Directors, and a newspaper clipping stated, it was a "confirmation of his successful management in the short time he has been in charge."

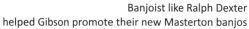

Banjoist like Ralph Dexter
helped Gibson promote their new Masterton banjos

Campbell also demonstrated "outside the box" thinking and came up with the idea of Gibson making economy or "budget brand" instruments. In 1925 the company introduced its first non-Gibson branded instrument, the "Oriole" banjo, and in 1930, the "Kel Kroydon" brand was also added. Campbell's idea was to offer a wider array of instruments at very affordable prices. Kel Kroydon included guitars, banjos and mandolins, and although they were cheaper than their Gibson counterparts they are highly sought after by collectors. Campbell also thought Gibson should "private label" instruments for other companies and around 1926 the company started making high-end banjos for the Trujo Banjo Company in San Francisco. In 1929 Campbell struck up a deal with Montgomery Ward, one of the largest mail order companies in the U.S., to produce several instruments that Wards called the "Recording King" and "Studio King" brands.

Frank B. Campbell
Sales Manager 1925-1930

In late 1929 Gibson started making the
Kel Kroydon brand of economy instruments

The TRUJO BANJO

Gibson also made high-end expensive
banjos for The Trujo Banjo Co. in
San Francisco

Frank Campbell was instrumental in launching the Oriole brand

Sales and Advertising

Frank Campbell was a very talented salesman and was influential in bringing Gibson from serious financial difficulties to record sales within two years. After 1923 Gibson's advertising clearly shows a significant shift from mandolins and guitars to banjos. In fact Gibson never advertised the Master Model F-5 mandolin after 1923 and 90% of the 1924-1929 ads featured Mastertone banjos Hart, Campbell, and the rest of Gibson's management team were so successful that the company had its greatest year ever in 1926 mostly due to the success of the Mastertone banjo line. Sales continued to grow steadily until one fateful day in October 1929...

1926 Mastertone banjo ad

1928 Mastertone banjo ad

A rare post-1925 ad for a Gibson mandolin appeared in the September 1928 issue of *Popular Mechanics* but showed an F-4 instead of an F-5

Gibson Instruments – 1920-1929

Model "DY - Army/Navy" Mandolin – 1920-1923

The DY Army/Navy mandolin was first introduced in 1918 but was discontinued in 1923. C.V. Buttelman wrote a small article in The Sounding Board Salesman which attempted to explain that a "cheap" mandolin didn't necessarily mean it was poorly made and recommended that the DY "presents good value at a comparatively low cost." Apparently the lack of sales of the DY coupled with the success of the A-Jr. prompted Gibson to discontinue this model.

1921 Price: $35.00
1923: Discontinued

Model "A-Jr." Mandolin – 1920-1929

The A-Jr. was one of six instruments in Gibson's Junior line that also included a guitar, three banjos and a mandolin-banjo. The A-Jr. mandolin and L-Jr. guitar were introduced in 1920, but the banjos and banjo-mandolin came later in 1923. The A-Jr. was an inexpensive "A" mandolin with almost no ornamentation, truss rod or adjustable bridge, but it did have a label with the Gibson name on it, and each one got a regular serial number. Even though the A-Jr. disappeared from Gibson's price lists and catalogs after 1925 the company continued to make them until 1930. It had a spruce top, birch back and sides, a mahogany neck and elevated finger-rest. The company's Junior brochure published in 1925 says the A-Jr. had a golden orange top finish, but all existing examples have a Sheraton Brown finish. The earliest examples have the same headstock shape as the other "A" mandolins, but got the "snakehead" design in 1922. Around 1927 Gibson switched back to the "paddle head" headstock shape which they also put on all of the "A" mandolins. Many examples of post-1925 A-Jrs. have a silk-screened "The Gibson" logo on the headstock, but pre-1925 A-Jrs. had no logo.

1921 Price: $35.00
1923-1924 Price: $39.00
1925 Price: $35.00
1926-1929: Does not appear on
  any price list

An early version of the A Jr. label that was glued on top of a DY label. Courtesy of Walter Carter

The round label only used on the Junior line of instruments

Style "A-0" Mandolin – 1926-1929

The model A-0 mandolin first appears in Gibson's 1926 Catalog P and on their June 1926 price list as the replacement for the A-Jr. However existing instruments indicate that Gibson didn't make any A-0s until 1930 after the A-Jr. was discontinued. More on the A-0 in Chapter 21.

Style "A" Mandolin – 1920-1929

Most of the "A" mandolins from the early 20s were very similar to those of the late teens including the Sheraton Brown finish. Gibson started installing their new patented truss rods in 1921 and adjustable height bridges the following year. Also in 1922, all the Style "A" mandolins got a completely new tapered headstock design. This earned it the nickname "snakehead" because its shape was similar to a venomous snake's triangular-shaped head. Although L. A. Williams and A. J. Reams's mandolin design patent from 1917 was the first time the tapered headstock design appeared, it may not have been the impetus for the change that occurred in 1922. The snakehead mandolins of this era are highly sought after by collectors because they were only made for a short period of time and have a unique style that is very appealing to the eye. Like the A-Jr. many "A" mandolins retained the snakehead shape after 1925, but around 1927 they went back to the early 20s design, usually referred to as the "paddle head."

1920 Price: $55.00
1921-1923 Price: $45.00 (4/1923 price increase to $55.00)
1924 Price: $55.00 (12/1924 price decrease to $50.00)
1925-1929 Price: $50.00 ($52.50 with case)

Style "A-2" Mandolin – 1920-1923 and 1925-1927

After the introduction of the A-2z in late 1923, the A-2 was discontinued for two years . Then it reappeared in 1925 but was finally discontinued permanently two years later. Pre-1923 A-2s had the standard paddle head shape of the other "A" models, but post-1925 A-2s had the snakehead feature. Even though the last time the A-2 appears on a Gibson price list is February of 1927, there are very few post-1925 extant examples making it difficult to determine exactly when Gibson stopped making this model.

1920 Price: $70.00
1921-1923 Price: $55.00 (4/1923 price increase to $65.00)
1924: Discontinued
1925-1927 Price: $70.00

Style "A-2z" Mandolin – 1923-1925
Sometime around the fall of 1923 Gibson replaced the A-2 with a new model, the A-2z, but it only lasted a short period of time and was discontinued in 1925. The main difference between the A-2z and the A-2, is the A-2z had a two-ply black and ivoroid binding on the top and the rosette was two rings of three-ply black/ivoroid/black celluloid with a thicker ivoroid ring in between. It had a single-bound back, soundhole and fingerboard, pumpkin top finish and a dark brown finish on the back, sides, and neck. All A-2z mandolins were snakeheads and are very collectible because of how few were made.

1924 Price: $70.00
1925: Discontinued

Style "A-3" Mandolin – 1920-1923 (not shown)
The ivory top A-3 was a short-lived model that Gibson made from 1918 until 1923. The company did not replace the A-3 with another model because General Manager Harry Ferris was adamant about reducing the number of different instruments the factory was making. Gibson never made another model A-3 after 1923.

1920 Price: $80.00
1921-1923 Price: $65.00 (4/1923 price increase to $75.00)
1924: Discontinued

Style "A-4" Mandolin – 1920-1929
Gibson's top-of-the-line "A" mandolin went through a series of changes during the 1920s. Early 20s A-4s retained the fingerboard extension that no other "A" model had, but Gibson started using curly maple for the back and sides on some examples. Some had the three-color sunburst top finish with the back having a two-color red and brown sunburst. In 1923 the A-4's headstock was changed to the snakehead design and retained the fleur-de-lis inlay below "The Gibson" logo. Several examples from the snakehead era had abalone shell inlays rather than white mother-of-pearl. Some A-4s had Virzi Tone Amplifiers installed in them during the Loar era (1922-1924). After 1926 A-4s went back to pre-1923 design specification including the paddle head shape, no multi-ply celluloid binding on the top edge or around the soundhole, and mostly mahogany for the back, sides and neck.

1920 Price: $90.00
1921-1923 Price: $65.00 (4/1923 price increase to $90.00)
1924-1927 Price: $90.00 ($94.50 with case)
1928-1929 Price: $80.00 ($85.30 with case)

Style "F-2" Mandolin – 1920-1929

In what can be only described as some kind of weird experiment many F-2s during the Loar-era have a celluloid tortoise shell binding on the back, but the normal ivoroid binding on the top edge, soundhole, and fingerboard. F-2s before this era did not have a back binding so the reason for this added feature is puzzling. There are examples of Loar-era F-2s with Virzis, but other than these unusual features and the addition of a truss rod and adjustable bridge, the rest of the F-2 mandolins stayed pretty much the same throughout the decade.

1920 Price: $125.00
1921-1923 Price: $100.00
 (4/1923 price increase to $125.00)
1924-1925 Price: $125.00
1926-1929 Price: $110.00

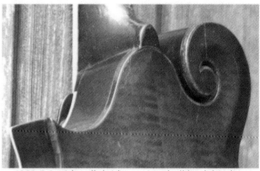

1923 F-2 with celluloid tortoise shell back binding

Style "F-4" Mandolin – 1920-1929

During the 1920s the F-4 was one mandolin model that did not change very much at all. There was the addition of the truss rod and adjustable bridge (1921 and 1922 respectively). The double flower pot inlay disappeared in the early twenties and post-Loar F-4 mandolins had the single flower pot design. Other than some variations in the sunburst finish that's about all that changed during the entire decade.

1920 Price: $165.00
1921-1923 Price: $100.00 (4/1923 price increase to $150.00)
1924 Price: $150.00
1925 Price: $110.00
1926-1929 Price: $150.00 ($157.50 with case)

Note: Style F-2 and F-4 mandolins had the same dimensions as 1910-1919 instruments.

Master Model Style "F-5" Mandolin – 1922-1929

It's hard to describe in mere words how revolutionary the F-5 design was compared to any other mandolin that had ever been made. It was truly the pinnacle of Gibson mandolin design and remains the most copied to this day. The earliest known F-5 has a label signed and dated by Lloyd Loar on June 1, 1922. As far as anyone knows Gibson didn't make any more until November 1922. The first advertisement for the F-5 was a two-page, full-color spread that appeared in *The Cadenza* magazine's March 1923 issue. In the fine print it stated "advance orders received before this announcement have taken all instruments ready to ship and the announcement was twice delayed to permit accumulation of a sufficient supply." The F-5 featured so many groundbreaking innovations that it pushed mandolin design to the extreme. Although it was advertised as having a 15-fret neck (15 frets clear of the body) the neck actually attached to body between the 13th and 14th frets. Adding an elevated fingerboard extension and increased neck angle gave the F-5 incredible volume and carrying power. The combination of the f-holes, top carving and the new bracing gave it a bright well-balanced tone from the lowest note to the highest.

Around July 1923 Gibson added two layers of binding around the side of the rims so a total of three-plys were visible from the top and from the sides. Some early F-5s got a new headstock inlay design commonly called "the fern" which is highly regarded as one of Gibson's finest design features. All the F-5s made from June 1922 until December 1924 were signed and dated by Lloyd Loar and over 240 are known to still exist which accounts for over 80% of the total number of Master Model Style 5 instruments made during Loar's tenure. Considering the fact that between 1935 and 1943 Gibson shipped a total of 117 F-5s, its initial success was pretty good but then seemed to fade quickly along with the popularity of the mandolin in general.

F-5 Mandolin dimensions:
Body width: 10"
Body length: 13 3/4"
Body depth: 1 3/4" at the rim
Nut width: 1 5/64" +/- 1/64"
Scale length: 13 15/16"
Overall length: 26 3/4"

Triple side binding that was added to the F-5 in mid-1923. Courtesy of Lowell Levinger

1922 Price: $200.00
1923-1929 Price: $250.00

Additional F-5 Specifications:
Hand-carved Adirondack spruce top
Flamed maple back, sides and 3-piece 15-fret neck
3-ply bound fingerboard and headstock (extra 2-ply binding added to the sides of the fingerboard)
3-ply bound top and back (extra 2-ply binding added to sides of the top rim 7/23/1923)
Elevated celluloid tortoise pickguard with 3-ply binding
Some Loar-era F-5s had "The Gibson" and flower pot pearl inlay (designs did vary)
  including "the fern" headstock inlay with 3-ply binding
Rosewood adjustable bridge
Mother-of-pearl nut
Ebony fingerboard with single pearl dots at 5th, 7th, 10th, and 15th frets, double dots at 12th fret
Waverly 4-on-a-plate nickel-plated engraved tuners with screw-on pearl buttons
Nickel-plate tailpiece with "The Gibson" stamped on cover (some F-5s had gold hardware)
5-ply celluloid pickguard support with nickel-plated threaded rod and mounting block
26 nickel-silver frets including fingerboard extension
Finish: see section below

1925 post-Loar F-5s are commonly referred to as a "fern" because of the headstock inlay design. Courtesy of Walter Carter

Style H-1 Mandola – 1920-1929

Gibson changed the Sheraton Brown finish of the late teens to a sunburst finish in 1923. They added an adjustable bridge in 1921 and a truss rod in 1922. The only thing that changed in the design of the H-1 mandola was a different rosette. Gibson stopped using the two inlaid rope rings and changed it to two three-ply ivoroid/black/ivoroid rings instead. After 1924 Gibson started silk-screening "The Gibson" logo on the H-1 instead of using inlaid pearl. Most of the mid-to-late 20s H-1s had a black top finish and retained the dark mahogany finish on the back, sides and neck.

1920 Price: $75.00
1921-1923 Price: $60.00 (4/1923 price increase to $75.00)
1924-1929 Price: $75.00 ($78.75 with case)

Style H-2 Mandola – 1920-1923 (not shown)

The H-2 became an obsolete model because they just weren't selling and the popularity of mandolas and mandolin orchestras was dying out. In an effort to reduce the number of different instruments they were making, Gibson discontinued the H-2 in 1924 .

1920 Price: $100.00
1921-1923 Price: $80.00
 (4/1923 price increase to $90.00)
1924: Discontinued

Note: Style H-1, H-2 and H-4 mandolas had the same dimensions as 1910-1919 instruments.

Style H-4 Mandola – 1920-1929

Like the F-4, the H-4 did not change very much during the 1920s. There was the addition of the truss rod and adjustable bridge and similar changes to the headstock inlay designs.

1920 Price: $180.00
1921-1923 Price: $145.00 (4/1923 price increase to $175.00)
1924-1929 Price: $175.00 ($183.75 with case)

The Gibson Mandola
---Tenor Voice of the Mandolin Choir

Master Model Style "H-5" Mandola – 1924-1929
Although the first Master Model H-5 mandola was signed and dated by Lloyd Loar on April 2, 1923, it didn't appear on any Gibson price list until January 1924, indicating that the company only made one in 1923. This supports the theory that Lloyd Loar may have worked on the initial design, but all subsequent instruments were then made using the specifications from the prototype. Gibson didn't make any more H-5 mandolas until March 1924, and there are only 21 Loar-signed H-5s known to exist. The H-5 had a 13-fret neck as compared to the 15-fret fret neck on the F-5. The H-5 had smaller f-holes and a shorter neck than the F-5 possibly because Loar thought it sounded better that way. The Loar-era H-5s had the fern inlay on the headstock four years before Gibson changed the F-5 inlay to the same design.

1924-1929 Price: $260.00 ($273.00 with case)

H-5 Mandola dimensions:
Body width: 11 1/8"
Body length: 14 3/4"
Body depth: 2 1/8" at the rim
Nut width: 1 1/4"
Scale length: 15 3/4"
Overall length: 29 1/4"

Additional H-5 Specifications:
Carved Adirondack spruce top
Flamed maple back, sides and 3-piece 12-fret neck
3-ply bound top, back, and headstock
Single-bound fingerboard
Elevated celluloid tortoise finger-rest with 3-ply binding
Ebony headstock veneer with inlaid pearl "The Gibson" logo and
  fern design
Rosewood adjustable bridge
Ebony fingerboard with single pearl dots at 5th, 7th, 10th, and
  15th frets, double dots at 12th fret
Mother-of-pearl nut
Waverly 4-on-a-plate nickel-plated engraved tuners with screwed-on
  pearl buttons
Nickel-plate tailpiece with "The Gibson" stamped on cover
  (some H-5s had gold hardware)
3-ply ivoroid/black/ivoroid pickguard support with nickel (or gold)
  threaded rod and mounting block
21 nickel-silver frets including fingerboard extension

Style K-1 Mando-cello – 1920-1929

Early 1920s K-1s had the Sheraton Brown finish but around 1924 and after, Gibson started using the black top finish. Instead of using a mother-of-pearl inlaid logo Gibson started silk-screening it like they started doing with all of the lower-end models. With the exception of the truss rod and adjustable bridge the K-1s of this era look very similar to the black top K-2s of 1910 to 1914.

1920 Price: $90.00
1921-1923 Price: $75.00
1924-1929 Price: $80.00 ($84.00 with case)

Style K-2 Mando-cello – 1920-1923 (not shown)

Just as they did with the H-2 mandola, Gibson dropped the K-2 mando-cello in 1924 after a 20-year run.

1920 Price: $120.00
1921-1923 Price: $95.00
 (4/1923 price increase to $115.00)
1924: Discontinued

Style K-4 Mando-cello – 1920-1929

There are very few surviving examples of K-4 mando-cellos from the 1920s, which seems to indicate that this model simply didn't sell very well. However there is at least one K-4 that had a Virzi Tone Amplifier installed during the Loar era. Some K-4s from the 20s had the double flowerpot headstock inlay; others had the standard single flowerpot design.

1920 Price: $195.00
1921-1923 Price: $155.00 (4/1923 price increase to $225.00)
1924-1929 Price: $200.00 ($210.00 with case)

Note: Style K-1, K-2 and K-4 mandolas had the same dimensions as 1910-1919 instruments.

 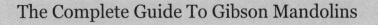

Master Model Style "K-5" Mando-cello – 1924-1929

The Master Model K-5 was a complete departure from any other mando-cellos Gibson had made prior to the Loar era. The earliest known Loar-signed K-5 is dated 10/13/1923, but it's certain that Gibson built the prototype at least a year earlier. The photo of the so-called "Bauer Quintet" first published in *The Cadenza* magazine in December 1922 shows a K-5 indicating that Gibson had built it approximately two months earlier. The K-5 did not appear in Gibson's Catalog N which was published at the end of 1923. It first appears on a January 1924 price list but wasn't shown in a catalog until late 1924. Ted McHugh's original specifications clearly establish that the K-5 was originally designed to have the same body as Gibson's L-4 arch-top guitar. Most experts have agreed that the L-5 was designed first and then Gibson decided to use its body design for the K-5 but that isn't the case. The earliest K-5 pre-dates the L-5 by at least six months and may have been the inspiration for designing the L-5 as a logical addition to the Master Model line. It also had the same price tag as the L-5 at $275.00, and it appears that the K-5 was too expensive and did not sell. There are only six known Loar-signed K-5s and it's likely that total number K-5s ever built was no more than 12 to 15. The K-5 had a unique tailpiece that combined a trapeze guitar tailpiece and a crown-top mandolin-style string holder that floated above the body. The K-5 also had an unusually long headstock and the tuning machines only covered a little over half the entire length.

K-5 Mandolin dimensions:
Body width at lower bout: 16"
Body width at upper bout: 11 5/8"
Body width at waist: 9 3/8"
Body length: 20 1/4"
Nut width: 1 5/8"
Scale length: 24 3/4"
Overall length: 40 5/8"

1924-1929 Price: $275.00
($304.50 with case)

Additional K-5 Specifications:
Carved Adirondack spruce top
Flamed maple back, sides and 3-piece 14-fret neck
Single-bound ivoroid fingerboard and headstock
3-ply bound top and back
Elevated celluloid tortoise pickguard with 3-ply binding
Ebony headstock veneer with "The Gibson" and flower pot pearl inlay
  (inlay designs did vary)
Rosewood adjustable bridge
Ebony fingerboard with single pearl dots at 5th, 7th, 10th, and 15th frets,
  double dots at 12th fret
Bone nut
4-on-a-plate nickel-plated engraved tuners with screwed-on pearl buttons
Nickel-plate trapeze tailpiece with "The Gibson" engraved on cover
Elevated celluloid tortoise shell pickguard with 3-ply binding
Celluloid pickguard support with nickel threaded rod and mounting block
21 nickel-silver frets including fingerboard extension

First published in December 1922, the so-called Bauer Quintet with all four members being Walter Bauer. On the left the prototype K-5

Gibson Style "J" Mando-bass – 1920-1929

The mando-basses of the early 1920s differed very little from those made before 1920, but after 1924, Gibson changed the Sheraton Brown finish to a black top with dark mahogany brown stained back, sides, and neck. They also discontinued using inlaid pearl for the logo, and switched to a silk-screened The Gibson logo.

1920-1923 Price: $170.00 (4/1923 price decrease to $160.00)
1924-1926 Price: $150.00
1926 Price: $150.00 ($157.50 with case)

Gibson Finishes – 1920-1929

Oil Varnish
Some sources believe that before Gibson started using nitro-cellulose lacquer they actually used an oil-based varnish. This may seem like a rather strange deviation during the transition from spirit varnish to lacquer, but conventional compressed air spraying equipment was still in its infancy. Extant instruments from the late teens through the Loar era show that Gibson brushed on a dark shellac which acted as a sealer over the water-based stained surfaces. Then an oil varnish was brushed on over it. Brushing these coats caused drips and run-off that are often visible on the inside of the back and/or the underside of the f-holes. In addition they added a clear spirit varnish top coat that was possibly French-polished or applied by hand rather than sprayed. Well-known experts believe that the spirit varnish top-coat(s) were buffed to a fine sheen using pumice which was essentially the same process used for violin finishing.

Cremona Brown
In 1921 Gibson started experimenting with 3-color sunbursts that were yellow, red, and brown. The first instrument to have a 3-color sunburst was a very bizarre-looking F-4 that earned the nickname "skunk burst." The back had bright yellow edges that graduated from orange to a red stripe down the center. Noted Gibson historian and author Joe Spann discovered that the three-color sunburst was developed by Fred Miller who was the foreman of Gibson's finishing department. Miller had been working for Gibson since 1915, so it's very likely that he was the person responsible for the development of the more refined 2-color sunburst finishes the company used from 1915 till 1921. Miller invented a new 3-color sunburst finish he called "Cremona Brown," which had an amber-colored center that radiated out to increasingly darker shades of brown toward the edges. The first instrument Miller used this finish on was an F-4, and it was so well-liked by everyone at Gibson that they started using it in on all the Style 4s. To the casual observer, the early Cremona Brown finishes on the tops and backs don't appear dramatically different from the earlier two-color process, but the rims typically had more prominent amber/yellow.

Although the Cremona Brown finish has become synonymous with the Loar-era Master Models some did not have it. There are extant Loar-signed F-5s with the tri-color yellow/red/brown sunburst.

The 3-color sunburst is also the subject of much debate, as there are varying opinions on how Gibson achieved this beautiful new and improved finish. The general consensus is that the company only used hand-rubbed water-based wood dye for the red and brown shading and left the center section un-dyed. Then, on the entire top, they applied orange shellac to fill the center section and seal the wood. One of the main reasons for this process is that light-colored wood dyes tend to show darker patches more prominently. This is not particularly displeasing to the eye as compared to the darker-colored dyes but the darker streaks in the yellow areas are much more noticeable and not very attractive. The second possibility is that Gibson did use a yellow dye for the center section; when the red dye was added and blended into the yellow it turned orange. The orange tended to hide the dark streaks a bit more than the yellow did.

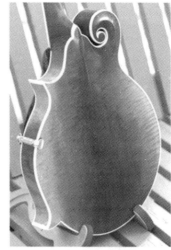

One early attempt at a 3-color sunburst was on a 1921 F-4 which earned the nickname "skunk burst." Courtesy of Dan Beimborn

There were other significant changes made to the finishes Gibson used in the 1920s. The first conventional hand-held spray guns became more prevalent in the early 1920s, which allowed manufacturers to start using an entirely new type of finish – nitrocellulose lacquer. Nitrocellulose is a naturally-occurring starchy by-product of cotton processing. As early as the 1860s it was discovered that nitrating cellulose (treating it with nitric acid) caused it to become highly explosive. It was originally called "gun cotton, because in a powder form it was six times more explosive than traditional gun powder. In 1868 American inventor John Wesley Hyatt plasticized nitrocellulose with camphor, allowing it to be formed into a hardened thin film or thick sheets. He named it celluloid, which is still the name used today. It's considered to be the first commercial plastic material that was used for everything from photographic film to hair brushes. In the early 1920s the DuPont Corporation developed the first nitrocellulose lacquer called "Duco," that was made by dissolving nitrocellulose in a solvent we now know as lacquer thinner. It was first used in the automobile industry because the drying time was a fraction of the time it took varnish to dry. Very soon lacquer became the most widely-used finish for wood products as well.

Some believe that Gibson may have started using a mixture of nitrocellulose lacquer with some shellac. But lacquer thinner prevents shellac from fully hardening, leading to an unwanted softness of the finish. Another formula Gibson may have used was dissolving the nitrocellulose and shellac mixture in amyl nitrate which gave it a distinct banana odor leading to the nickname "banana lacquer." Amyl nitrate doesn't inhibit the hardening of the shellac as much as lacquer thinner and can speed up drying time because it evaporates quickly. The problem was that its fumes were highly volatile causing dizziness, lowered blood pressure and relaxation of the involuntary muscles. Someone inhaling these fumes would become intoxicated and disoriented. Gibson realized that all the inherent problems with these finishes out-weighed the benefits, and by the end of the 1920s they started using pure nitrocellulose lacquer.

Matchless finish, with just enough ornamentation to emphasize the richness of the beautiful Cremona-brown shaded varnish.

Above: A short excerpt from Catalog N about the Cremona Brown finish being a "shaded varnish." Right: The illustration of the back of the F-5 showing the finish on the figured maple

Gibson Parts & Accessories – 1920-1929

In 1924 Gibson decided to publish a separate accessories catalog rather than include all of that information in their main-line catalogs. They published a second accessories catalog in 1928, but neither of these catalogs contained many illustrations. This leaves a lot of guesswork in order to determine what each part or accessory was and who made them.

Instrument Cases

By 1924 Gibson stopped carrying cases made by the Felsberg Company, formerly Maulbetsch & Whittemore. Geib & Schafer became Gibson's sole supplier of instrument cases from 1924 until after World War II. Gibson used two basic G&S case designs, the "Mastercraft" brand Gibson called "Faultless" and the G&S "Utility" cases, which is what Gibson called them too. The Faultless cases had two options for linings - the "Faultless V" had a green felt lining and the "Faultless S.P." had green plush lining. Gibson only offered the plush-lined cases for the "F" mandolins, the H-4 and H-5 mandolas and the K-4 and K-5 mando-cellos. All the rest were either felt-lined Faultless or Utility cases. The Utility cases were made of a thick strawboard material, or as it's commonly known, "chip-board," and were covered with Keratol. In 1923 Gibson had G&S make special "Faultless S.P." cases for the Master Model Style 5 instruments. They were rectangular like a suitcase with a form-fitting interior plush-lined compartment. These cases were twice the price of the "Faultless V" cases, and today a Loar-era G&S Faultless 440 F-5 case can sell for thousands of dollars. In 1926 a one-of-a-kind G&S double mandolin case was made for a pair of sequentially numbered F-5s. It's the only one known to exist.

The cover of Gibson's 1924 accessories catalog

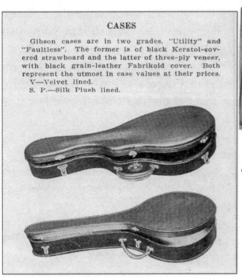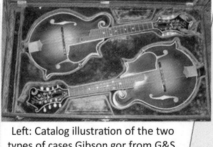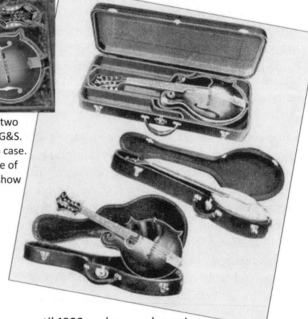

Left: Catalog illustration of the two types of cases Gibson gor from G&S. Above: Custom-made double F-5 case. Right: 1926 Catalog P cases, one of the only catalogs in the 20s to show parts illustrations.

Tuners

Gibson continued using tuning machines made by Louis Handel & Co. up until 1922 and were also using economy tuners made by Dinsmore & Jager. After Gibson stopped using Handel tuners Waverly Musical Products became their new supplier. In fact, the first Loar-signed Master Model F-5 from June 1922 has one of the first sets of Waverly tuners (if not the first). Early on, Waverly's tuners were a bit crude-looking mainly because the plating (gold or nickel-silver) was insufficient to prevent it from flaking off over time. The quality of the parts and machining was good, and they had several distinctive design features including fleur-de-lis-shaped ends, engraved plates and mother-of-pearl buttons that screwed onto the shafts. Gibson used Waverly tuners on all of their high-end instruments including all the Style 5s.

Waverly also made tuners with a rounded tab on the ends of the base plates where the mounting screws were located and usually had ivoroid buttons. However several extant F-2s from this transitional period had nickel-plated metal buttons. Gibson usually used these tuners on their lower-priced mandolins, mandolas, mando-cellos, and guitars. The company continued to use the D&J economy tuners that had simple rectangular mounting plates with square ends made with un-plated or nickel-plated brass.

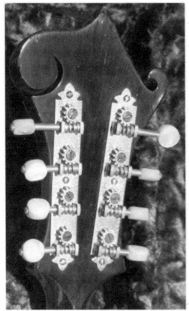

In 1925 Gibson started mounting all their tuners upside down. The tuners were mounted so that the worm gear (the spiral end of the shaft) was above the cog (the gear at the bottom of the string post) otherwise known as "worm-over," instead of "worm-under" like they had been doing for the previous 25 years. This seems to indicate that the company decided to discontinue using D&J tuners and gave Waverly the vast majority of their business. The reason for this change is unclear as the tuners Waverly made prior to 1925 were mounted worm-under, but the worm-over versions had the worm gear reversed which enabled the tuners to work the same way. To raise the pitch of the string the tuner buttons were rotated counter-clockwise on both versions. The real diffi-culty in determining this supposition that is neither manufacturer marked the tuners with a logo or patent date. Gibson never included any illustrations of the D&J tuners after 1918 and never included illustrations of the Waverly mandolin tuners in any catalog or brochure. Neither company was ever mentioned by name. Conversely, they did specifically identify their banjo tuners as being made by A. D. Grover & Sons, and it's likely that Waverly never provided Gibson with the "cuts" or illustrations for use in their sales literature.

One of the first sets of Waverly tuners Gibson used were on a 1922 Loar-signed F-5 mandolin

Above top: The lesser expensive Wavely F-tuners without screw-on buttons
Below: The rounded end style Waverly tuners

Gibson's 1928 Parts & Accessories catalog included lots of information about tuners except any illustration

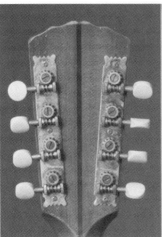

Comparison between "A" mandolin tuners
1921 Handels mounted "worm-uner" (avove left)
and 1928 Wavelry rounded-end "worm-over" (above right)

Strings

In the early 1920s Gibson was still using the string envelope design they had been using since 1912 In about 1924 they changed the design of the envelope, but for some very strange reason these newer envelopes had the picture of a bowl-back instrument in the upper right-hand corner. It took about a year until someone realized that given Gibson's long history of being anti-potato bug, this graphic was totally inappropriate. So in 1925, they came up with their new "Mastertone" brand of strings, which coincided with the introduction of the new banjo line. From 1920 to 1928 Gibson still had all their strings made by an outside supplier, but then that all changed in 1929.

1912-1922 Gibson string envelope

1924-1925 string envelope with bowl-back mandolin illustration

1926-1928 Gibson Mastertone strings

In 1929 Gibson started manufacturing their own strings in-house. They introduced the "Mastertone Deluxe" brand of strings and these were described in one catalog as having "all windings [are] of new 'Mona-steel' – developed and perfected July 1929." The Mona-steel name was a derivation of "monel," which was a corrosion-resistant nickel alloy invented by David Browne in the early 1900s. Browne was chief metallurgist for the International Nickel Company, and this new alloy was named after the company's president, Ambrose Monell. Gibson set up an entire string manufacturing department and started buying large quantities of Monel wire from American Steel & Wire Company in Chicago. After July 1929 Gibson introduced the "Mastertone Deluxe – Mona-steel" brand of strings which the company promoted as "the ultimate in trueness, brilliancy, clarity and volume." Then, in the early 1930s, Gibson dropped the "Mastertone Deluxe" name and their strings became simply the "Mona-steel" brand.

In 1929 Gibson started making their own strings. The first brand was the Mastertone Deluxe

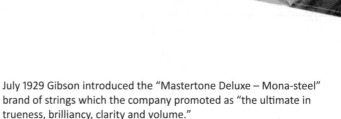

July 1929 Gibson introduced the "Mastertone Deluxe – Mona-steel" brand of strings which the company promoted as "the ultimate in trueness, brilliancy, clarity and volume."

All string envelope pictures courtesy of Rod McDonald

Pickguards

From 1918 to 1922 Gibson's pickguards were mounted on the instruments using two pins that attached it to the side of the fingerboard and a single pin that inserted into a hole in the treble side of the bridge base. The supports were made with a small half-moon-shaped celluloid riser with a threaded rod arm that extended from the spacer to a threaded celluloid block that was glued to the underside of the pickguard. When Gibson started using the McHugh adjustable bridge, they eliminated the bridge pin on the pickguard as well as changing its shape. Gibson was still using the patented Laurian cam clamp to attach the pickguards to the side of the instrument. Starting in 1922 the new Master Model Style "5" instruments got a new five-ply mount that did not use the cam clamp, but screwed into the side of the instrument. The pickguard support had nickel-plated metal parts, but was also available in gold to match custom-order instruments that had all gold hardware. Gibson finally eliminated the cam clamp altogether in 1925 and replaced it with a notched solid nickel-plated mount.

F-5 pickguard mount of alternating black & white celluloid

F-4 pickguard nickel-plate brass with threaded rod & nut

Picks

In the 1920s Gibson only carried a few picks for mandolins, mandolas, and mando-cellos. The "Kork Grip" picks were still available, but the rest were plain celluloid tortoise shell and were available in medium and stiff. In 1928 Gibson started offering banjo picks that were "genuine tortoise shell" with a price tag to match. The only illustrations of picks in any catalog or brochure during the 1920s was an accessories booklet Gibson published in 1928. The company did add one unusual pick, the #61, that initially had no detailed description. It does appear in many 1930's catalogs and described as "brown - tortoise celluloid, beveled edges with rubber grips. Although the pick design was patented by Louis C. Knackstedt in 1914. Gibson didn't start carrying them until the late 20s. Knackstedt's design was rather ingenious because the rubber grips were inserted through three holes in the top of the pick so both the thumb and index finger would come into contact with them and prevent the pick from slipping.

Gibson's 1928 accessories catalog included lots of illustrations of picks including the #61 (upper left corner)

The pick designed and patented by Louis C. Knackstedt in 1914

Gibson Publishing - 1920-1929

Gibson Catalogs

Gibson published two large full-line catalogs in 1920 and 1921, Catalogs "L" and "M," but after that the size of their catalogs was cut in half. Sales Manager C.V. Buttelman had taken over as the person responsible for the catalog content, and he eliminated all the pages that contained the so-called "gospel according to L.A. Williams" that had filled half of Gibson's catalogs from 1910 till 1921. In 1923 Gibson published its landmark Catalog N, the first full-line catalog to include the new Master Model F-5 mandolin. Given the fact that Catalog N had the new company name "Gibson, Inc." printed on it, this catalog was published no earlier than December 1923, a year and a half after Gibson built the first F-5. This seems to indicate that Gibson was very slow in bringing the F-5 to market. The rest of the Style "5" instruments didn't appear until the following year when the company published Catalog O. In the 1920s Gibson published separate catalogs and brochures for their banjos versus all the rest of their instruments. They published mandolin and guitar catalogs in 1926, 1928 and 1929 – designated letters P, Q and R. 1928's Catalog Q featured a mandolin on the cover, but oddly it wasn't the F-5, it was an F-4.

The last of Gibson's big catalogs was 1921's catalog M

1928's Catalog Q featured a mandolin on the cover but it wasn't the F-5, it was an F-4.

Above: Clipping from Catalog N with the new company name "Gibson, Inc." was published in December 1923, 18 months Gibson built the first F-5
Right: Catalog N also included a full-color full-page spread for the new Master Model

The Gibsonite was referred to as a "new publication devoted to the interests of Gibson"

Publications:

In 1921 C.V. Buttelman came up with the idea of publishing a pseudo-newsletter called *"The Gibsonite."* Although it was in the form of a newsletter, complete with volume and issue numbers, it was actually published as a series of two-page ads in *The Cadenza* magazine from January 1921 to October 1923. In an article, *The Gibsonite* was referred to as a "new publication devoted to the interests of Gibson" and Buttelman said "that almost every month, we are able to announce another step in the march of Gibson progress." Volume 1 No. 1 featured an

announcement about Gibson's latest innovation, the adjustable bridge, "a truly Gibsonic feature." It also had a short section that called Gibson's mandolins "the Strad of Mandolins," and pre-dates the use of that phrase for the Master Model F-5 by more than two years. In typical Buttelman style, the content and writing style was up-beat and light-hearted and even included some amusing cartoons.

"The Gibson Way" according to C.V. Buttelman was full of love, romance and Gibson mandolins

SOMETHING NEW

Almost every month we are able to announce another step in the march of Gibson progress. This month it is the

GIBSON ADJUSTABLE BRIDGE

A truly Gibsonic feature, now standard equipment on all Gibson Mandolins. Easy action—high action—whatever you require, instantly secured. Write for circular.

Gibson Mandolin-Guitar Co.
500 Parsons St.   Kalamazoo, Mich.

Volume 1 No. 1 of *The Gibsonite* featured an announcement about Gibson's latest innovation, the adjustable bridge "a truly Gibsonic feature."

Vol. 3 No. 7 of *The Gibsonite* included the announcement of Gibson's Master Model F-5

Gibson continued to publish its in-house magazine *The Sounding Board Salesman* with Buttelman as editor. The publication had grown steadily and many issues exceeded 48 pages. Buttelman was trying to motivate Gibson's teacher/agents using things like amusing cartoons and informational articles like "The Art of Playing and Teaching the Mandolin," written by Zarh Myron Bickford, a very well-known and respected musician and author of a best-selling method book. Buttelman wanted Gibson agents to be up on the latest and greatest goings on in Kalamazoo including announcements about new innovations like the patented adjustable bridge and truss-rod. He was hoping to use the magazine to educate Gibson's agents as well as applaud the efforts of agents who demonstrated creative ways to promote Gibson instruments like store window displays. He also organized many sales meetings called "round-ups," where agents would get together to discuss everything related to sales and listen to mandolin groups and special guest speakers. L. A. Williams continued to use the publication to apply pressure on their sales representatives by instituting sales quotas, charging agents for multiple copies of Gibson catalogs and continually haranging agents who failed to meet his expectations of successful selling. Williams berated sales reps who tried to blame others for their failures, which of course was exactly what he was doing. After Buttelman's departure from Gibson in January 1924, the company discontinued publishing *The Sounding Board Salesman*.

Volume 1 No. 1 of *The Mastertone* magazine from October 1926

Volume I   October, 1926   No. 1

Your Window is Your Best Salesman

Here is an example of an effective Gibson window trim by J. W. Jenkins' Sons, Kansas City, Mo. Windows like this create widespread interest. Foremost merchandisers all agree that care and thought in devising new and original windows...the effort, as they not...displayed, but also bui...progressiveness. There...window, as it all depen...out different effects.

After the change in management at Gibson in 1923, Sales Manager Frank Campbell decided that Gibson needed a new in-house publication and he came up with the name, *The Mastertone,* capitalizing on the popularity of the Mastertone banjo line. The first issue was published in October 1926 and was solely intended as a special publication for Gibson dealers. Campbell specifically mentions that magazine issues "will not be mailed to competitors in the same city – only to Gibsonites." *Mastertone* also included features on new design innovations, prominent Gibson players like Nick Lucas, Carson J. Robison and Jack Rose, as well as a question and answer section and announcements about Gibson instruments being used on the radio and for recordings. Some issues even contained articles "of interest to mandolinists."

The cover of the December 1929 issue featured Nick Lucas in the movie The Gold Diggers of Broadway

Page Twenty   *The MASTERTONE*

Of Interest to
The Mandolinist

The
Get-Together Corner *for* Mandolinists

In 1929 Campbell gave *The Mastertone* a bit of a face-lift including a redesigned cover and new graphics and became "Mastertone," without "The." He started selling copies to the general public for 15 cents and also sold advertising space to other companies, some of which were considered competitors like Standard Musical String Co. who advertised their "Kleertone" brand of guitar strings. However the magazine was published during an era when Gibson was so focused onbanjo sales that they contained almost no mandolin content.

Something New and Better
**KLEERTONE
GUITAR STRINGS**
A Set Includes
One Plain, High-Tension Wire and Five Specially Balanced and Durably Wound Strings, All Fitted with Non-Slip Ball Ends
Now Adopted by
Leading Manufacturers and Players

TRIAL SET 50c

Standard Musical String Co.
122 Cypress Ave., New York City

Even though their were a competitor Standard Musical String Co. advertised their "Kleertone" brand of strings in *Mastertone Magazine*

Gibson, Inc. – 1930-1939

After the stock market crash in October 1929, it wasn't long before Gibson felt the effects of the Great Depression. In December 1930 Guy Hart laid off a significant percentage of Gibson's workforce including his right-hand man, Frank Campbell. Hart promoted Neil Abrams as his assistant and production manager and together they would guide the company through the worst economy in U.S. history. Gibson's high-end instruments like the Style 5 Master Models weren't selling, so Hart and Abrams started experimenting with all kinds of different designs and models in order to determine what would appeal to their customers. What Depression-era customers wanted were quality instruments at very affordable prices. Hart was aware of Gibson's success with previous economy models like the Junior line from the 1920s, so it was clear that cheaper instruments was the way to go. In 1930 Gibson introduced the Style A-0 which at $35.00 was their least expensive mandolin, but it didn't sell very well. Then in 1931 Gibson introduced the somewhat obscure model C-1 flat-top mandolin that at $25.00, it was half the price of the "A" mandolin. The company called it "a genuine Gibson at this very low price," but it was a complete failure because the price was too high for such a simple design. Gibson discontinued it within a year. However Hart and Abrams may have thought they were onto something, so in 1933 Gibson introduced the A-00. It was a higher quality mandolin but had the same $25.00 price tag as the C-1. The A-00 was priced just right and quickly became the company's best-selling mandolin.

Neil Abrams
Assistant to the General Manager

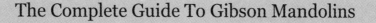

Also in 1933 Hart and Abrams came up with an idea that not only proved to be incredibly successful, but literally saved the company from closing its doors for good. The company introduced a whole new line of instruments that didn't carry the iconic Gibson name, but an entirely new brand named after the city Gibson had called home since its inception, "Kalamazoo." They advertised the Kalamazoo instruments as "the world's greatest value." The first Kalamazoo mandolin was only $12.50, half the price of the C-1, even though it was essentially the same design. When first introduced there was only one mandolin model, a flat-top called the "KM," short for "Kalamazoo mandolin." In 1934 the KM became the model "KM-11." Gibson also introduced an arched-top mandolin, the "KM-21." In addition to the Kalamazoo mandolins, they also made four different banjos, three guitars, plus economy versions of the entire mandolin family of instruments. In 1935 they introduced the Kalamazoo "KH-21" mandola, the "KK-31" mando-cello, and even a Kalamazoo mando-bass called the "KJ." Sales of the Kalamazoo instruments were so good that they out-sold their Gibson counterparts by a very wide margin. They were very good quality instruments, built by a premiere instrument manufacturer, but sold at a fraction of the cost of a name-brand Gibson. By the end of the 30s the company had sold over 60,000 Kalamazoos.

Neil Abrams was also responsible for resurrecting the almost defunct relationship between Gibson and Montgomery Ward and grew it into a very successful branch of the business. Montgomery Ward was Gibson's single biggest customer during the 1930s with total sales in excess of 14,000 instruments and amplifiers. Gibson also started making many other brands of inexpensive mandolins including Cromwell, another Gibson in-house brand and private-label brands like Capital, Hayden and Henry L. Mason. The Washburn and Fascinator branded mandolins were made for the Tonk Brothers in Chicago.

Some of the other brands Gibson made during the 1930s: Montgomery Ward "Recording King" mandolin; The Fascinator brand was made for the Tonk Bros.; Hayden was the brand name used by L.D. Heater and the Coast Wholesale's Henry L. Mason brand.

However Gibson did not ignore their name-brand instruments, and in 1933 they introduced a brand new "A" mandolin, the A-50. Then in 1934 they introduced several new mandolin designs including three new "F" style models, the F-7, F-10 and F-12, plus two more "A" models, the A-75 and the Century Model Style A-C. Unfortunately Hart and Abrams failed to follow their initial instincts and totally misread the dire economic conditions in the U.S. When the new "F" and "A" models didn't sell, they discontinued most of them within three years. Mandola and mando-cello sales weren't doing well either, so in 1935 they introduced an economy mandola designated the Style H-0. This helped sales a bit, but in turn Gibson decided to discontinue the H-1 and H-5 mandolas, the K-5 mando-cello as well as the Style J mando-bass because they weren't selling at all. The 1930s also saw the decline of the banjo as the dominant fretted musical instrument it had been in the 1920s, and by the mid-1930s the guitar emerged as the most popular instrument for the "swing era." The 1930s was also the decade when electrified instruments were introduced, including the first electric mandolin.

The swing era ushered in the "big band" and gave rise to the popularity of the guitar

For some reason Gibson kept pushing the notion that the mandolin was going to make a comeback. A January 1935 article published in *Mastertone Magazine* stated that "Indications all point to a strong 'come-back' of the mandolin to popularity, even greater than before." They also claimed that "a student can show more rapid progress in the mastery of the mandolin than any other instrument," and even went so far as to assert that even "a deaf person can learn to play the mandolin and always produce true tones." Proof of this supposed resurgence was, as Gibson claimed, "the number of mandolin orchestras new in evidence in Cleveland."

In reality the mandolin had faded from the public's eye and Gibson essentially relegated them to being second-class citizens. Almost all of Gibson 1930s-era catalogs listed all the mandolins last behind guitars and banjos. Gibson's management remained fairly astute about the changes in the musical instrument market and were able to maintain their place as the predominant instrument manufacturer in the United States. Gibson guitars, both arch-top and flat-top acoustic models from the pre-WWII era are considered some of the finest instruments ever made. That's not to say that the company wasn't building high quality mandolins, but the main reason Gibson stayed afloat in the 1930s was due to the enormous success of Gibson guitars as well as the Kalamazoo line and the instruments made for Montgomery Ward.

In 1937 the U.S. economy appeared to be on the rise and musical instrument sales were increasing, so Gibson started hiring new employees and expanding the factory. Unfortunately the economy took another nose-dive in 1938 and in 1939, the company had to layoff many factory workers just as they had done in 1930. Gibson managed to make it through the Great Depression, which was not the case with many other musical instruments manufacturers who went out of business. Gibson was hopeful that the 1940s would be much less difficult, but it turned out to be just as hard if not harder.

c1930 Gibson factory workforce. Courtesy of the Kalamazoo Public Library

Gibson Instruments – 1930-1939

A-0 Mandolin – 1930-1933

As mentioned in Chapter 17, Gibson's 1926 catalog and price list showed the introduction of the A-0 as the replacement for the A-Jr., but Gibson didn't make any A-0s until 1930 after the A-Jr. was discontinued. The A-0 was nearly identical to the A-Jr. except that it had a standard white oval "guarantee" label just like all the other mandolins. Gibson finally eliminated the incorrect patent date that had appeared on their labels for nearly 20 years. Early A-0s did not have a truss rod or an adjustable bridge, but Gibson added them soon after their initial introduction. Some of the first A-0 truss rods were not adjustable and were put in place merely to strengthen the neck, but not to correct bowing. Early versions also had the same Sheraton brown finish as the A-Jr. models, but later ones had a black top finish, sometimes black back, sides and neck as well. Realizing that the economic conditions of the early Great Depression demanded even less expensive instruments, Gibson discontinued the A-0 in a little over two years in favor of the A-00.

1930 Price: $36.75 (June 1930 price decrease to $35.00)
1933: Discontinued

The transition from the "paddle head" with "The Gibson" logo (left) to the 1930s "open book" headstock shape with the new Gibson script logo

"A" Mandolin – 1930-1932

The "0" and "00" model designations were intended to convey the fact that those models were less fancy and less expensive than the standard "A" or any other "A" with the number one or higher after the letter. This seems to be the reason why Gibson discontinued the plain "A" mandolin in 1933. When Gibson introduced the A-00, the "A" was twice the price and too expensive for the average buyer. The few examples of early 30s "A" mandolins that do exist look the same as they did in the late 1920s, with a black-top finish and dark brown back, sides, and neck. There are some rare examples of early 30s "A" mandolins that have the open-book headstock shape with a silkscreened "The Gibson" logo, but in 1932 the company dropped "The" from the logo and there appears to be no existing "A" mandolins with the open-book headstock and the 1930s-style "Gibson" script logo.

1930 Price: $52.50 (June 1930 price decrease to $50.00)
1933: Discontinued

A-00 Mandolin – 1933-1939

The Great Depression was forcing Gibson to offer mandolins at very low prices, so they discontinued the A-0 and replaced it with an even cheaper model, the A-00. What's rather perplexing is the fact that the A-00 had a truss rod, single bound top, a sunburst finish and yet its price was $10.00 less than the A-0. The earliest A-00s had oval-shaped soundholes but did not have an elevated finger-rest. They had a small celluloid tortoise shell pickguard glued to the top. Even though the first catalog illustration of the A-00 had the 20s style paddle head headstock shape and logo, existing instruments have Gibson's iconic "open-book" headstock shape, with a silkscreened "Gibson" script logo because the company had dropped "The" from their logo in 1932. Concurrently with the introduction of the A-00 was the complete changeover to this new open-book headstock shape which was used on all of the "A" models and has remained the standard shape for almost all Gibson instruments until today. In 1934 the A-00 along with almost every other Gibson "A" mandolin was redesigned with f-holes instead the round or oval holes like all of their mandolins from the previous three decades. The f-hole version of the A-00 had an elevated finger-rest. It went on to become Gibson's best-selling mandolin in the 1930s.

1933 Price: $25.00
1936 Price: $26.25
1937 Price: $30.00
1938 Price: $31.50
1939 Price: $33.00

The oval soundhole version of the A-00 only appeared in one Gibson brochure published in 1933

In 1934 when Gibson redesigned the A-00 adding f-holes and an elevated finger-rest, they discarded the flat-back and started using an "arched" back. They did not carve the backs like the other "A" model and introduced the "arco-arch" process. Gibson would take a thin piece of wood, either maple or mahogany and steam-press into a mold that formed the shape of the arch. It was a very economical way to cut costs and enable them to sell the A-00s at a very competitive price. They also employed thias process for almost all of the off-brands like Kalamazoo and Cromwell.

Additional A-00 specifications:
Carved spruce top
1933: Flat back, usually mahogany but sometimes maple
1934-1939: Arched (not carved) back with one brace
Single bound top and no back binding
1933: Single bound oval sound hole
1934-1939: Unbound f-holes
Nickel-plated "cloud" tailpiece
Non-adjustable ebony bridge
Waverly tuners with black buttons
Finish: Two-color brown and red sunburst top, brown back, sides, and neck

A-1 Mandolin – 1933-1939

After a 15-year absence Gibson reintroduced the model A-1 in 1933. The 1930s era A-1s went through many design changes. Gibson's 1933 small pocket-sized catalog was the first to show the reintroduced A-1 with an oval sound hole like the early 20s version. Since there seems to be no existing examples of this version, it's possible that Gibson didn't actually make any. The 1934 version of the A-1 had f-holes, the open-book headstock with the silkscreened logo, bound top and back, 20s era tailpiece, sunburst finish and four-on-a-plate Waverly tuners with ivoroid buttons.

In 1937 Gibson completely changed the design of the A-1 and introduced a new "wide body" version, as it's called, which had an 11 1/4" wide pear-shaped body and an increased scale length of 14 1/2" vs. their standard 13 7/8" scale. This wide-body version is not highly regarded by most Gibson mandolin enthusiasts and not nearly as collectible as the earlier 10 1/4" version. Four years later Gibson got rid of the wide-body design and reintroduced the pre-1937 version of the A-1.

1933 Price: $35.00
1936 Price: $36.75
1937 Price: $37.50
1938 Price: $39.38
1939 Price: $41.25

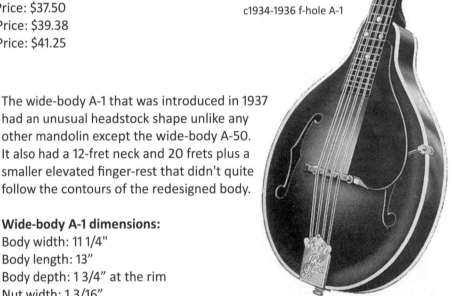

c1934-1936 f-hole A-1

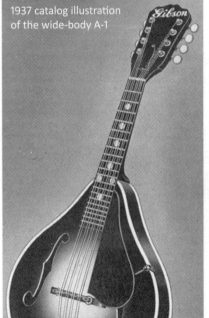

1937 catalog illustration of the wide-body A-1

The wide-body A-1 that was introduced in 1937 had an unusual headstock shape unlike any other mandolin except the wide-body A-50. It also had a 12-fret neck and 20 frets plus a smaller elevated finger-rest that didn't quite follow the contours of the redesigned body.

Wide-body A-1 dimensions:
Body width: 11 1/4"
Body length: 13"
Body depth: 1 3/4" at the rim
Nut width: 1 3/16"
Scale length: 14 1/2"
Overall length: 25 1/2"

Note: Gibson did not change the case part number for the wide-body A-1. Catalogs list the Geib & Schafer "Challenge" case no. 101 for both the standard width "A" mandolins and the wide-body versions.

A-4 Mandolin – 1930-1934

Gibson continued to make a few A-4 mandolins in the early 1930s, but like the company's other expensive mandolins, the A-4 was doomed to failure because of the Great Depression. Existing shipping records show only two A-4s shipped after it was discontinued, one in 1935 and the other in 1936, but ostensibly it had been discontinued in 1934, and the post-1934 instruments were just left-over stock. The illustrations of the A-4 that appeared in Gibson's early 1930s catalogs were the same as they had used in the 1920s, which was also the case for all of the other mandolins they discontinued in the early part of the decade.

A-4

1930 Price: $84.00
(June 1930 price decrease to $80.00)
1935: Discontinued

Early 1930's
oval-hole A-50

A-50 Mandolin – 1933-1939

In 1933 Gibson introduced a new mandolin model, the A-50. During this era Gibson started naming their instruments based on what they cost, so the A-50 got its name because it cost $50.00. Like the A-1, the A-50 started out as an oval hole "A" model, but then changed to an f-hole design in 1934. Then in 1937 it was completely redesigned like the A-1 and got the wide 11 1/4" pear-shaped body and a longer scale length. The A-50 sold fairly well in spite of the fact that it was $15.00 more than the A-1 and proved to have real staying power, lasting well beyond the 1930s.

1933 Price: $50.00
1936 Price: $52.50
1937 Price: $50.00
1938 Price: $52.50
1939 Price: $55.00

1937 catalog illustration of the wide-body A-50

Wide body A-50 dimensions:
(same as wide-body A-1)

Additional A-50 Specifications:
Inlaid pearl script logo
Inlaid pearl fleur-de-lis
Varying fingerboard inlay shapes
  (similar to the F-7)
Bound top, back and fingerboard
Bound elevated finger-rest

1934-1936 f-hole
version of the A-50

A-75 Mandolin – 1934-1937

In 1934 Gibson produced an even fancier "A" model, the A-75, which cost $75.00 another direct result of its model designation. Gibson started naming many of their instruments based on their price in 1934. The A-75 had an inlaid mother-of-pearl logo with a large fleur-de-lis below it and an ivoroid bound top, back, and fingerboard. Gibson finished it with a three-color sunburst on the top and the back, and the rim and neck were dark brown. These additional features were really not enough to justify the price tag, so the A-75 only lasted until 1937 because it wasn't selling nearly as well as the less expensive "A" models.

1934 Price: $75.00
1936 Price: $78.75
1938: Discontinued

Century Model A-C Mandolin – 1934-1937

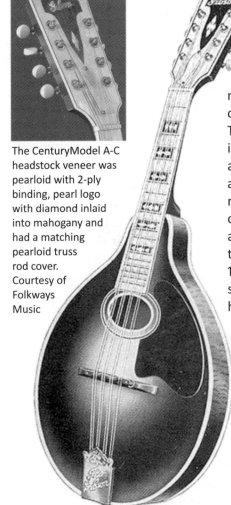

The CenturyModel A-C headstock veneer was pearloid with 2-ply binding, pearl logo with diamond inlaid into mahogany and had a matching pearloid truss rod cover. Courtesy of Folkways Music

In the summer of 1933 Gibson was one of hundreds of exhibitors at the Chicago World's Fair, which was called "The Century of Progress," chronicling the 100-year history of the industrial revolution. Gibson had been experimenting with a faux-pearl plastic material called Pyralin or more commonly, "pearloid." To commemorate the World's Fair Gibson introduced several "Century" instruments with art-deco ornamentation with pearloid fingerboards and headstock veneers inlaid with a combination of mother-of-pearl and mahogany. Some consider the Century models to be a bit ostentatious. The pearloid material is often referred to as "mother-of-toilet-seat," a less than complimentary reference to bathroom fixtures. The A-C holds the distinction of being the only carved-top "A" mandolin with an oval sound-hole made after 1933. It was not that expensive, even though it had many fancy features including a sunburst finish on the top, back, neck and even the back of the headstock. It also had a two-ply white/black binding on the headstock and fingerboard as well as a matching pearloid truss rod cover. Gibson also used figured maple for the backs, but the A-C backs were not carved or arched, just flat. They were often one piece of wood as opposed to two book-matched pieces glued at the center like an F-4 or F-5. In spite of being only $5.00 more than an A-50, the A-C did not seem to appeal to most customers and was discontinued in 1937. However Gibson did continue to make the Century L-C guitar, well after that.

1934 Price: $55.00
1936 Price: $57.75
1937: Discontinued

C-1 Mandolin – 1931-1932

In 1930 Gibson decided to manufacture its first flat-top style "A" mandolin. They introduced a new brand of instruments called "Kel Kroydon" which included two mandolin models, the KK-20 and KK-21. Unfortunately the company over-priced these "budget" instruments and had to discontinue them in less than a year. Times were tough but in typical Gibson fashion they didn't throw anything away and decided to turn the Kel Kroydon design into a Gibson-branded version called the C-1. In order to keep manufacturing costs low, the C-1, like the Kel Kroydons, had no truss rod, no adjustable bridge, a cloud tailpiece and very plain ornamentation. Gibson's catalogs described it as "a popular priced mandolin within the reach of all." One of the oddest features of the C-1 was described as a "built-in finger-rest," which was actually just the shape of a pickguard painted on the top. Although catalog illustrations show a flat-top head-stock shape, existing C-1 mandolins had the 1920s-era paddle head. Gibson priced the C-1 at $25.00, $5.00 more than the KK-20, but it was still over-priced and the C-1 was another very short-lived model lasting only about a year. Once Gibson decided to make the A-00 as its least expensive entry level model, the C-1 became totally obsolete.

1931 Price: $25.00
1932: Discontinued

Artist's rendering of a Kel Kroydon
KK-20 mandolin Included here
for reference purposes

Kel Kroydon – 1930-1931

The name Kel Kroydon has been a Gibson "history mystery" because for decades, because no one has had any idea where the name came from. The Kel Kroydon line was Gibson's first attempt at a full-line inexpensive alternative to their name-brand instruments. The only information about the two mandolin models comes from a May 1930 price list that included the KK-20 and KK-21 models. Several examples of KK-20 mandolins do exist but no KK-21 has ever surfaced in the past 85 years and this might indicate that Gibson never made any. There are no known illustrations of the KK mandolins because they never appeared in any dealer catalog. Both the KK-20 and KK-21 were flat-top and flat-back mandolins with the same body shape as a standard Gibson "A" model. They were a no-frills, bare-bones instrument and did not have a truss rod, adjustable bridge and had very plain ornamentation. The labels inside these instruments did say "for professionals" and "made by Gibson, Inc." which unusual for any off-brand instruments.

F-2 Mandolin – 1930-1934

In the early part of the Great Depression the F-2 was just too expensive and unnecessary because the F-4 was Gibson's flag-ship oval hole Style "F" mandolin, so the F-2 was discontinued. In late 1930 F-2s were among the first mandolins to get a sprayed sunburst top finish (see the section at the end of this chapter). Even though there were a few F-2s shipped after 1934, they were just left-over stock from 1934 or earlier. Like the A-0 and A-4, Gibson never made another F-2 after 1934.

1930 Price: $115.50
(June 1930 price decrease to $110.00)
1934: Discontinued

F-4 Mandolin – 1930-1939

The F-4 proved to have lasting appeal for Gibson's customers and was the best-selling Style "F" Artist mandolin of the 1930s. The F-4 got a few design changes during the 30s, most notably the elimination of the fingerboard extension in 1934. The F-4 fingerboard was redesigned to a shorter length with a rounded end that came to a point in the middle, sometimes called a "scalloped end." Unlike the 20s F-4s, Gibson only finished the tops of the 30s F-4s in sunburst with dark brown stained backs, rims and necks. They also eliminated the headstock binding and changed the flower pot headstock inlay to a large diamond-shaped piece. Hoping to boost its sagging sales Gibson slashed the price of the F-4 to $105.00 in 1936 and it seemed to work. The U.S. economy was on the rise in 1937 which was probably more of a factor in increased sales of the F-4. Many hoped it was a sign that the Great Depression was coming to an end but the economy got bad again in 1938, and instrument sales tumbled to all-time lows. However Gibson continued to make the F-4 up until WWII.

1930 Price: $157.50 (June 1930 price decrease to $150.00)
1936 Price: $105.00
1937 Price: $110.00
1938 Price: $115.50

Master Model F-5 Mandolin – 1930-1939

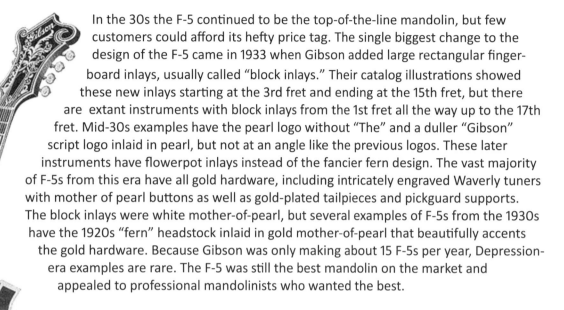

1930 Price: $262.50
(June 1930 price decrease
   to $250.00)
1936 Price: $262.50
1937 Price: $250.00
1938 Price: $262.50

In the 30s the F-5 continued to be the top-of-the-line mandolin, but few customers could afford its hefty price tag. The single biggest change to the design of the F-5 came in 1933 when Gibson added large rectangular fingerboard inlays, usually called "block inlays." Their catalog illustrations showed these new inlays starting at the 3rd fret and ending at the 15th fret, but there are extant instruments with block inlays from the 1st fret all the way up to the 17th fret. Mid-30s examples have the pearl logo without "The" and a duller "Gibson" script logo inlaid in pearl, but not at an angle like the previous logos. These later instruments have flowerpot inlays instead of the fancier fern design. The vast majority of F-5s from this era have all gold hardware, including intricately engraved Waverly tuners with mother of pearl buttons as well as gold-plated tailpieces and pickguard supports. The block inlays were white mother-of-pearl, but several examples of F-5s from the 1930s have the 1920s "fern" headstock inlaid in gold mother-of-pearl that beautifully accents the gold hardware. Because Gibson was only making about 15 F-5s per year, Depression-era examples are rare. The F-5 was still the best mandolin on the market and appealed to professional mandolinists who wanted the best.

F-7 Mandolin – 1934-1939

In 1934 Gibson introduced three new Style "F" Artist mandolins, the F-7, F-10 and F-12. Each model had the same basic design elements as the F-5, but with varying ornamentation. The F-7 was similar to the L-7 guitar which borrowed its inlay design from the Nick Lucas Special guitar. The fingerboard had different geometric shapes at each fret and a fleur-de-lis below the Gibson logo on the headstock. The main differences between the F-7 and F-5 is that the former had a shorter fingerboard that was square on the end and had no fingerboard extension. It also had a single bound top, back, fingerboard, headstock, and a bound elevated finger-rest that was the same shape as an "A" mandolin, rather than the fancier F-5 pickguard shape. Even though the F-7 had nicely figured maple backs and rims but the necks were usually mahogany and Gibson only finished the top in sunburst. Unlike the F-10 and F-12, the F-7 sold almost as well as the F-4, but ultimately it was decided to discontinue it in 1939.

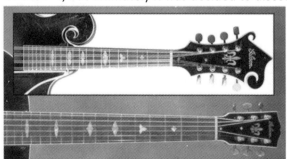

Comparison between F-7 and L-7 fingerboard inlays

1934 Price: $135.00
1936 Price: $131.25
1937 Price: $125.00
1938 Price: $131.25

F-10 Mandolin – 1934-1936

Rather than naming the new Style "F" models based on their price, their models mirrored the introduction of three new arch-top guitars designated L-7, L-10, and L-12. The F-10 and F-12 were more ornate than the F-7 and had similar design features as their guitar counterparts. The most striking feature of the F-10 was its "black ebony" finish that covered the entire mandolin. Unlike the F-7, it did have a fingerboard extension like the F-5. Gibson's management quickly realized that the high price they were charging for the F-10 and F-12 offered very little to attract customers. Professionals who wanted the best bought anF-5. Scaled-down versions like the other Style Fs were not going to be successful in the depressed economy of the 1930s. Shipping records show that the last F-10 shipped in 1937 had a serial number that dated to 1935 indicating it was just left-over inventory suggesting that Gibson only made F-10s for a little over a year.

1934 Price: $150.00
1936 Price: $157.50
1937: Discontinued

F-12 Mandolin – 1934-1936

The F-12 is one of the rarest mandolins from this era simply because they didn't sell and Gibson made very few. The only examples that have surfaced look just like the catalog illustration. Gibson described the F-12 as being "only surpassed by the Master Model F-5 – here is grace, beauty and dependability for those who want something special in a mandolin, but cannot afford the F-5 model." Even at $75.00 less than an F-5, the F-12 was not affordable to the average 1930s customer, and like the F-10, did not interest professional players. However an existing F-12 is very valuable and highly sought after by collectors because of their rarity.

1934 Price: $175.00
1936 Price: $183.75
1937: Discontinued

EM-150 Electric Mandolin – 1937-1939

One of the milestones in Gibson's storied history was the introduction of electrified instruments starting in 1935. Gibson was not the first company to offer an electric mandolin, but in 1937 a couple of years after the company started making its first electric instruments, they introduced the EM-150. Essentially the EM-150 was an "A" mandolin with a single pickup with one volume and one tone control and a standard 1/4" output jack. In 1937 Gibson was awarded its first patent for a pickup and although Guy Hart's name was on it as the inventor, he had nothing to do with its design or development. Walter Fuller, Gibson's most highly regarded electronics engineer, is widely credited with its design. Fuller's design became known as the "Charlie Christian" pickup, named after the legendary jazz guitarist who was the first well-known player to use a

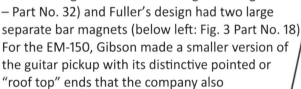

Gibson ES-150 electric guitar in a big band. His design was not revolutionary, but was quite similar to the pickup that was invented by Art Stimson for National/Dobro. Although both patents were awarded in 1937, Stimson had applied for his patent in 1934. Fuller's idea was to change the horseshoe magnet configuration that Stimson designed (diagram lower right – Part No. 32) and Fuller's design had two large separate bar magnets (below left: Fig. 3 Part No. 18) For the EM-150, Gibson made a smaller version of the guitar pickup with its distinctive pointed or "roof top" ends that the company also used on their electric tenor guitars and banjos. Gibson usually sold the EM-150 as a set with the EH-150 amplifier, the same way they sold most of their electric instruments.

Walter Fuller

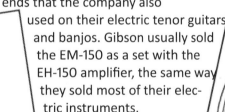

Art Stimson "horse shoe" magnet pickup. Patent No. 2,078,350

1937-1939 Price: $77.50
(with 15 ft. cord)
EH-150 Amplifier
Price: $75.00

Patent No. 2,087,106 for the "Charlie Christian" pickup

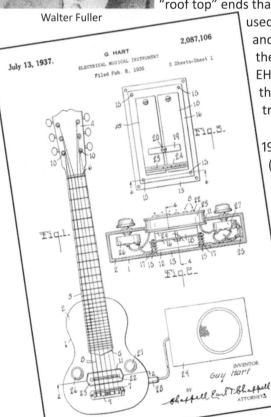

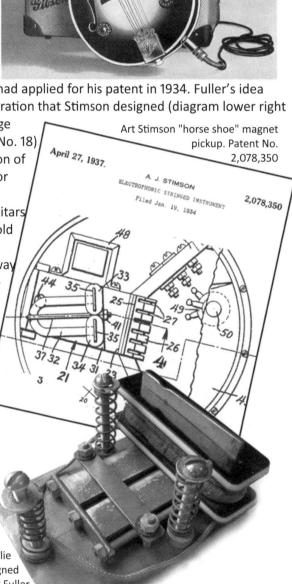

The guts of a "Charlie Christian" pickup designed by Walt Fuller

EM-100 Electric Mandolin – 1938-1940

In 1938 Gibson introduced a less expensive electric mandolin model but the early EM-100s were actually the company's way to get rid of left-over parts. Almost all of the EM-100s shipped in 1938 were made from excess off-brand electric mandolins like the Cromwell model "EGM" and the Capital "EJM." Cromwell was Gibson's own in-house brand they had started making in 1934, and when they decided to introduce electrified Cromwells in 1937 they made the EGM. The Cromwell EGM was such a complete flop that Gibson only shipped 15 of them and after only two months then abandoned the whole project. The Capital EJM was made for J. W. Jenkins Music in Kansas City and they bought a grand total of two. The main reason they were so unsuccessful is an EGM retailed for $62.50, only $15.00 less than a name-brand Gibson EM-150. Gibson never discarded left-over parts, so in 1938 the company buffed off the Cromwell logo, put Gibson on the headstock and sold them as EM-100s for only $49.00. By the time an illustration of the EM-100 appeared in Gibson's 1939 Catalog AA, the relabeled instruments were used up and they continued making them with very few changes to its design. The new EM-100 had a pickup that was very similar to the one on the EM-150 only it had rounded ends and no ivoroid trim around the edges. Its affordable $49.00 price tag resulted in much better sales than the Cromwells and Capitals and Gibson sold almost as many as the top-of-the-line EM-150.

1938-1939 Price: $49.00 (with 10 ft. cord)
1940: Discontinued
EH-100 Amplifier Price: $55.00

1938 Gibson-made Capital EJM electric mandolin
The main difference between the Capital and the
Gibson EM-100 was that the Capital had a pointed-top
headstock shape with the Capital logo and enlarged f-holes.

H-0 Mandola – 1935-1939
Gibson firmly believed that there was still a market for mandolas in the 1930s, but needed a less expensive model that would be on par with the A-00 mandolin. They were still promoting themselves as a company that "does more to advocate, encourage and help in the forming mandolin orchestras than any other firm." The H-0 was introduced in 1935 even though it did not appear in a catalog until late 1936. That same year they shipped the last of the H-1 mandolas and then discontinued that model. The company made only ten H-1s in 1936, but shipped 30 H-0s in 1937 proving that an economically-priced mandola was a good idea. From 1935 to 1943 Gibson sold more H-0s than the rest of the other mandola and mando-cello models combined. The H-0 had the same dimensions as the H-1, but its ornamentation and construction was the same as the A-00 mandolin, including a sunburst top, dark brown flat back, sides and neck. It was single-bound only around the top edge.

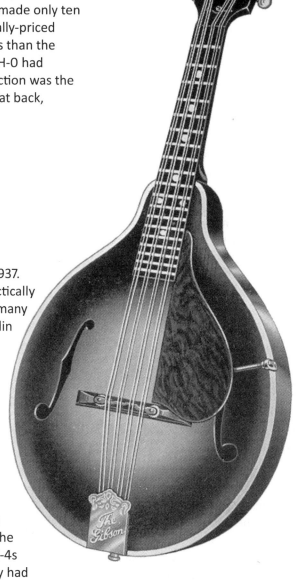

1935 Price: $35.00
1936 Price: $36.75
1937 Price: $37.50
1938 Price: $39.38
1939 Price: $41.25

Style "H-1" Mandola – 1930-1936 (not shown)
As mentioned previously, Gibson discontinued the H-1 mandola in 1937. At more than double the price of the H-0, sales of the H-1 were practically non-existent. In 1936 Gibson made the mistake of raising prices on many instruments to the detriment of sales. The popularity of the mandolin orchestra had gone by the wayside and no one was interested in buying expensive mandolas and mando-cellos. An illustration of the H-1 did not appear in a single catalog during the entire decade of the 1930s.

1930 Price: $78.75 (June 1930 price decrease to $75.00)
1936 Price: $78.75
1937: Discontinued

Style "H-4" Mandola – 1930-1939 (not shown)
Sales of the H-4 mandolas were even worse than the H-1 during the 1930s. Gibson was selling only two per year and most, if not all, of the H-4s shipped after 1935 were old stock. The serial numbers of the H-4s shipped in the late 30s date to the early 30s, which means that they had sat around the factory for years and Gibson had stopped making them around 1934. Like the H-1, no illustration of the H-4 ever appeared in any catalog during the 1930s.

1930 Price: $183.75 (June 1930 price decrease to $175.00)
1936 Price: $183.75
1937 Price: $175.00

Master Model H-5 Mandola – 1930-1936

In the 1930s sales of the Master Models H-5 and K-5 were even worse than the H-4 and K-4, so those models were discontinued in 1936 along with several other instruments in the mandolin family. The guitar was the most popular fretted instrument of the decade and few people wanted to buy a $260.00 mandola. Gibson was only shipping about one H-5 per year and the instruments shipped after 1934 were just left-over stock, so Gibson had effectively discontinued it in 1933 or 1934. The H-5 did appear in Gibson catalogs from 1930 to 1934, but the illustration was the same one they had been using since 1924. The H-5 is not listed in 1936's Catalog X, but it was listed on the October 1936 price list. It's clear that the company just needed to sell the few remaining H-5s they had left in stock. Finding a surviving 1930s H-5 is just about impossible as no known extant instruments have surfaced.

1930 Price: $273.00 (June 1930 price decrease to $260.00)
1936 Price: $273.00
1937: Discontinued

K-1 Mando-cello – 1930-1939 (not shown)

Gibson continued offering the K-1 mando-cello throughout the entire decade of the 1930s, but they were shipping fewer than two per year. An illustration of the K-1 never appeared in any catalog and only a brief description was included to let customers know it was still available. A price drop in 1937 didn't have any positive effect on sales and for some reason Gibson increased the price of the K-1 in 1938 which killed-off sales completely. Only five K-1s were shipped between 1937 and 1940.

1930 Price: $84.00 (June 1930 price decrease to $80.00)
1936 Price: $84.00
1937 Price: $80.00
1938 Price: $84.00
1939 Price: $88.00

K-4 Mando-cello – 1930-1938 (not shown)

Like the other mando-cello models, Gibson was only shipping about one K-4 per year and although the company persisted in offering this model, it appears that they only made a handful in the early 1930s and all subsequent orders were filled from old stock. The last K-4 was shipped to Dave Apollon, a very well-known mandolinist, on February 24, 1938, but its serial number 87705 dated to 1931, which meant it had been sitting around the factory for seven years. Although the K-4 appeared on Gibson price lists until 1938, no illustration of it was included in any 1930s-era catalog. For all intents and purposes it had been discontinued as earlyt as 1932.

1930 Price: $210.00 (June 1930 price decrease to $200.00)
1936 Price: $210.00
1937 Price: $200.00
1938 Price: $210.00

Dave Apollon

Master Model K-5 Mando-cello – 1930-1936

The Master Model K-5 mando-cello suffered the same fate as the H-5 mandola because Gibson simply couldn't sell a $300.00 mando-cello regardless of how beautiful and well-made it was. The K-5 was the only mando-cello model shown in catalogs during the first half of the 1930s, but like the H-5, Gibson was still using the original illustration from 1924. With the exception of two K-5s shipped in 1937, shipping records show that the company wasn't selling any K-5s. One of the two had a serial number that dated back to the Loar-era (1924) and the other had a 1934 serial number and may been one of the only K-5s Gibson built in the 1930s By comparison a customer could buy a Kalamazoo KK-31 mando-cello for $27.50 - one tenth the cost of a K-5.

1930 Price: $288.75 (June 1930 price decrease to $275.00)
1937: Discontinued

Gibson-made
Kalamazoo KK-31
mando-cello
Price $27.50

The Gibson Mando-Bass

— *The Regal Monarch of The Fretted Instrument World.*

No other instrument can compare with the Gibson Mando-Bass for the deep but brilliant foundation tones demanded in modern music.

For both solo and rhythm playing it opens a rich field of opportunity for the ambitious musician. Orchestra leaders everywhere are catering to the public favor by adding the bass to even such small combinations as five or more instruments.

GIBSON MANDO-BASS
STYLE J

Price $150.00
Cover Extra

The deep, profound pulsations of the mando-bass are the very heart and soul of true rhythm. Without it, the other instruments in the combination lose much of their effectiveness. The mando-bass is often featured for solos and for "hot breaks" in the orchestra.

Although unusually easy to master, there are not at present nearly enough bass players to meet the demand.

Beautifully finished and an instrument that will make you the center of attention wherever you go. Played with pick in either sitting or standing position. Its range is just one octave below the four lowest guitar strings and has the same tuning as the bass-viol. Forty-two inch scale with fretted fingerboard.

"J" Mando-bass – 1930-1939

In 1933 Gibson stopped listing the price for the Style "J" mando-bass, their price lists only said, "Write for Price." This was mainly due to the fact that they would only build one if they got an order. In addition, the Kalamazoo "KJ" mando-bass was less than half the price, so Gibson only sold/shipped a total of four Style J mando-basses from 1935-1939 compared to 37 Kalamazoo KJs shipped in the same time period. Gibson stopped including an illustration of the Style J mando-bass in their catalogs in 1938.

1930 Price: $157.50
(June 1930 price decrease to $150.00)
1934-1939: "Write For Price"

Gibson Finishes

The most significant change in Gibson's finishes was the transition from hand-rubbed to sprayed sunbursts. It appears that the company first started spraying the sunburst top finishes on mandolins before their other instruments. There are examples of F-2s from late 1930 or early 1931 that have sprayed sunburst tops but there also examples of c1931-1933 instruments that have hand-rubbed finishes. The complete transition occurred in 1934 and it included all of Gibson's instruments including guitars. The beauty and artistry of hand-rubbed finishes is undeniable as no two instruments were ever the same, while the sprayed sunbursts are more uniform and vary much less from one instrument to the next. The sprayed version was a three-color process as it had been with the hand-rubbed finishes. The center section was amber that transitioned to red and then to a dark brown. Only the high-end instruments like the F-5, H-5 and K-5 had a sunburst finish on the top, rim, back and the back of the neck. Most of the rest of the mandolin models like the F-4 and F-7 only had a sunburst top. A typical sprayed sunburst consisted of laying down the amber center area and then using a hand-held mask, the finisher then sprayed the red in a circular pattern around the edge of the mask at a slight angle. Spraying the second color at an angle allowing a finer mist to go under the edge of the mask and border the lighter color to create a blended effect. This process was repeated with the brown to center section Opinions vary as to which type is better, but most will agree that nobody did a sunburst finish better than Gibson.

A spray booth at the Gibson factory with finisher spraying lacquer out of a 55 gallon drum

Comparison between a hand-rubbed sunburst (left) and a 30s-era sprayed sunburst

Gibson Parts & Accessories – 1930-1939

Tuners

In early 1930 Gibson started using guitar tuners made by A. D. Grover & Son, Inc. Its founder, Albert D. Grover had died in 1927, so his son Walter was running the company. Walter Grover was a very aggressive salesman and succeeded in convincing Gibson to use Grover tuners on most of their high-end guitars (they were already Gibson's sole supplier of banjo and ukulele tuners). Waverly Musical Products and their General Manager, Herbert Lomb, were Grover's biggest competitor, but they continued to supply all of the tuners Gibson used on mandolins, mandolas, mando-cellos, and even their lower-priced guitars. There is no evidence to suggest that Gibson ever used any Grover tuners on these instruments with the exception of some economy 3-on-a-plate guitar tuners in the mid-1930s.

Walter Grover, President of A.D. Grover & Son

Herbert Lomb, General Manager of Waverly Musical Products

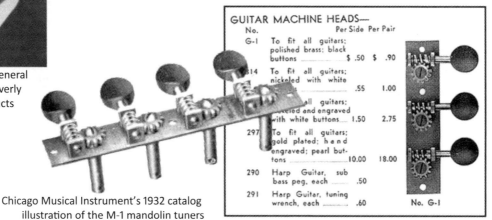

Chicago Musical Instrument's 1932 catalog illustration of the M-1 mandolin tuners

GUITAR MACHINE HEADS—			
No.		Per Side	Per Pair
G-1	To fit all guitars; polished brass; black buttons	$ .50	$ .90
14	To fit all guitars; nickeled with white	.55	1.00
	all guitars; …eled and engraved …ith white buttons	1.50	2.75
297	To fit all guitars; gold plated; hand engraved; pearl buttons	10.00	18.00
290	Harp Guitar, sub bass peg, each		.50
291	Harp Guitar, tuning wrench, each		.60

No. G-1

1933 catalog "cut" of Waverly G-1 guitar tuners and appears to have a missing mounting screw hole from being re-touched

In 1933 Gibson included one illustration of Waverly's economy guitar tuners in a pocket-size catalog titled "The Music Pals of a Nation," and assigned them a new part number G-1. It appears that Gibson erased the Waverly logo by retouching the illustration, making it appear that the tuners were missing one mounting screw hole. Gibson also added two new part numbers for the Waverly mandolin tuners, M-1 and M-12, but did not include any illustrations of either. The illustration shown here is from Chicago Musical Instrument's 1932 catalog of the M-1 tuners, which were brass with black buttons. Gibson only used them on the economy models like the C-1 and A-00, plus some off-brand mandolins like the Kel Kroydon and Kalamazoos. This illustration does show the Waverly logo. Why they decided to assign those particular part numbers is unknown, because prior to 1933 Gibson kept using the same numbers for the tuners even though it appears that they had switched vendors at least twice.

All of this changed in 1937 when the Kluson Manufacturing Company in Chicago managed to supplant Waverly as Gibson's sole supplier of mandolin tuners. The company was founded in 1925 by John Kluson, a machinist by trade. Early, on Kluson was just a small machine shop that made metal music stands, folding chairs, and even desk accessories. In December 1936 John Kluson filed for his first tuning head patent. The most significant improvement in his design was the brackets that were bent in a "U" shape, now commonly referred to as "bent tab tuners." Standard un-bent tabs had the tendency to get out of alignment causing the worm gears to bind up preventing them from turning smoothly. Over-tightening them often caused the worm gear shaft to break. Kluson's bent tab design solved this problem by stabilizing the brackets so they wouldn't slip or bend and he was awarded the patent on October 11, 1938.

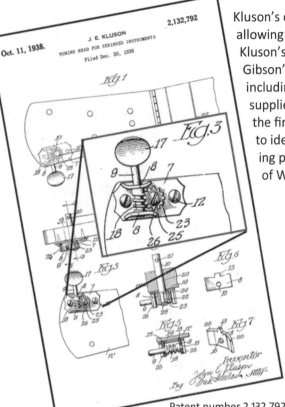

Kluson's design also simplified the assembly process, thus reducing labor cost and allowing the company to offer their tuning heads at very competitive prices. In fact Kluson's prices were so competitive that he not only managed to secure all of Gibson's business, but most of the other instrument manufacturers as well, including Martin, National and Regal. By 1939 the company became Gibson's sole supplier of tuning heads for all their instruments. Gibson's 1937 Catalog Y was the first to show any illustration of mandolin tuners since 1918. Kluson's are easy to identify not only because of the bent tab design, but also because the mounting plates had semi-circular clipped corners instead of the plainer square ends of Waverly's design.

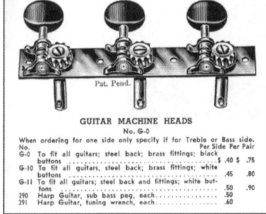

Gibson's 1937 Catalog Y showing the "patent pending" Kluson tuner illustration but still listing the same part numbers as the Waverly tuners

GUITAR MACHINE HEADS
No. G-0

When ordering for one side only specify if for Treble or Bass side.

No.		Per Side	Per Pair
G-0	To fit all guitars; steel back; brass fittings; black buttons	$ .40	$ .75
G-10	To fit all guitars; steel back; brass fittings; white buttons	.45	.80
G-11	To fit all guitars; steel back and fittings; white buttons	.50	.90
290	Harp Guitar, sub bass peg, each	.50	
291	Harp Guitar, tuning wrench, each	.60	

Patent number 2,132,792 for Kluson's "bent tab" tuner design. Figure 3 is enlarged to show more detail

Also from Catalog Y - the entire section of mandolin accessories including the new M-10 Kluson tuners

MANDOLIN SUPPLIES

MANDOLIN PICK GUARDS

No.		Each
860	To fit arched top models; elevated; brown celluloid; nickel attachments	$ 2.50
863	To fit all arched top models; elevated; brown celluloid bound with white ivoroid	5.00
865	For F-5 model; elevated; brown celluloid bound with black and white; gold plated attachments	8.00

MANDOLIN AND MANDOLIN-BANJO MACHINE HEADS

No. M-10

No.		Per Side	Set of Two
M-10	To fit all makes and models with exception of F-2, F-4, F-7, F-10, F-12 and F-5 mandolins; steel back with brass fittings; white buttons	$ .55	$ 1.00
299	To fit all models and makes except F-2, F-4, F-7, F-10, F-12, F-5 mandolins; nickel with metal buttons	.80	1.50
304	To fit F-2, F-4, F-7, F-10 mandolins; nickel; metal buttons	2.50	4.25
305	To fit F-12, F-5, mandolins; gold plated, engraved; pearl buttons	11.00	20.00

		Each	Set of Four
334	Machine head to fit Mando-Bass	$7.20	$28.80

MANDOLIN TAILPIECES

No. 780

No.		Each
780	To fit Style A-00; nickel, detachable cover	$ .30
780-C	Cover for No. 780	.20
780-B	Base for No. 780	.20
782	To fit all makes and models; nickel; engraved; detachable cover	.60
782-C	Cover for No. 782	.35
782-B	Base for No. 782	.35
784	For F-12, F-5 models; De Luxe gold plated; engraved; detachable cover	3.25
784-C	Cover for No. 784	$ 2.00
784-B	Base for No. 784	2.00

MANDOLIN, MANDOLA AND MANDO-CELLO BRIDGES—Adjustable

No. 520

No.		Each	Doz.
520	To fit all makes of arched top mandolins; ebony offset saddle	$1.00	$10.00
520-A	Ebony offset saddle for No. 520	.50	5.00
520-B	Ebony base with thumb screws and studs for 520	.50	5.00
518	For all Mandolas; ebony with offset saddle; same shape as No. 520	1.65	16.50
518-A	Offset saddle for No. 518	.75	7.50
518-B	Ebony base with thumb screws and studs for No. 518	.90	9.00
519	For all Mando-Cellos; ebony with offset saddle; same as No. 520	2.00	20.00
519-A	Offset saddle for No. 519	1.00	10.00
519-B	Ebony base, studs and thumb screws for No. 519	1.00	10.00

Instrument Cases

Geib & Schafer remained Gibson's sole supplier of instrument cases throughout the 1930s. There were a total of five different options for mandolin, mandola and mando-cello cases, plus the #159 waterproof canvas bag for the Style J mando-bass. The least expensive "Challenge" cases were made of black waterproof leatherette (a cheaper version of Keratol) with purple flannel lining that Gibson only offered for the A-00 mandolin (case #101); "utility" cases had a chip-board shell covered with Keratol and flannel-lined, which were the next step up for the "A" mandolins (case #102); the "Faultless V" was the heavy-duty hard-shell case with velvet lining for the "A" mandolins (case #362); the "Faultless SP" was also a hard-shell case, but with silk plush lining for the "F" mandolins. There were actually two versions of the Faultless SP. The #371 form-fitting version that mirrored the shape of the "F" mandolins and the #440 rectangular suitcase-style case with the individual interior compartments which was more than double the price of the #371.

For the mandolas Gibson offered the #135 Challenge case for the lower-priced models – H-0 and H-1, and the #378 Faultless V hard-shell fitted case. The only case made for the H-4 and H-5 were the form-fitting #388 Faultless V. There were no Challenge cases available for the mando-cellos. The #394 Faultless V was for the K-1, the #394 Faultless SP for the K-4, and the #515 Faultless SP for the K-5, which was also the same case for the L-5 guitar.

Top right: G&S #440 rectangular suitcase-style case that was double the price of the #371 case (below right)

Strings

Gibson continued making their own strings in the 1930s and the Mona-steel name became synonymous with Gibson. In 1933 they added "hand-polished strings" as another option. The mandolin A and E strings were the same price as the unpolished Mona-steel strings, but the wound G and D strings were nearly twice the price because the wire wrap was polished flat, or what is now referred to half-round. In 1934 they introduced their bronze strings, which were not actually made of bronze as this was just the name Gibson used for their economy strings. The company used three main suppliers for all the wire used in manufacturing their instrument strings. Based in Harris, New Jersey, the company Driver Harris supplied Gibson with many different types of wire in various gauges. American Brass Company was their main supplier of the wire for the bronze strings. American Steel & Wire was their supplier of monel wire.

Gibson factory workers making strings

Tailpieces

In 1937 Kluson Manufacturing started making all of Gibson's metal hardware including their tailpieces. The illustrations for these parts first appeared in Gibson's 1937 catalog Y. They also supplied other hardware like pickguard supports.

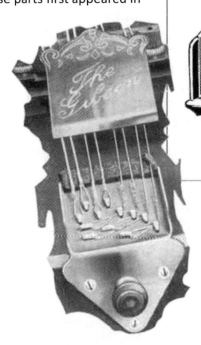

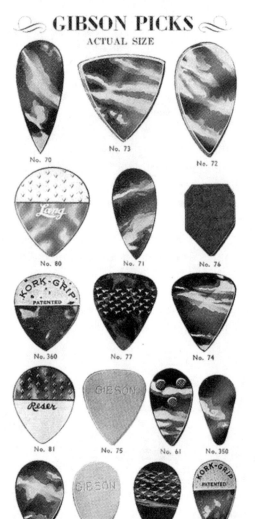

Picks

Gibson started expanding their line of instrument picks in 1933, including some celebrity-endorsed picks like the Eddie Lang and Harry Reser, plus several new styles that had Gibson's name embossed or stamped on them. Most of the company catalogs in the 1930s provided "actual size" illustrations, plus a part number, price and description. One of the most unusual picks they offered was the No. 76 "Genuine Gallolith" picks, which were shaped like home plate on a baseball diamond. Gallolith (the modern spelling is galalith, also called milk stone) was an imitation ivory material made from a milk by-product called casein. It was also used for a wide variety of other products including combs, knitting needles and even piano keys. Casein is still used today as a food additive because it is the organic protein found in milk, which makes it ideal for high protein foods and beverages.

Gibson Publishing – 1930-1939

Gibson Catalogs

Gibson published more catalogs, brochures and other literature in the 1930s than in any other era. In 1930 they published a 68-page catalog that is referred to as the "Blue Cover," because it was a full-line catalog that had no letter designation like all preceding catalogs. It was the last catalog Sales Manager Frank Campbell produced before being laid-off in December 1930. The banjo was the featured instrument, and it included new models like the ornate "All American," which was their most expensive banjo at $550.00, an astronomical sum for a rapidly collapsing economy. The design of All American seemed

HG-24

to have been inspired by the equally ornate banjos the company made for the Trujo Company. By this time mandolins always appeared last in Gibson's catalogs as the instrument's popularity had steadily declined during the 1920s. The company only offered three "F" and three "A" mandolins, plus mandolas, mando-cellos, and the Style "J" mando-bass. In 1931 Gibson only issued a small fold-out brochure entitled "The Road To Happiness," existing copies of which are quite rare. It was the first time the C-1 flat-top mandolin appeared, as well as the only publication to contain an illustration of the rather odd HG-24 that was described as having an "amplifying double tone chamber, really two guitars in one." All three HG models and the C-1 mandolin were complete failures and Gibson discontinued them within two years. In 1932 the company went back to the letter designations and issued

Why the Experts say:

"Only A

Gibson

Is Good Enough"

catalog U. This catalog has the distinction of having both the letter designation and the year it was published, which Gibson did not do on the vast majority of their catalogs. The following year Gibson issued another small "pocket-size" catalog called "Music Pals of a Nation." It also had no letter designation and is sometimes referred to a Catalog V, because the company skipped that letter and issued Catalog W in 1934. The 1933 brochure is a significant piece of Gibson ephemera because it contained illustrations of many new instrument models including the re-introduced A-1 and the early oval soundhole versions of the A-50 and A-00 mandolins

WHY YOU SHOULD PLAY A GIBSON

There are many reasons why you should play a Gibson — the fact that there are thousands of happy, satisfied Gibson owners throughout the world, and that Gibson instruments are made in the largest plant of its kind, are mighty strong reasons — BUT — the thing you are interested in is, "Will A Gibson Satisfy Me? It Is My Money I Am Spending, And I Am The One Who Is Going To Play The Instrument."

—and we do say to you, without reservation or fear of contradiction that a Gibson will give you the greatest value for your money and greater satisfaction in every respect than any other instrument made. There is nothing halfway about a Gibson — other instruments may be outstanding in one or two different ways, but a Gibson is PERFECT IN ALL WAYS.

Gibson gives you a guarantee that really means something — regardless of where you are, how you play, or how long you have had your Gibson, you are entitled to Gibson service. Would a company dare back up their instruments like that if they did not absolutely know them to be the finest made? That is why we say to you, "Get A Gibson And Know What Real, Lasting Satisfaction Means."

As you look through this book, you will see many reasons why Gibson will give you the greatest value for your money — for instance, consider the Gibson Truss Rod neck construction. What happens if you buy an instrument without a Truss Rod and the neck bends out of place? You have to spend your money all over again — but not with a Gibson, from the lowest priced to the highest, they have that famous Truss Rod construction that provides adjustment of the neck — and remember, every Gibson guitar neck joins the body at the 14th fret.

You owe it to yourself to play nothing but the best — a Gibson.

VISIT THE GIBSON FACTORY

You are welcome — Kalamazoo is on the main Highway, Railroad and Bus lines from Detroit to Chicago. Plan now to visit the home of these famous instruments — it will be a thrill of your lifetime.

Gibson kept up with the ever-changing instrument market, as all of their catalogs and brochures after 1931 featured guitars first, then banjos, followed by the mandolin family of instruments. The guitar was quickly becoming the instrument of choice for the "Swing Era." Catalog W was the first publication to introduce the F-7, F-10 and F-12 models as well as two more "A" models, the Century Model Style A-C and the A-75. It also contained new illustrations for all the other "A" mandolins that now featured f-holes. Catalog X came out in late 1936, and although it did not contain any new mandolins, Gibson's new H-0 economy mandola appeared for the first time. No illustrations of any other mandolas or mando-cellos were included because Gibson had discontinued several of those instruments. It was also the first publication to

introduce the company's new slogan "Only a Gibson is Good Enough," which has since become one of the company's most well-known catch phrases. 1937's Catalog Y was the first to introduce the EM-150 electric mandolin, as well as the wide-body versions of the A-50 and A-1. In 1938 Gibson published another full-line catalog, designated letter Z. It did not include numerous instruments that been discontinued the year before like the F-2 mandolin and the Master Models H-5 mandola and K-5 mando-cello. They also issued another small brochure with a blue cover that made the claim that Gibson started in 1892 (see previous page). This is another contradiction in dates proving the current 1894 date is wrong. Catalog AA came out in 1939 and contained many striking new instruments like the "Premiere" guitars that featured cutaways, the first classical guitars – Style GS, and the first illustration of the lower-priced EM-100 electric mandolin.

Mastertone Magazine

Gibson's in-house magazine, *Mastertone* had been introduced by Frank Campbell in October 1926, but following his departure, Guy Hart's new right-hand man, Neil Abrams, continued publishing it. Although the popularity of the mandolin was fading away, some issues of *Mastertone* contained articles and clippings of interest to mandolinists. The January 1935 issue had a full-page article entitled "The Mandolin and Its Possibilities." Although no credit is given to its author, it featured H. Russell Truitt, a prominent Pittsburgh mandolin teacher and Gibson salesman. The article makes a few questionable statements like "indications all point to a strong come-back" of the mandolin's popularity and would be "even greater than ever before." It went on to say that "when we say that the mandolin is headed for a strong revival of popularity, which automatically includes the mandola, mando-cello, and mando-bass. In reality, this was nothing more than a pipe dream.

H. Russell Truitt

In some issues of *Mastertone* Gibson inserted small sheet music inserts which were mostly guitar music, but also the occasional mandolin arrangement, like "Dreaming" which was sent out with the with the April 1935 issue. Although it's not clear why, Gibson stopped publishing *Mastertone* magazine in January 1938. However the company also published several instruction books in the mid-30s but they were all guitar-related. In 1939 Guy Hart decided to publish sheet music arrangements under the name Mastertone Publishing. This particular venture was not successful and was discontinued soon after. Another issue contained a comicbook style pictorial about the adventures of Dave Apollon, mandolinist and Russian soldier in Siberia.

Mandolin solo called "Dreaming" was an insert in the July 1935 issue of *Mastertone* magazine

The amazing adventures of Dave Apollon mandolinist and Russian soldier.

Gibson, Inc. – 1940-1949

For Gibson, the 1940s was another era full of ups and downs. Massive changes were on the horizon for both the company itself as well as its management. The decade did not start well for Gibson as they lost their single biggest customer, Montgomery Ward. They also discontinued another in-house brand, Cromwell, simply because they weren't selling, and for the most part, stopped making all of the other off-brands like Washburn and Capital. By WWII they were only making two "budget brands," Kalamazoo and the Mastertone Special line of very inexpensive guitars, lap-steels (electric slide guitars) and amplifiers. With the exception of the A-50, all of the company's mandolin models were discontinued after the outbreak of World War II.

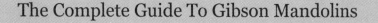

1942 ad featuring Gibson's line of electric steel guitars and players like Roy Smeck and Alvino Rey

Fortunately they were selling hundreds of electric Hawaiian guitars and amplifiers which really helped keep Gibson afloat. In the late 1930s and early 40s Guy Hart had instituted a policy that every spare part laying around the factory was to be used for assembling "Specials," or as they were also known, "floor sweeps." Sales flyers from 1941 listed several of these models, including the Special No. 3 and No. 5 guitars and the EG-00, all of which were Hawaiian lap-steels made from left-over Montgomery Ward parts, as well as the Special No. 7, a 17" wide arch-top guitar that was often a strange mix of parts including banjo headstock veneers and fingerboards from other discontinued instruments. A March 4, 1941 price list offered the Special No.7 for $38.50, one quarter the price of Gibson's least expensive arch-top. In an effort to get rid of all remaining wide-body A-1 mandolins they slashed the wholesale price to $20.00.

Can't You See There's War On?

Many sources have claimed that Gibson stopped making musical instruments during the war, but that's completely false. Gibson had to dedicate a large portion of their manufacturing capabilities toward the war effort in order to produce many diverse parts and components like electronics for aircraft and a slew of plastic and metal parts. They did continue making musical instruments throughout the entire war and even introduced new models. Unfortunately the manufacturing processes needed for the war effort proved to be financially disastrous for the company. During WWII Gibson was in real financial trouble and was losing $100,000 a month!

Maurice H. Berlin
President of CMI

Then in May 1944, more than a year before the war ended, Gibson was bought by the Chicago Musical Instrument Company (CMI). That company was founded in 1919 by Maurice H. Berlin, and he had grown it into one of the largest musical instrument distributors in the world. "M.H." as he was known, was a well-known and well-respected music industry executive who wanted to get into the instrument manufacturing business. Although Gibson and CMI had never done business before 1944, Berlin set his sights on purchasing Gibson, and as it turned out his timing was perfect. A number of factors led to this change of ownership. Chief among them was that Judge John W. Adams, co-founder of the company, majority stockholder, and Gibson's president for nearly four decades, was 85 years old and wanted to retire. Partially because of Gibson's financial difficulties, Berlin was able to acquire a majority interest in the company. Guy Hart was promoted to president, but after CMI his reign would be very short lived.

April 1944 ad in *Metronome* magazine congratulating employees for a job well done

I Gotta Gal from Kalamazoo

Prior to WWII Gibson employed approximately 1500 people, but after the war started most of the men who worked there had to leave and fight overseas. Like many other companies, Gibson started hiring women to replace the mainly male workforce and in this way were able to continue making instruments. Wartime instruments, especially those with the "Only A Gibson Is Good Enough" "banner" logo on the headstock, are highly sought after by collectors. Gibson introduced some great new guitar models like the J-45 and J-50 flat-top acoustic guitars which sold quite well. In 1939 the company started making a complete line of orchestral instruments including violins, violas, cellos and basses and were able to continue making these instruments throughout the war. Unfortunately, as far as mandolins are concerned, by the end of WWII the factory was only making A-50s and not a single other model. In 1944 Gibson shipped only four left-over F-4s, and not one F-5. They had discontinued every

Gibson's workforce during WWII was almost entirely made up of women

other mandolin, mandola, and mando-cello model at the outbreak of the war. It was probably Berlin who suggested that they revert to the more popular pre-1937 A-50 design and, coupled with a price cut, this resulted in an explosion in sales. Gibson shipped nearly three times the number of A-50s from 1945 to 1949 than they had in the previous 10 years combined!

Just after CMI had acquired Gibson, Berlin did something that to this day is a real mystery. Gibson was building far fewer instruments compared to all the parts and components for the war department, but somehow Berlin thought it would be a good idea to have Gibson build "prototype" instruments for National/Valco. CMI had become National's exclusive distributor in 1941, and in July 1944 Gibson built several new National-branded prototype instruments and shipped them directly to CMI for M.H.'s approval. They included both acoustic and electric arch-top guitars, acoustic flat-tops and four mandolin models. The mandolins were designated models NM-00 and NM-50. Although none of these mandolin prototypes have ever surfaced since 1944, the model designations clearly indicate they were simply relabeled A-00s and A-50s, with National's name on them. The "NM" prefix stood for National Mandolin. Apparently the whole idea was not at all appealing to Louis Dopyera, who at the time was president of National and Valco. One can only imagine Dopyera looking over these instruments in Berlin's office and saying. "Well, maybe," "No," "Absolutely not," "Not interested," or words to that effect. This didn't seem to deter Berlin from having Gibson make even more instruments

Gibson shipping ledger entries for some of the National prototype instruments including the NM-50 and NM-00 mandolins

for National. From July 1944 to September 1945, Berlin had Gibson produce 25 different prototype instruments with National's name on them and according to Gibson's shipping ledgers, a total of nearly 100 were all sent to CMI.

Stranger Than Fiction

In 1946 CMI published a price list called the "Tentative Postwar List of National Instruments, Amplifiers and Cases." The list included "several pre-war models, plus several new carved and flat-top Spanish guitars and three mandolins." It may be purely conjecture, but Berlin must have been trying to ram these Gibson-made models down Dopyera's throat. That strategy didn't work either. Very few of these instruments have ever surfaced and the model designations don't really provide enough clues to ascertain exactly what they were. The list does break down the instruments into categories like

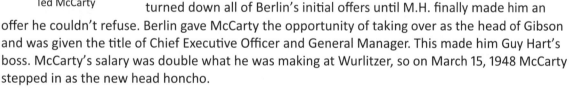

"carved top guitars," "flat-top guitars" and "carved mandolins," so clearly Gibson didn't make any National-branded flat-top mandolins akin to the Kalamazoo KM-11 or KM-12. Like so many of the Gibson-made brands of the pre-war period, most of the National model designations did not match up to existing Gibson models, so knowing exactly what was what is mostly guess work. The three mandolins listed had completely new model names and included the N-31, N-51 and N-51B. The "B" suffix indicated it had a "blonde" or natural finish, while no letter suffix meant it was a sunburst finish. Gibson's shipping ledgers show that four N-31 mandolins were shipped to CMI in April 1945, they never shipped anything called an "N-51" or N-51B." Ultimately National didn't want any of these instruments and opted to have Gibson only supply components like guitar bodies, necks and fingerboards that National assembled into finished instruments. Gibson never supplied any mandolin parts to National.

National's Tentative Post-War Price List with enlarged area showing the proposed Gibson-made mandolin models N-51, N-51B & N-31

The Hired Gun

Ted McCarty

M. H. Berlin gave in and dropped the whole Gibson/National idea because he had much bigger issues to solve. As mentioned earlier, Gibson was hemorrhaging money to the tune of $1.2 million a year and although Berlin had promoted Guy Hart to president of Gibson, he was clearly not the person Berlin felt was capable of turning things around. Although war-time production had really hurt the company financially, it was Hart who was responsible for how badly the company was doing, so Berlin decided it was time for a big change in management. In 1948 Berlin decided that Ted McCarty was the right man for the job, but by all accounts McCarty was not interested. He had been working for the Wurlitzer Company for 12 years, working his way up from accountant to head of merchandizing for all of that company's retail stores. McCarty wanted to get out of the music business altogether, but Berlin relentlessly pursued him. McCarty turned down all of Berlin's initial offers until M.H. finally made him an offer he couldn't refuse. Berlin gave McCarty the opportunity of taking over as the head of Gibson and was given the title of Chief Executive Officer and General Manager. This made him Guy Hart's boss. McCarty's salary was double what he was making at Wurlitzer, so on March 15, 1948 McCarty stepped in as the new head honcho.

John Huis

Heads Are Going to Roll

Ted McCarty immediately identified some major problems with how Guy Hart had been running Gibson. The company was very top-heavy and McCarty saw clearly that they had too many middle and upper management personnel. The "dead-heads," as McCarty called them, had to go. He started cleaning house which apparently included giving Guy Hart his walking papers, as well as firing many of Gibson's other executives. McCarty was also very concerned that the transition from a mostly female workforce during WWII back to the post-war male-dominated workforce was causing problems with the quality of the products Gibson was producing. There were an inordinate number of instruments being returned for repair or replacement and it was costing the company a lot of money. McCarty's solution was to re-hire John Huis, who had worked for Gibson for many years prior to WWII, and make him Factory Superintendent. Within two short months McCarty had taken Gibson from losing $100,000 a month to turning a profit, a truly miraculous achievement. By the end of the decade the company was not only profitable, but they were also turning out the high-quality instruments that had been the hallmark of the Gibson name for nearly 50 years.

F-12 Artist Mandolin – 1950-1959

During the 1950s the United States was experiencing a booming economy, but sales of Gibson's "F" mandolins were only slightly higher than during the Great Depression. In spite of enormous growth in the music industry, the mandolin still was not a very popular instrument. There was no call for it in bebop jazz, pop and certainly not the newest craze, rock and roll. Mainstream country music was mostly dominated by guitars and even though "The Father of Bluegrass," Bill Monroe was a very popular mandolinist and performer, bluegrass's popularity has always been centered in the South and not as popular nationwide as it is today. Gibson was only selling about 40 F-12s as F-5s per year. The only noticeable change on the F-12 was the lack of the tulip inlay on the headstock which the late 1940s version had.

1950 Price: $275.00
1952 Price: $290.00
1956 Price: $325.00
1957-1959 Price: $350.00
Case No. 371: $32.50
Case No. 440: $43.50

The "Father of Bluegrass" Bill Monroe with his Gibson F-5. Courtesy of Centerstream Publishing

EM-150 Electric Mandolin – 1950-1959

The EM-150 was also not included in Gibson's 1950 brochures even though they were manufacturing them. From the late 1940s until the end of the 1950s, the EM-150's basic design did not change. When it appeared in the company's 1956 catalog, the description simply stated that the "EM-150 is an electric version of the A-50 having a reinforced top to accommodate the built-in pickup." What this really meant was that the EM-150 had a heavy laminated top which was thick plywood heat pressed into the arched shape. Gibson did this with most of the acoustic-electric instruments both as a cost-cutting measure and a way to solve the problem of having braces under the top getting in the way of mounting the pickup. The heavy plywood tops would not warp or crack and were very strong.

1950 Price: $152.00
1952 Price: $160.00
1956 Price: $175.00
1957-1959 Price: $185.00
Same cases as A-40 and A-50

Florentine Electric Mandolin – 1954-1959

The Florentine electric mandolin debuted in 1954 and was the first and only solid-body electric mandolin Gibson ever produced. It was certainly not an inexpensive instrument. A 1957 Florentine electric cost $205.00, for only $247.50, a customer could get a gold-top Les Paul electric guitar. The Florentine had a solid mahogany body with arched contours that mirrored the design of the A-5 prototype Gibson made in 1953. It had a four-pole P-90 pickup with Alnico 5 magnets that is commonly referred to as a "soap bar" pickup because it did not have the "dog eared" cover and was a simple rectangular shape with rounded edges. The pickup was mounted inside a cavity in the top in the neck position or just below the end of the fingerboard. A large cavity in the back allowed the volume and tone controls to be mounted through the top and the output jack was mounted to a plate on the side. All of the wiring was accessed in the back cavity by removing a plastic cover. It was a smaller version of the same design Gibson used for Les Paul solid-body guitars. There is no comparison between the success of the Florentine and the Les Paul. Gibson was selling thousands of Les Pauls although they were only selling about 50 Florentine electrics a year.

1954 Price: $179.50
1956 Price: $195.00
1957-1959 Price: $205.00

1958-1959 Price: $435.00

EMS-1235 Double Mandolin – 1958-1959

The EMS-1235 model designation was used for the double mandolin as well as several other instruments with different configurations of two necks on one body. The catalog illustration shows two six-string guitar necks and Gibson referred to the shorter one as "a mandolin neck with six strings," but a more accurate description would be an "octave guitar" because it's tuned one octave above a regular guitar. The company claimed "the Gibson Double Mandolin lends conspicuous quality to any performance...character that commands attention." Every EMS-1235 was "custom-built to order only," as the catalog specified, because of the wide variety of options available to customers. The photo illustration shown here is of an actual double mandolin (an EMS-1235 with a regular six-string guitar and a standard eight-string mandolin neck). Both the "Double 12" and the EMS-1235s had semi-hollow bodies that were 1 7/8" deep. The top and back were "German carved," a term that refers to a contour profile that has a large flat center with a sloping contour around the edges only. Although the guitar side of the instrument had Gibson's new Tune-O-Matic bridge, the mandolin side had a standard height adjustable mandolin bridge. The double-necks also had Gibson's newest pickups, the humbucker. Gibson made a smaller 4-pole version of the electric guitar PAF humbucker for the EMS-1235. PAF stands for "patent applied for" because pre-patent pickups had a sticker that stated such. This design was patented by Seth Lover, one of Gibson's brightest electronics engineers, but it took over four years for the patent to be awarded in July 1959. The PAF moniker has now become synonymous with these early Gibson humbucking pickups.

EMS-1235 Specifications:

German-carved spruce top

Maple back and rim

Mahogany neck

Rosewood fingerboard with 24 frets

Double parallelogram guitar fingerboard inlays

Standard pearl dot inlay on mandolin fingerboard

3-ply top binding, single-bound back and fingerboard

Block pearl inlay logo on both headstocks

Finish: Available in white, sunburst or black

Mandolin Electronics: Single 4-pole PAF humbucker pickup in
  neck position

One volume and one tone control

Guitar electronics: Twin PAF pickups with pickup selector switch,
  one volume and one tone control

Single 1/4" output jack

3-way toggle switch mounted above guitar bridge. Bottom
  position – guitar neck only. Center position – both necks.
  Top position – mandolin neck only

EMS-1235 Dimensions:

Body width: 17 1/4"

Body length: 20"

Body depth: 2" at rim

Overall length: 41 1/2"

Guitar scale length: 24 3/4"

Mandolin scale length: 13 7/8"

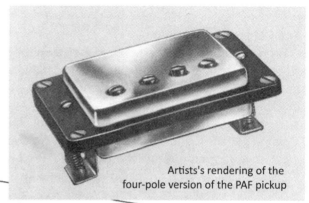

Artists's rendering of the
four-pole version of the PAF pickup

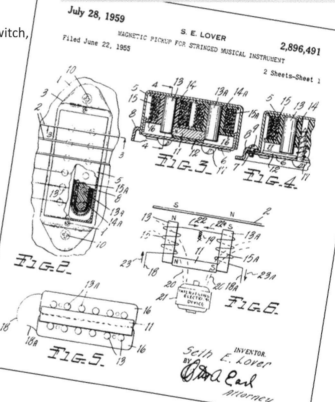

1959 Patent No. 2,896,491 for Gibson electronics
engineer Seth Lover's PAF humbucker pickup

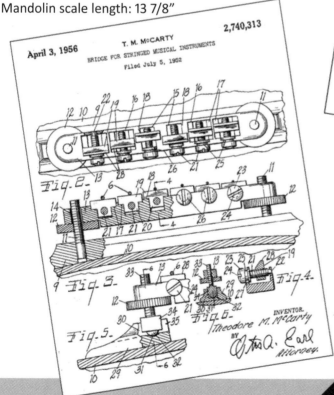

1956 Patent No. 2,740,313 for Ted McCarty's
  Tune-O-Matic bridge

Gibson, Inc. – 1960-1969

The Golden Era Ends

Gibson experienced unprecedented growth in the 1960s, and by the middle of the decade they were shipping 100,000 instruments and amplifiers per year. America's taste in music was diversifying into a wide array of genres including rock and roll, folk, country and western, jazz and even classical music. The popularity of the electric guitar was steady but Gibson's acoustic guitar sales exceeded all of their instruments by a pretty wide margin. They saw an explosion in sales of classical guitars, even though by today's standards, their classical guitars are not considered to be very good instruments. The growing popularity of country and western music was fueling acoustic guitar sales, but had no effect on sales of mandolins. Gibson was actually selling many more banjos than mandolins and even when sales peaked in 1964 they only sold 338 A-40s. By comparison they sold over 3500 C-0 classical guitars that same year. In 1960 Gibson just added an additional 60,000 square feet of manufacturing space and purchased another building in Kalamazoo four years later which increased manufacturing space by another 60,000 square feet. Gibson's growth was exceeding the national average by 400 percent!

1966 catalog illustration
of the C-0 classical guitar

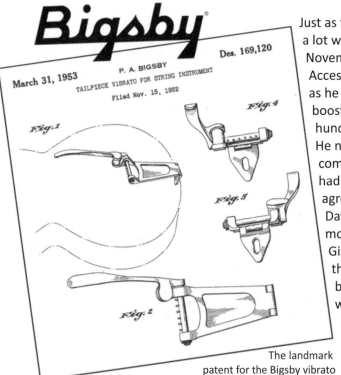

The landmark
patent for the Bigsby vibrato

Just as things seemed as though they couldn't get any better, they got a lot worse in 1966 when Ted McCarty resigned as president. In November 1965 McCarty got a call from Paul Bigsby, founder of Bigsby Accessories, because he wanted to sell the company. Paul, or "P.A." as he was known, was good friends with McCarty who had greatly boosted Bigsby's patented guitar vibrato sales by installing them on hundreds of Gibson guitars. P.A. was 65 years old and in poor health. He needed to retire, but told McCarty that he did not want to sell his company to a big corporation like CMI/Gibson, the way Leo Fender had sold his company to the CBS Corporation a year earlier. McCarty agreed to purchase the company independently, and on New Year's Day 1966 the entire Bigsby plant was loaded onto a truck and moved to Kalamazoo. Apparently what transpired next was that Gibson's upper-management, namely M.H. Berlin, told McCarty that he could not be president of Gibson and of his own company because it would be a conflict of interest. McCarty's response was to resign as president of Gibson in March 1966. John Huis, McCarty's right-hand man and partner in Bigsby, also resigned.

Without the leadership of Ted McCarty, Gibson was in total disarray. Within a very short period the company went from being very profitable to losing $1,000,000 a year. Finally in February 1968, nearly two years after McCarty's resignation, M.H. Berlin promoted CMI's Vice President of Manufacturing, Stanley E. Rendell, to being the new president of Gibson. Most sources and Gibson enthusiasts alike pinpoint this change in management as the end of the golden era and the beginning of a steady decline in the quality and innovation of Gibson instruments. Stan Rendell concentrated on making Gibson more efficient, but many of the changes he instituted resulted in a marked drop in quality. For example, Rendell's solution to the increased number of instruments being returned for repair was to make the parts heavier and thicker, which

Stanley E, Rendell

prevented problems like breaking necks and cracking tops, but also made the instruments sound terrible. Apparently M.H. Berlin didn't seem to care because he was so bitter about McCarty's resignation. He was quoted as saying that Rendell was responsible for more new products, more improvements in quality and more new policies of benefit to the company, its employees and Gibson customers than during the rest of the company's entire history. Nothing could have been further from the truth.

Dark Times Ahead

In December 1969 M.H. Berlin lost his controlling interest in CMI to a South American enterprise, Ecuadorian Company Limited or ECL Industries, Inc. ECL was a large corporation that brewed beer and manufactured concrete among other things, and for some reason they wanted to get into the musical instrument business. CMI's stock price had been at an all-time low and ECL was able to buy up a majority share in order to gain a controlling interest in CMI. M.H. Berlin was 84 years old and had turned over the day-to-day management to his son Arnold. Within a few months ECL changed the name of the company to Norlin Industries whose name came from combining part of ECL's president Norton Stevens's first name and Arnold Berlin's last name. They never even consulted M.H. and he was devastated to learn that CMI, the company he founded in 1919, no longer existed. Gibson simply became a wholly-owned subsidiary of Norlin.

Publishing and Advertising

Gibson continued publishing the *Gibson Gazette* and for the first time in many years there was mandolin-related content including two covers featuring Homer and Jethro, a musical comedy team, and mandolin virtuoso Dave Apollon. Jethro

Jethro Burns was a funny and entertaining performer who was also an incredible mandolin player. His mandolin of choice was Gibson's A-5 Florentine and he became so well-known for playing that particular one that it's still referred to as the "Jethro Burns Model." Dave Apollon was still a very well-known mandolinist whose career started in the 1930s and Gibson still valued his connection to the company. They also featured him in their magazine as well as an advertisement, the first mandolin ad the company had placed since the 1920s.

The cover of March 1960 issue of the Gibson Gazette featuring the musical comedy team of Homer & Jethro

The Summer 1961 cover featured Dave Apollon who was known as "The World's Greatest Mandolin Virtuoso"

"The Magic of the Mandolin" was a slogan Gibson used for this 1961 ad featuring Dave Apollon

Gibson Instruments – 1960-1969

A-5 Florentine Mandolin – 1960-1969

In 1959 Gibson presented Jethro Burns with a custom-made A-5 mandolin that had a longer fingerboard without a scalloped extension and pearl dot inlays. It also had a flowerpot inlay below the logo on the headstock. Instead of the standard sunburst finish, Gibson did a solid red finish which prompted Burns to nickname it "Red." Although Homer and Jethro primarily did musical comedy, Burns was an incredible player and his custom-made A-5 now resides at the Country Music Foundation in Nashville. Despite the fact that he played his A-5 in countless performances, it did not help increase sales.

1960 Price: $275.00
1962 Price: $300.00
1964 Price: $345.00
1967 Price: $450.00
1968 Price: $495.00

A-40 Mandolin – 1960-1969

After Ted McCarty's departure in 1966, Gibson's prices skyrocketed by an average of over 50 percent. For the first time, the company starting charging more for the A-40N (natural finish) than the A-40 sunburst version. Remarkably these across-the-board price hikes helped sales and increased profit margins. The A-40 remained Gibson's best-selling mandolin throughout the 1960s, but shortly after the ECL acquisition and the change in management the A-40 was relegated to the scrap-heap and discontinued in 1970.

1960 Price: $112.50
1962 Price: $125.00
1964 Price: $147.50
1967 Price: $225.00
1968 Price: $245.00 (A-40)
1968 Price: $255.00 (A-40N)

A-50 Mandolin – 1960-1969

In terms of longevity and consistency of sales the A-50 was the workhorse of Gibson's mandolin line. After WWII until it was discontinued in 1970, the company sold over 5400 A-50s, 4000 of which were sold between 1946 and 1956. The general popularity of the mandolin did not see a significant turnaround until many years later. The A-50, along with most of Gibson's other mandolin models, was discontin-ued in 1970. Even though the price of the A-50 had more than doubled between 1960 and 1969, it remained one of Gibson's all-time best-selling mandolins.

1960 Price: $145.00
1962 Price: $160.00
1964 Price: $182.50
1967 Price: $275.00

F-5 Artist Mandolin – 1960-1969

After 40 years, 1966 marked the first year Gibson published a full-color illustration of the F-5 in their catalog and it finally showed an accurate depiction of the design the company was producing. It included the correct crown-top tailpiece with the an engraved logo, all gold-plated hardware, block inlays from the first to the 19th fret and the flowerpot headstock inlay. The F-5 has always been the mandolin of choice for bluegrass players. From Bill Monroe to Ricky Skaggs, the F-5 has defined the sound of bluegrass for many generations. A well-known bluegrass mandolinist said that the F-5 is truly the Stradivarius of mandolins because no matter if you are in the front row of the orchestra or the last row of the third balcony, you can hear its bright punchy tone carry over everything.

1960 Price: $550.00
1962 Price: $600.00
1964 Price: $680.00
1967 Price: $1000.00
1968 Price: $1095.00

F-12 Artist Mandolin – 1960-1969

The pictures of the mandolins in Gibson's 1966 catalog were photo-illustrations or photographs that are touched up to make them sharp, clear and vibrant. It was the first time Gibson used this process and since then, it has been standard practice for all their catalogs. The differences between the F-12 and the F-5 remained the same. The F-12 had an unbound headstock with the tulip inlay, dot neck, no fingerboard extension and a five-ply laminated finger-rest instead of the three-ply bound pickguard found on the F-5. In the 1960s the F-12 sales on average amounted to only 25 per year, mainly due to its cost being more than double the price of most of Gibson's high-end flat-top guitars.

1960 Price: $395.00
1962 Price: $435.00
1964 Price: $495.00
1967 Price: $845.00
1968 Price: $895.00

EM-150 Electric Mandolin – 1960-1969

Very few changes were made to the EM-150 during the 60s except its price. While a customer in 1968 could buy a Les Paul Standard guitar, it was only $40.00 more than the price of an EM-150. An SG Standard guitar was $20.00 less than an EM-150 and like most of the other mandolin models the EM-150 was discontinued in 1970. Today an EM-150 from the late 60s is worth less than $1000, a 1968 Les Paul is worth four to five times that amount.

1960 Price: $195.0
1962 Price: $215.00
1964 Price: $245.00
1967 Price: $325.00
1968 Price: $355.00

EM-200 Florentine Electric Mandolin – 1960-1961

In 1960 Gibson changed the model number of the Florentine electric and called it the EM-200. Based on the catalog descriptions, the design had not changed nor did the catalog illustration. The reason for the model name change remains a mystery. Some speculate that the name change coincided with a new pickguard design that wrapped around the pickup, but apparently this did not to occur until 1966.

1960 Price: $225.00

Florentine Electric Mandolin – 1962-1969

The EM-200 model designation lasted only two years. Then in 1962, Gibson reverted to the Florentine Electric name without the EM-200 designation. The biggest change came in 1966 when the company redesigned the pickguard. The new style pickguard wrapped around the entire pickup but the pickup was still mounted in the body. In the 1950s Ted McCarty had invented the "floating pickguard" for several electric guitar models and they had the pickup mounted to the pickguard and suspended above the body of the instrument. The new pickguard on the Florentine electric did not suspend the pickup but was elevated above the body. Oddly, Gibson's 1966 catalog description does not even mention this feature.

1962 Price: $250.00
1964 Price: $285.00
1967 Price: $345.00
1968 Price: $375.00

 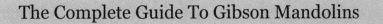
EMS-1235 Double Mandolin – 1960-1968

In 1960 Gibson's catalog listed the scale length of the mandolin neck on the EMS-1235 at 15 1/2", but the reason for increasing it over 1 1/2" is unclear. There are examples of double mandolins from the 1960s that have the standard 13 7/8" scale length, so it's likely that Gibson was offering two options. Extant double mandolins have a wide array of different configurations and features because they were all custom-built to each customer's specifications. Some had block inlays on the mandolin neck similar to an F-5 and others had small double parallelogram inlays that matched the guitar neck. Gibson usually used a standard rosewood mandolin bridge, but some had an aluminum saddle, while other examples have a custom Tune-O-Matic mandolin bridge. The Tune-O-Matic Bridge was designed and patented by Ted McCarty in 1952, but the patent wasn't awarded until 1956. Its design is still the standard used today on the majority of electric guitars. It provides the ability to adjust the height of the bridge as well as each individual saddle piece for optimum intonation.

The biggest change to the EMS-1235 came in 1962 when Gibson started making them with a thinner solid mahogany body instead of a semi-hollow body. It made all the double-neck instruments lighter and less expensive to manufacture, but the company actually raised the price. Post-1962 solid-body double mandolins usually had matching double parallelogram fingerboard inlays and a pearl tulip inlay below the logo which matched the guitar neck. Gibson built the custom double-neck instruments up until about 1968. By that time the double mandolin's price was nearly twice what it had been in 1950.

1960 Price: $495.00
1962 Price: $600.00
1963 Price: $640.00
1967 Price: $750.00
1968 Price: $810.00

1966 photo-illustration of the solid-body
"Double 12" is just for reference purposes only

Gibson, Inc. – 1970-1986 – The Norlin Era

The Norlin era can be characterized as 16 years of corporate greed, mismanagement and lack of vision that resulted in Gibson nearly going bankrupt. Stan Rendell may have been an expert in manufacturing efficiency but did not possess the creative genius of his predecessor and lacked the ability to enable Gibson to produce new and innovative products. He was convinced that Gibson was building the finest instruments ever made but in reality they were producing instruments that lacked the quality of instruments from earlier eras, and the new designs were often unappealing and widely considered the worst the company has ever produced. Most of the instruments the company introduced during his

tdid not sell and were discontinued in a fairly short period of time.Gibson had completely lost the hands-on management style that had been such an integral part of their prior success. In the 1970s musical instrument sales were down industry-wide and for Gibson, they were even worse. Dozens of Asian companies were flooding the market

A small number of the multitude of Asia imports from the 70s

with cheap knock-offs of Gibsons and Fenders. It was crippling the American instrument manufacturing industry. Norlin's response was to make extensive cuts in the number of different instruments Gibson was manufacturing. They also discontinued several iconic instruments like the Firebird, Flying V and ES-350 electric guitars, the entire line of Gibson lap steel and pedal steel Hawaiians, the A-40 and A-50 acoustic mandolins and the EM-150 and Florentine Electric mandolins.

Norlin had little regard for the welfare of its Kalamazoo employees and considered the higher wages to be an unnecessary cost of doing business that was eating into their profits. Rendell was a staunch anti-unionist and did not like the fact that the union was dictating a lot of the ways the company was run. They eliminated individual incentives for employees including a profit-sharing plan and factory morale kept sinking lower and lower. In 1974 Norlin started moving all instrument manufacturing to Nashville where labor was cheaper and workers did not have to join a union if they didn't want to. The vast majority of Gibson's Kalamazoo workforce, some of whom had been with the company for decades, did not follow. The Kalamazoo factory remained open until 1984, but was a mere shell of its former glory. The few remaining employees resorted to manufacturing products like water-beds as a last ditched effort to keep the factory open and not lose their jobs.

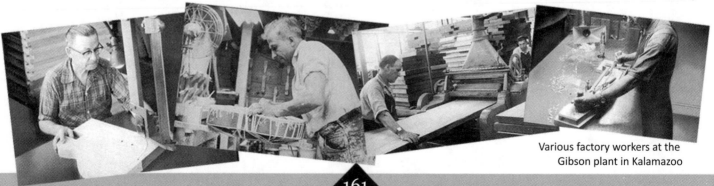

Various factory workers at the Gibson plant in Kalamazoo

You Couldn't Burn Money Faster

All of the cost-cutting measures and attempts to make the company profitable failed. Under Norlin's management Gibson was hemorrhaging money so quickly that one employee remarked that "you couldn't burn through money faster than Norlin went through it." Things had become so that Gibson's 1970 mandolin brochure has the photographs of the A-50 and EM-150 reversed as well as the F-5 and F-12. Gibson's address is listed in Lincolnwood, Illinois as if the Kalamazoo headquarters didn't even exist. They introduced many new instruments, most of which were complete failures, including the first acoustic guitars built in Nashville, the Mark Series. Sales were abysmal mainly because the guitars sounded terrible and didn't even look like Gibson guitars. In a vain attempt to garner more interest in the Mark Series, Norlin paid for celebrity endorsements from Peter Frampton and John Sebastian with catch phrases like "Frampton's Right on the Mark."

1970s ad campaign for the Mark Series guitars featuring Peter Frampton

What Were They Thinking?

There was a whole host of bizarre new instrument designs introduced during theNorlin era including the Les Paul Signature model that looked more like a Rickenbacker guitar than a Les Paul. The L-5S model wasn't even close to the design of a traditional arch-top acoustic/electric L-5CES. They also introduced two new mandolin models, the A-9 and A-12. Like so many of Gibson's 1970s designs, they looked nothing like a traditional "A" mandolin and were so ugly that they earned the nickname "lump scroll" mandolins. Even if someone had a good idea for a new product, the bureaucracy was such that it took dozens of meetings and memos just to get anything approved. There was no clear way to determine in what direction the company was going. Norlin's management had Gibson discard so many of their proven products and seemed to care very little about the company's heritage and the traditions had made the company so great. Norlin was choking on their own bureaucracy which was filled with too many mid-level managers and upper-management executives who did little more than sit in an office. Gibson had become very top-heavy, a problem that Ted McCarty dealt with in 1948, but Norlin did nothing about it. In 1979 the unthinkable happened. Norlin merged Gibson, Inc. into Norlin Industries, Inc. and Gibson ceased to exist as a company and became nothing more than a brand name. Finally in 1986, just three months away from being bankrupt, Norlin was sold for only $5,000,000. In retrospect, CBS had also done a terrible job running Fender, but at least they had sold that company for twice Gibson's selling price.

1970s-era L-5S that was unlike any L-5 acoustic-electric guitar

Gibson Instruments – 1970-1986

A-5 Mandolin – 1971-1978

Shortly after Norlin acquired Gibson they discontinued the A-5 Florentine double cutaway design and introduced an entirely different mandolin. Incongruously they also called it the model A-5 but this version was a bizarre mix of different mandolin features. It had an oval soundhole like its predecessor, a fingerboard extension that was so long it nearly reached the opposite side of the soundhole and had a total of 30 frets. The headstock shape was like that of an "F" mandolin and although the body was more akin to an "F," than an "A," it lacked the traditional spiraling hand-carved scroll found on an F-5 or F-12. This design has since earned the nickname "lump scroll" because that's what it looked like - a lump. Back in the 1930s, Gibson used a very similar design for one of their off-brand mandolin models, the Cromwell GM-6 but it's unlikely that it had anything to do with the development of 1970's A-5. The reason for the company giving it an "A" model designation is perplexing but not all that surprising given the chaotic management of the company.

1971 Price: $595.50
 (November 1971 price increase to $645.00)
1975 Price: $999.00
1978 Price: $1299.00

The Gibson-made Cromwell GM-6
"lump scroll" mandolin

A-12 Mandolin – 1971-1979

1971 also marked the year that Gibson stopped making several traditional "A" mandolins including the A-40, A-50 and EM-150. Rendell seemed to think very highly of the new A/F combination and decided Gibson should also make an f-hole version and call it the A-12. It did not have a floral inlay design below the logo and an unbound elevated finger-rest which were used on the A-5. Even though it outsold the A-5, Gibson discontinued it in 1979. After Stan Rendell resigned, no one at Gibson thought the lump-scroll models were worth keeping as part of the product line.

1971 Price: $395.50 (November 1971 price increase to $425.00)
1975 Price: $799.00
1978 Price: $1079.00

A-5 and A-12 specifications:
Carved spruce top
Carved maple back and maple rims
Rosewood fingerboard with extension and pearl dots
12-fret neck – 30 frets
"Gibson" script logo and floral design inlay in headstock
Single-bound top, back and fingerboard
Nickel-plated hardware
Cremona Brown with yellow sunburst finish (that's what the catalog says)

A-5 and A-12 dimensions:
Body width: 10"
Body length: 13 3/4"
Body depth: 1 3/4"
Overall length: 28"
Nut width: 1 1/8"

A-40 Mandolin – 1970 (discontinued)

A-50 Mandolin – 1970 (discontinued)

F-5 Artist Mandolin – 1970-1979

As it had been for many years, the F-5 continued to be Gibson's top-of-the-line mandolin. However during the 1970s, F-5s had the reputation of being over-built. In a vain attempt to make more durable instruments that wouldn't require any warrantee work, the tops and backs were thicker and the top braces were wider and higher. The result was a dull muted sounding mandolin that lacked the punch and volume normally associated with F-5s. The company still used the less fancy Gibson block logo and tulip inlaid in the headstock but in 1975, the F-5 got new ornate fingerboard inlays and the headstock that featured the pre-WWII "The Gibson" script logo and flowerpot inlay below it Gibson continued to make the F-5 up until 1979 at which time the new improved F-5L became the only mandolin Gibson made.

1971 Price: $995.00 (November 1971 price increase to $1045.00)
1975 Price: $1499.00
1978 Price: $1799.00

F-12 Artist Mandolin – 1970-1979

F-12s from the early 70s were the same design as the 1960's version. In the mid-70s Gibson redesigned the F-12 and added some more fancy features that were reminiscent of the original 1930s design. The headstock also featured "The Gibson" script logo and the same floral design they used on the A-5. Gibson also changed the necks on the F-5 and F-12 to 12-frets clear of the body and a longer fingerboard extension that had a total of 30 frets. The F-12 also got binding on the fingerboard and headstock as well as a triple-bound elevated tortoise shell finger-rest. In 1979 it was discontinued at the same time as the F-5.

1971 Price: $795.50 (November 1971 price increase to $845.00)
1975 Price: $1249.00
1978 Price: $1499.00

EM-150 Electric Mandolin – 1970 (discontinued)

EM-200 Florentine Electric Mandolin – 1970 (discontinued)

F-5L Mandolin – 1978-1986

After nearly a decade of mismanagement and misguided attempts to introduce new designs, Gibson decided to reinvent themselves. Noted Gibson historian and master luthier Roger Siminoff approached Gibson with the idea of building F-5s the way they did in the 1920s. In particular, Siminoff proposed that Gibson should build them to the original specifications of the Lloyd Loar-signed Master Model F-5 and call it the F-5L in honor of Loar. In typical fashion Stan Rendell completely rejected the idea, saying Siminoff was "way off-base." Fortunately Rendell resigned shortly thereafter and Siminoff remained persistent in trying to convince Gibson to create this "re-issue" F-5. Finally in 1977, Siminoff presented the concept to Plant Manager, Jim Duerloo and several other members of management. Siminoff demonstrated how important the original design of the F-5 was including the process of tap-tuning the tops, backs and tone bars (or braces) the way Lloyd Loar had done over 50 years earlier. Gibson's response was "Well, let's get going." Siminoff and a team of Gibson craftsman went to extraordinary lengths to insure that the new F-5L would be as close to the original as possible. They employed brand new technology like top deflection machines and strobe-tuners that precisely measured the resonance response of the tops and backs. Three F-5L prototypes were built and presented at the June 1978 NAMM (National Association of Music Merchandizers) convention. The F-5L was an immediate hit and turned out to be the only mandolin Gibson produced after 1980 until the company was sold by Norlin.

1979 Price: $2399.00

1980 ad for the F-5L with Lloyd Loar in the background

F-5L Specifications:

Tap-tuned carved spruce top
Tap-tuned curly maple back with
  matching curly maple rims
Single-bound ivoroid top, back and fingerboard
Three-ply bound headstock
Pearl "The Gibson" logo and abalone "Fern" inlay on headstock
Ebony fingerboard with pearl dot markers
Gold-plated Grover tuners with pearl buttons
Gold-plated hardware including engraved tailpiece
Ebony adjustable bridge
Ebony end-pin with pearl dot
"Antique Sunburst" finish

Dimensions:

Same as c1923 Master Model F-5

Gibson Guitar Corporation – 1986-Present

In January 1986 three partners purchased the musical instrument division of Norlin Industries and formed the Gibson Guitar Corporation. Henry Juszkiewicz, David Berryman and Gary Zebrowski were able to acquire both Gibson and Epiphone for only $5,000,000, a fraction of what the company is worth today. They quickly went about the task of restoring Gibson's reputation as a premiere musical instrument manufacturer. Their appreciation for Gibson's heritage led to the reintroduction of some of Gibson's best-known guitars including the dot-neck ES-335, the flame-top Les Paul and others. The company was growing again and was enjoying 20 to 30 percent annual increases in revenue and profits. The company relied heavily on the popularity of its most iconic instruments like the Les Paul and the F-5L mandolin. After the closing of the Kalamazoo factory in 1984 all instrument manufacturing was done in Nashville.

Only one month after the acquisition, the company's management and employees were present at a very special event. Bill Monroe's original 1923 Lloyd Loar-signed F-5 mandolin was restored by Charlie Derringer, Gibson's master craftsman and repairman. Monroe's F-5 was thought to have been damaged beyond repair after being smashed into many pieces. Derringer proved to be an indispensable member of the company's continued efforts to make mandolins in Nashville. In 1987 Gibson acquired the Flatiron Mandolin Company in Bozeman, Montana. Flatiron was founded by Steve Carlson, a master luthier who had been building mandolins since the early 1980s. Flatiron had the reputation for manufacturing very good instruments and Gibson wanted them to build their mandolins. Carlson sold his company and went to work for Gibson.

For a while the Bozeman factory was actually making both Gibson and Flatiron mandolins. In 1988 Carlson helped reintroduce the classic "A" style mandolin including the A-5L and A-5G models. The A-5L like the F-5L was designed to mimic the Lloyd Loar A-5 prototype, Gibson's first "A" mandolin to have f-holes. He wanted to use the design of the original prototype but also mirror the fine appointments of the F-5L including tap-tuning the tops and backs, fancier ornamentation and a hand-stained sunburst finish. He also added innovative features like an elevated fingerboard with an elongated extension and 28 frets as well as a neck that attached to the body at the 15th fret. Some say that Carlson's designs had one major flaw. The neck joint was not a tapered dovetail which had been the standard for all Gibson acoustic instruments. Instead, Carlson used a mortise and tenon joint which was not as strong and could cause the instrument to go out of tune due to the joint slipping.

Mortise and tenon joint (upper left) versus the tapered dovetail neck joint

Carlson was also responsible for hiring Bruce Webber who furthered the mandolin renaissance at Gibson's acoustic division in Bozeman after Carlson's departure in 1993. Also in 1993 Gibson acquired Original Musical Instruments (OMI), makers of Dobro wood-bodied resonator guitars. Then in 1997 Gibson decided to consolidate almost all of their acoustic instrument manufacturing under the name Original Acoustic Instruments (OAI) a subdivision of the company. They relocated Dobro from Huntington Beach, California and also moved mandolin manufacturing from Bozeman into a separate manufacturing facility in Nashville to make mandolins, resonator guitars as well as banjos.

When Gibson had introduced the original F-5L in 1978 they decided to have their mandolin builders sign a label inside every mandolin the same way that Lloyd Loar had done decades earlier. There was a long succession of master craftsmen who signed instruments including Wilbur Fuller, who helped with the development of the F-5L in 1978, Jim Triggs (1986-1989), Steve Carlson (1987-1993), Bruce Webber (1993-1997), Charlie Derrington (1998-2004) and the current master luthier at Gibson, David Harvey (2008-present).

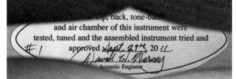

A David Harvey signature label from 2011

In 2004 Charlie Derrington was appointed head of Gibson's acoustic instrument production in Nashville. One of the first things he did was to change the neck joints back to Gibson's standard tapered dovetail. Derrington's philosophy was "about putting forth the bluegrass message to the masses" as it was clear that the rising popularity of this genre was fueling mandolin sales. Bluegrass mandolinists love the Gibson F-5 because of its punch, clarity and carrying power. Gibson did make some other mandolin models like the A-9 and F-9 as well as some custom instruments like the OM-5C octave mandolin and K-5C cutaway mando-cello, but it quickly became apparent that their customers were more interested in the iconic F-5 than any other design.

Starting in the late 1990s Gibson offered dozens of variations of the Les Paul, their most popular electric guitar, and decided to design and build many variations of the F-5 as well. There was the F-5 Master Model, the "Fern," Goldrush and Victorian. Customers could get F-5s in a wide array of finishes like gold-top, pelham blue, peacock sunburst, gold pearl, ruby rush and charcoal. They also built artist signature models like the Sam Bush, Ricky Skaggs and Doyle Lawson. The majority of these models were built as limited edition, short-run, non-production instruments, usually referred to as "custom shop" instruments. They carried some hefty price tags ranging from $6,000-$19,000.00.

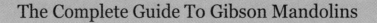

The Gibson Bluegrass Showcase that was located at the Opry Mills Mall until the flood of 2010

In 2003 Gibson opened the "Bluegrass Showcase" at the Opry Mills Mall in Nashville. For the first time customers could see first hand how mandolins were made. The company had its craftsman working behind large windows which allowed the public to see the inner workings of the acoustic instrument manufacturing department. This facility also included a retail store and restaurant and even some live music. Unfortunately in May 2010, Nashville suffered one of the worst floods in its history causing an estimated $2.3 billion in damages including the Opry Mills Mall and the Bluegrass Showcase. Gibson was forced to abandon the site entirely and move production to another building. The company also decided to dispense with the "Bluegrass Division" name and mandolins were built in Gibson's "custom shop." The custom shop had been in place for many years and they were almost exclusively building one-off custom-made instruments and prototypes. Mandolin production seemed to decline after this point as Gibson was mainly offering only the limited edition models.

During the last two decades or so hundreds of small "boutique" mandolin builders have sprung up all over the world offering instruments of exceptional quality at prices that are often well below Gibson's. In 2014 Gibson offered the 120th anniversary F-5 with an enormous price tag of $60,000.00. Although Gibson did issue a mandolin price list in May 2015 that included five different "F" models, the internet page on Gibson's website that should show their 2016 mandolins simply comes up blank. One Gibson retailer has to put a disclaimer on their website "Gibson does not allow us to list our inventory or prices on the web." The company is still building mandolins but it appears be only in limited quantities.

What does the future hold for Gibson mandolins? This is a difficult question to answer. We can only hope that the company that established itself in the early 20th century as the world's premiere manufacturer of carved top mandolins and guitars returns to its rightful place as the world's most famous mandolin manufacturer.

Remember... *"Everyone a Gibson-ite"*

Gibson Instruments – 1986-Present

A-5L – 1988-2012

Gibson started making the A-5L soon after they acquired The Flatiron Company. Steve Carlson had been building a Flatiron A-5 model that mirrored the techniques used to produce the F-5L. He designed and built them using 1920s-era processes including tap tuning the tops and interior air chamber, more ornate trim like an F-5 and a vintage Cremona Brown sunburst finish. The A-5L had flamed maple backs, rims and neck. For a time the company's factory was making both the Flatiron A-5s and Gibson A-5Ls. It was advertised as "…65 years in development."

No Pricing Information Available

A-5G – 1988-1996

The A-5G had the same basic design and construction as the A-5L, but was less ornate. It had a three-ply bound top, but the back, fingerboard and headstock had a single binding. "The Gibson" logo was inlaid in pearl with an abalone fleur-de-lis on the headstock. It had a muted brown sunburst finish on the top, but the back, rim and neck were a solid dark mahogany color. The A-5G also featured Steve Carlson's design including a full 15-fret neck with elevated fingerboard and fingerboard extension allowing for a total of 29 frets.

No Pricing Information Available

A-9 – 2003-2012 (no picture available)

The A-9 model designation had been used by Gibson in the 1970s, but this less ornate version of an "A" mandolin had a standard symmetrical body. It had a single black top binding, but no binding on the back or fingerboard. It had no inlays on the headstock but did have the 1920s-style tapered snakehead shape. No Pricing Information Available

F-5G – 1993-Present

Like the A-5G, the F-5G was a less ornate F-5 model. It had a three-ply bound top, but the back, fingerboard and headstock had no single binding. "The Gibson" logo and flowerpot design were inlaid in pearl on the headstock. It had a muted brown sunburst finish on the top, but the back, rim and neck were a solid dark mahogany color. It also had nickel-plated hardware instead of the customary gold hardware on other top-of-the-line F-5s.

2015 Price: $5799.00

F-5L – 1986-2002

Gibson continued making the F-5L that had been developed in 1978 by Roger Siminoff and Jim Deurloo. This model is sometimes referred to as the "Loar Reissue" (the "L" in F-5L). It had the vintage "The Gibson" pearl logo and the Loar-era fern inlaid in abalone. 20s-era Cremona Brown sunburst finish on the top, back, rim and neck and all gold hardware. All of the other specifications adhered very closely to the 1978 version until it was discontinued in 2002.
No Pricing Information Available

F-5 Master Model – 1999-Present (aka Varnish Master Model)
The Master Model version of the F-5 was essentially the same design as the F-5L but had a period-correct varnish finish from the Loar-era. It also had silver-plated hardware and came with a rectangular plush-lined case, also like the original specifications of a Loar-era F-5. Gibson's 1999 brochure states that the varnish is "hand-brushed," but oddly lists it as also having a "hand-applied French polish," which is not a technique Gibson had ever used.

2009 Price: $14,499.00
2015 Price: $18,299.

F-5 "The Fern" (aka F-5 Fern) **– 2003-Present**
In 2003 Gibson introduced the F-5 "The Fern" after it discontinued the F-5L. It had all of the same basic design elements as its predecessor including "The Gibson" pearl logo and the Loar-era fern inlaid in abalone on the headstock. The sunburst finish was more akin to a 1930s-era F-5 rather than the 1920s-era Cremona Brown and Gibson referred to this finish as a "fern burst." There are a few variations on the model name and it was last listed as an F-5L "The Fern" in 2015.

2015 Price: $8799.00

Ricky Skaggs Distressed Model - 2008-2012

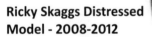

It took over a year for Gibson to develop this signature model F-5 named after the world-renowned bluegrass mandolinist. Skaggs wanted Gibson to build it to replicate the specifications of his original 1923 Loar-signed F-5. The Cremona Brown sunburst was aged to give it the appearance of an 85-year old mandolin that had been played many, many times resulting in the "distressed" moniker. This model also featured a "speed neck" including a 1 1/16" wide nut and a thinner profile or neck shape, which were specifically designed to copy the narrower neck dimensions of Skagg's F-5. It was only offered in limited quantities of 30 instruments at a time that were "personally inspected by Ricky to insure it meets his rigorous standards for tone, playability and appearance."
No Pricing Information Available

F-5 Sam Bush Signature Model – 2000-Present

This artist-endorsed model was supposedly designed to copy an old F-5 Sam Bush had owned for many years. His F-5 dated from the 1930s, but had been repaired and modified many times over the years. It had no fingerboard extension and only 21 frets. The mother-of-pearl inlays were apparently original to a 30s-era F-5 including a Gibson script logo and flowerpot design on the headstock and large block inlays in the fingerboard. 2015 Price: $9999.00

Doyle Lawson Signature Model F-5 – 2013-Present

Gibson called the Doyle Lawson Signature as "another groundbreaking mandolin" that was developed as a "collaboration between another contemporary master musician and our elite luthiers." It featured a unique headstock inlay design of stems, leaves and flowers with a pearloid truss rod cover that had Lawson's signature engraved and filled in black. They also used another unusual fingerboard design with 21 frets with the 21st fret sitting on a very short centered extension. By some accounts the Doyle Lawson signature model does not sound as good as a typical high-end F-5 and is generally not well regarded.

2015 Price: $10,299.00

F-5 Goldrush – 2006-Present
Luthier David Harvey designed and built the Goldrush version of the F-5 starting in 2006 and he used a "golden amber finish" which was accentuated by a dark binding on all the edges. It incorporated the headstock inlay design of the F-5 Fern as well as the high-end gold hardware. The fingerboard has an unusual 23 frets with a slanted stair-step design in place of the longer, rounder F-5 fingerboard extension.

2015 Price: $7699.00

120th Anniversary F-5 – 2014
Gibson pulled out all the stops for its 120th Anniversary F-5 which carried a hefty $60,000.00 price tag. The ornamentation designed and built by David Harvey was unprecedented in the entire history of the F-5. It included a stunning tree-of-life fingerboard inlay design and a headstock that had no logo but a torch and wire inlay design that hadn't been used by Gibson since the pre-1910 era F-4 mandolins. Harvey went even further by adding a pearl script Gibson logo in the fingerboard extension and the triple-bound pickguard had ornate floral shapes and a large pearl banner with the inscription "120 Years – 1894-2014." All of the very fancy pearl inlay was beautifully offset by an all-black finish reminiscent of the early 1930s F-10.

2014 Price: $60,000.00

F-9 – 2003-Present
When first introduced in 2003 the F-9 was a "no-frills" mandolin that was somewhat similar to the F-12 of the post-WWII era, the first "F" model to be produced by Gibson under the management of Ted McCarty. Early versions had a muted brown satin sunburst finish with a dark single-bound top and no other binding. The headstock only had the plainer Gibson script logo without any other inlay and a squared-off fingerboard that was not elevated. Later on Gibson gave the F-9 a bit of a facelift including a brighter sunburst finish on the top, back and rim plus a single ivoroid top binding.

2015 Price: $4799.00

Gibson Instrument Shipping Totals - 1935-1979

Shipping Totals - 1935 - 1945

Model	1935	1936	1937	1938	1939	1940	1941	1942	1943	1944	1945
A-00	268	318	330	224	198	174	225	159	16	4	
A-00N							22	34	8		
A	0	2	1	0			2	1			
A-1	230	291	298	179	132	97	118	72	54	29	
A-3	1	1	0	0							
A-4	1	1	0	0							
A-40											
A-50	108	80	126	131	124	92	109	46		54	200
A-75	16	19	16	0							
A-C	22	43	41	9	1						
EM-100				16	53	23					
EM-125							37	29	2	1	0
EM-150	0	0	53	83	52	26	37	11	2		
F-2	2	1	1	0			1				
F-4	34	42	28	19	26	30	35	19		4	0
F-5	15	12	21	20	8	6	12	17	6		0
F-7	30	31	32	25	26						
F-10	4	9	5	0							
F-12	8	6	1	0							
H-0	6	5	30	29	16	12	14	6	7		
H-1	9	10	0	0	1						
H-4	2	3	2	2	1	3			1		
H-5	2	1	2	1		1					
K-1	3	0	2	1	1	1		2			
K-4	1	1	1	4	1						
K-5	0	0	2	0							
J	1	1	0	1	1					1	
Electric Mandola					2			1			
Electric F-5				2	1						
Electric H-5					1						
H-0 Electric							1	1			
Elec. Mando-cello			1								
A-1 12-string		1									
A-1 Electric		1	1								

Gibson Instrument Shipping Totals - 1935-1979

Shipping Totals - 1946 - 1956

Model	1946	1947	1948	1949	1950	1951	1952	1953	1954	1955	1956
A-00				4							
A-40			225	280	220	369	247	522	339	235	330
A-40 Black			4								
A-50	552	827	561	359	206	295	307	313	220	187	179
A-50 Electric			11								
EM-150			34	88	84	65	91	158	158	122	121
Florentine Electric									57	72	53
F-4			2								
F-5		1			5	22	18	22	14	16	22
F-5N		2									
F-12			6	74	44	51	52	40	72	31	43

Shipping Totals - 1957 - 1967

Model	1957	1958	1959	1960	1961	1962	1963	1964	1965	1966	1967
EMS-1235		15	13	7	9	3	4	0	3	5	2
F-5	21	14	21	24	27	18	34	26	15	11	30
F-12	34	24	25	19	22	14	26	19	30	7	31
A-50	113	60	103	103	92	67	129	118	99	236	84
A-40	221	121	165	166	114	103	167	265	148	170	0
A-40N					67		61	73	45	11	17
A-5	14	18	18	22	19	31	40	53	27	45	43
Florentine Electric	45	25	54			42	39	63	53	22	41
EM-200 Florentine				28	41						
EM-150	126	58	81	58	84	51	87	77	49	40	27

 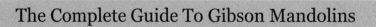

Gibson Instrument Shipping Totals - 1935-1979

Shipping Totals - 1968 - 1979

Model	1968	1969	1970	1971	1972	1973	1974	1975	1976	1977	1978	1979
F-5	29	50	32	43	42	124	180	195	115	136	23	6
F-5L											3	23
F-12	19	26	14	16	11	13	8	65	53	12	6	5
A-50	91	97	41									
A-40	222	149	55									
A-40N	60	44	16									
A-5	39	83	25	31	12	12	63	65	64	30	9	0
A-12				53	30	18	87	172	72	27	11	2
Florentine Electric	38	42	20									
EM-150	62	69	22									

Term	Definition
neck block	a wooden block with a tenon (slotted opening) used to secure the neck to the body of aninstrument
nut	the nut is small hard piece of material such as bone, ebony or mother-of-pearl that the sits at the top of the fingerboard (closest to the headstock) and is slotted for each string so they are the corect distance apart. It also is one of two achoring points that establishes the vibrating string length
oil varnish	a type finish like spirit varnish only using an oil-based solvent instead of alcohol
pin block	a solid piece of celluloid or other hard material that has tapered holes for holding pins to secure the strings; ususally found on a mando-cello or harp-guitar
position markers	usually mother-of-pearl dots or other decorative shapes positioned at specific areas of the fingerboard as a reference point
purfling	a narrow decorative edge inlaid into the top plate and often the back plate of a stringed instrument.
radius	generaly refers to the arch or curved top of the fingerboard and is measured in inches
rasp	a coarse file with a roughened surface for scraping, filing and shaping wood
reclaimed lumber	wood that has been taken from other wooden products such as furniture or achitecturtal woodwork
rim	the bent sides of a stringed musical instrument
rosette	aka soundhole rings; a decorative border around an instrument's soundhole
sandarac	a gum resin obtained from the alerce (cypress) of Spain and North Africa, used in making varnish.
shellac	resin from the lac bug that ground into thin flakes, dissolved in a solvent and used for making varnish or other instrument finishes
silk-screened	a process to print, decorate, or reproduce an image by pushing ink throug a silkscreen
soundhole	an opening(s) in the top of a musical instrument that allows the tone to be projected out of the body
spirit varnish	a type of finish that contains resins such a shellac, copal or sandarac dissolved in alcohol or "spirits"
Style "O" guitar	is an eight-string fretted musical instrument with four pairs of unison strings and tuned like a viola – C, G, D, A, E low to high.
sunburst	a type of instrument finish that mimics the rays of the sun; a center section of yellow or orange that gradually gets darker near the edges
tail block	a wooden block that is glued to the bottom of an instrument inside the body to secure the tailpiece and end pin
tailpiece	a metal piece attached to the bottom of a stringed instruments body to anchor the string s
tortoise shell	celluloid materiel that is colored to make it appear like the shell of a sea tortoise, aka faux tortoise shell
varnish	resin dissolved in a liquid for applying on wood or other materials to form a hard, clear, shiny surface when dry.
vaudeville	a type of entertainment popular chiefly in the US in the early 20th century, featuring a mixture of specialty acts such as burlesque comedy and song and dance.
veneer	a thin piece of hardwood that is glued over a substrate to give the appearance of solid wood
volute	a raised spine on the back of an instruments neck and used to strengthen the transition from the neck to the headstock
waist	the narrower portions of an instrument's body such as a guitar of "F"-style mandolin
wood dye	any number of different color liquids use to change the appearance of wood a different color
worm-gear	the part of a tuning machice that has a turning button on end and a spiral gear on the other
zither	a musical instrument consisting of a flat wooden sound box with numerous strings stretched across it, placed horizontally and played with the fingers and a plectrum.

Term	Definition
abalone	a smooth shining iridescent substance forming the inner layer of the shell of some mollusks, especially abalone used for ornamentation like pearl
blow gun	an early device for spraying finish by blowing a tube that draws the finish up a syphon and sprays out of a nozzle
boot jack	a yokelike device for catching the heel of a boot, as a riding boot, to aid in removing it.
bout	the wider portions of an instrument's body such as a guitar of "F"-style mandolin, upper boat (wide area close to the neck) or lower boat, typically the widest are of a fretted string instrument (closest to the bottom of the body - or tailpiece)
cam lever	a rigid bar pivoted about a fulcrum, used to transfer a force to a load and usually to provide a mechanical advantage
copal	resin from any of a number of tropical trees, used to make varnish
denatured alcohol	also called methylated spirits, is ethanol that is used as a solvent for spirir varnish
end pin	a peg that is usually ebony or other hardwood that extends from the tailpiece to secure a strap
f-hole	a particular type of soundole that shaped like a cursive letter f; found on many instruments of the violin and mandolin family as well as guitars
figured maple	aka tiger maple, fiddle-back maple, or flamed maple that contains contrasting light and dark lines.
fingerboard	a flat or roughly flat strip on the neck of a stringed instrument, against which the strings are pressed to shorten the vibrating length and produce notes of higher pitches.
finger-rest	synonymous with pickgaurd - invented by L.A. William in 1907 and is elevated above the body and helps to prevent pick sctraches\
fleur-de-lis	a stylized lily composed of three petals bound together near their bases. It is especially known from the former royal arms of Francebut used as ornamentation on may musical instruments
guard-plate	an early name for a pickguard or finger-rest, but refers to the type that is inlaid into the top if the body
harp-guitar	is an eight-string fretted musical instrument with four pairs of unison strings and tuned like a viola – C, G, D, A, E low to high.
headstock	also called the peghead, the wider top part of the neck that is ususally slanted where the tuning machines are mounted
inlay	decorative material such as pearl, abalone or other material that is glued into a cavity that matches its shape
intonation	accuracy of pitch in playing or singing, or on a stringed instrument such as a guitar.
ivoroid	ivory-colored celluloid
Keratol	a pyroxylin-coated waterproof material that is embossed with leather-like pattern used especially in covering instrument cases, suitcases and book covers
lute	a plucked stringed instrument with a long neck bearing frets and a rounded body with a flat front that is shaped like a halved egg.
machine-haeds	synonymous with tuners or tuning pegs - mounted on the headstock and turned to lower or raise the pitch of a string
mando-bass	is a four-string fretted musical instrument with four strings and tuned like an acoustic bass E, A, D, G low to high.
mando-cello	is an eight-string fretted musical instrument with four pairs of unison strings and tuned like a cello – C, G, D, A, E low to high.
mandola	is an eight-string fretted musical instrument with four pairs of unison strings and tuned like a viola – C, G, D, A, E low to high.
mandolin	is an eight-string fretted musical instrument with four pairs of unison strings and tuned like a violin – G, D, A, E low to high.
mastic	an aromatic resin exuded from the bark of a Mediterranean tree, used in making varnish
mother-of-pearl	aka pearl - a smooth shining iridescent substance forming the inner layer of the shell of some mollusks, especially oysters used in ornamentation.
multi-stringed	a stringed instrument having more than the standard number of strings such as a 7-string guitar

c1905-1906 "F" Mandolin with f-holes

Every so often a Gibson instrument will surface that even baffles the experts. Such is the case with this incredibly unusual Style "F" mandolin with f-holes. It is clearly the work of Gibson and yet it is very difficult to make sense out of the fact that it is a c1905 or 1906 Gibson mandolin with f-holes. Gibson did not officially make any mandolins with f-holes until the introduction of the F-5 in 1922. The experts who have examined this mandolin believe the top is original but it appears that the fingerboard is not. It would be easy to dismiss this mandolin as a fake or possibly a Gibson three-point "F" that had been re-topped (the top was replaced at a later date) but there is clear evidence that it is a genuine Gibson and the top is original to the instrument. It does not have a Gibson label but close examination of the interior reveals that it was "Order No." although the actual number that should follow is illegible. Gibson stopped stamping "Order No." in 1906 with the highest number recorded being 355 so this "prototype" pre-dates that year.

It has bent rims with kerfed liners with a separate neck block and tail block so it is "period correct" for a c1905 or 1606 "F" mandolin. The elaborate headstock inlay design suggests that it was based on the Style F-4 but the plain fingerboard pearl dots and unusual scalloped extension may indicate that the fingerboard was replaced. This established Gibson as the first company to ever put f-holes on a mandolin.

Gibson Customs and Prototypes

1905 Gibson Octave Mandolin

This rare and unusual instrument was built by Gibson in 1905, although they never advertised it or put it in any catalog or brochure. Some believe that Gibson may have made as many as five octave mandolins, but only one is known to exist. Most likely, it was made as a special order for one particular customer. L.A. Williams was so adamant about the correct instrumentation for a mandolin orchestra only including mandolins, mandolas, mando-cellos, guitars, and harp-guitars that it's a wonder Gibson ever manufactured an octave mandolin. Williams was an influential member of The American Guild of Banjoists, Mandolinists, and Guitarist, and was probably responsible for getting the Guild to bar the octave mandolin from mandolin orchestras in 1908. The Guild had appointed itself as the official organization governing the fretted instrument industry and claimed responsibility for closing many "fake" mandolin schools and determining what the proper instrumentation, method of playing, and the general principles that should be adopted by all American players and groups alike.

Octave mandolin dimensions:
Body width: 14 1/4"
Body length: 19"
Overall length: 34"
Scale length: 21 3/4"
Nut width: 1 3/8" +/- 1/16"

Courtesy of Frank Ford

Gibson Customs and Prototypes

1906 Custom 3-point Octave Mandolin

The octave mandolin was basically a smaller Style "K" mando-cello but was built nearly 10 years before the K-4 was introduced. It had the same body size as a mando-cello, but a shorter 10-fret neck and a shorter scale length so it should be considered an octave mandolin and not a mando-cello. Like its name implies it was tuned an octave below the mandolin It was constructed using the same materials as a Style "K-1," including a spruce top, birch back and sides, and what appears to be a cherry neck; "The Gibson" pearl logo, two sound hole rings, and binding around the top only. Unlike the "K-1," the octave mandolin had "Handel" tuners, and mother-of-pearl fingerboard inlays of various shapes at the 5th, 7th, 10th, 12th and 15th frets, and a bound fingerboard.

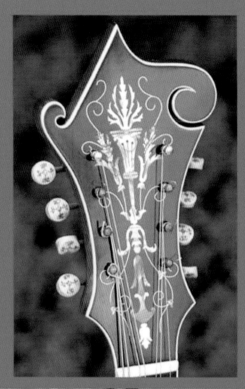

Gibson Customs and Prototypes

1916 12-string A-4 Mandolin

Gibson has always been a company that was willing to experiment as well as building just about any custom instrument a customer wanted. This 1916 A-4 is the earliest known 12 string mandolin the company ever made. Instead of the standard four pairs of strings like a mandolin it has four courses of three strings. It was custom-made for Al Bluhm who had Gibson custom engrave his name on the truss rod cover. It appears that Gibson used one set of standard Handel guitar tuners with the fancy inlaid buttons but had to cut off two separate pieces from another set to add the fourth and fifth tuners to each side. The rest of the mandolin appears to be a normal A-4 including the fingerboard extension but the width of the neck was increased slightly to accommodate the extra four strings.

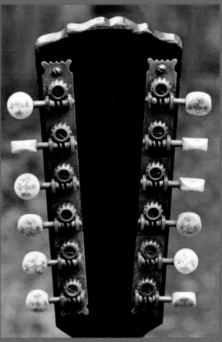

Courtesy of Lowell Levinger

Gibson Customs and Prototypes

1922 Lloyd Loar 10-string Mando-viola

In 1922 Lloyd Loar had Gibson build him one of the most unusual instruments they ever produced. It is referred to as a "mando-viola" although it has nothing in common with a viola per se. The body is the same as a Style "H" mandola but has a wide neck accommodating a total of ten strings (five double courses or pairs). It is believed that Loar used a variety of tunings when he played it including Eb - Bb - F - C – Eb (low to high) and the scale length was similar to a mandola at 15 5/8." In the photograph of Loar at the Gibson factory, he is posing in front of his workbench holding this instrument. But Loar actually had Gibson build two of these and was photographed playing the earler version with groups like the Fisher Shipp Concert Company. The first version had a Style H mandola body with an oval soundhole and a "paddle head" headstock . It may have been made prior to when he started working for Gibson. The second version was built in 1922 and it had f-holes and a "snakehead" headstock and is the one that Gibson-ites are familiar with. He also ordered a custom-made Geib & Schafer case the not only housed the mando-viola and his electric viola but also his "musical saw." The musical saw was a fairly popular novelty instrument that was essentially a hand-saw played with a violin bow across the edge and flexing the blade and to create various eerie metallic tones. Loar's "snakehead" mando-viola is the only known example of this instrument and was discovered by Roger Siminoff among Loar's personal belongings in 1994. It does have a Virzi Tone Amplifier installed which is no surprise since Loar absolutely loved them.

The second version of the Loar mando-viola has the unmistakeable "snakehead" headstock and f-holes . Courtesy of Darryl Wolfe

Lloyd Loar playing the first version of his 10-string mando-viola with an oval soundhole and "paddle head" design. His performing partner and wife was Sally Fisher Shipp.

1905 F-4 "Tree of Life" Mandolin
Courtesy of Elderly Instruments

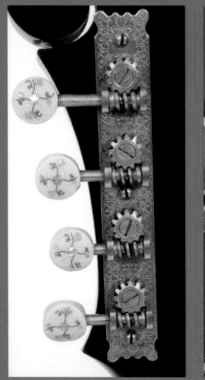

1905 A-3 Mandolin
Courtesy of Frank Ford

Above: 1905 F-3 Mandolin
Courtesy of Lowell Levinger

Right: 1906 F-3 Mandolin
Courtesy of Lowell Levinger

Above left: 1906 F-4 Mandolin
Courtesy of Lowell Levinger

1906 "black top" F-2 Mandolin
Courtesy of Gruhn Guitars

1910 "black top" A-4 Mandolin
Courtesy of Retrofret

1917 A-4 Mandolin
Courtesy of Folkway Music

1917 H-4 Mandola
Courtesy of
Elderly Intsruments

1922 H-4 Mandola
Courtesy of Frank Ford

1918 K-4 Mando-cello
Courtesy of
Elderly Instruments

Above 1919 "Sheraton Brown"
A-2 Mandolin
Right: 1921 "Sheraton Brown"
H-1 Mandola
"Sheraton Brown"
Courtesy of Folkway Music

1920 "Ivory-Top"
A-3 Mandolin
Courtesy of Folkway Music

Left: 1935 A-50 Mandolin
Courtesy of Folkway Music

Right: 1935 A-00 Mandolin
Courtesy of
Folkway Music

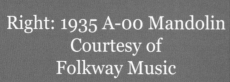

1950 F-12 Mandolin
Courtesy of Folkway Music

1952 A-40 Mandolin
Courtesy of Folkway Music

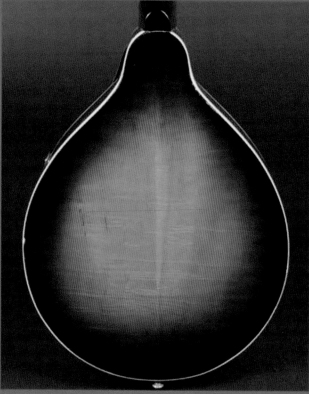

1955 EM-150 Electric Mandolin
Courtesy of Carter Vintage Guitars

1959 EMS-1235
Double Mandolin
Courtesy of Retrofret

Above: 1963 Florentine Electric Mandolin
Courtesy of Carter Vintage Guitars

Right: 1965 EM-200 Florentine Electric Mandolin
Courtesy of Retrofret

The Master Mandolin
F-5
Professional Special

The Master Mandola

H-5

Professional Special

Index